MAKING MONEY AT THE RACES

by DAVID BARR

Melvin Powers
Wilshire Book Company

12015 Sherman Road, No. Hollywood, CA 91605

Published by arrangement with Citadel Press
(a subsidiary of Lyle Stuart, Inc.)

Third paperbound printing, 1972
Copyright © 1959 by David Barr
Citadel Press, Inc., Publishers
A subsidiary of Lyle Stuart, Inc.
120 Enterprise Avenue
Secaucus, New Jersey 07094
Manufactured in the United States of America

ISBN 0-87980-268-5

CONTENTS

1 *How to Get Winners From the Consensus or Selectors* 9

2 *Making Profits From Consistent Horses* 25

3 *When to Play a Plater Dropped Down in Price* 29

4 *Beating 'Em With Best Bets* 37

5 *How to Beat the Half-Mile Ovals* 48

6 *Front Runners* 51

7 *Playing the Longshots* 61

8 *How Backing Five-Year-Olds Gives You an Edge* 75

9 *How to Make Money Betting Place* 80

10 *How Trainers Maneuver to Win* 88

11 *When to Watch the Jockey* 98

12 *Winning by Watching Scratched Horses* 110

13 *How to Get Winners by Consulting the Result Charts* 115

14 *Profits From Watching Workouts* 122

15 *Using the Speed Rate as a Time Gauge* 134

16 *Playing Horses That Show Preferred Distances* 146

17 *How to Find Formful Horses and Make Them Pay* 152

18 *Short and Sweet* 158

19 *Latching Onto Overlays* 164

20 *How Dutching Can Build a Bankroll Up Fast* 170

21 *How to Detect Hot Horses* 178

22   *Watch the Big Stables for Winners*   184

23   *Watching the Early Returners*   188

24   *Using Methodical Procedures for Profit*   191

25   *How to Beat the Optionals*   201

26   *Playing Favorites and Beaten Favorites*   205

27   *Solid All the Way*   216

28   *The Last Lap*   219

1.
HOW TO GET WINNERS
FROM THE CONSENSUS OR SELECTORS

Where does the average horse player get the horses he bets on? Most pick them cold from a list of entries or a scratch sheet. Lots of bettors watch the consensus as listed in a daily newspaper, or latch onto some paper's star handicapper, especially when he's hot. Gelardi of the New York *Daily Mirror,* often clicks with long ones, so he has many faithful followers. Some bettors favor the various "tout sheets" available for anywhere from a quarter to a dollar. It's hard to break a losing bettor's bad habits, for like the proverbial bad penny, those bad habits keep coming back.

All the above methods of selecting a horse must fail, unless a logical, business-like approach to the problem is applied. Just picking a horse from a scratch sheet, a list of entries, or a selector's choice is not sufficient. All newspaper handicappers usually display figures in the loss column for their first choice selections at the end of the year. All the other methods of simple selection must also lose money.

However, if the bettor works at the game methodically, if he applies common sense and the necessary good business logic that goes with it, failure can yield to success. With this in mind he can go ahead doing as he did before, but only at the right time. If he can sort out the good, sound selections from the bad, it is possible to make a profit out of such simple selection devices.

Three such methods will be described to help the reader. One of them is based primarily on the initial consensus selection. It was this method that turned up 100% winners for an entire month. Another of the methods uses the combination choices of the consensus and selector to produce a play. The third is a simple spot system based on selectors' selections. Used wisely, they should repay you for the time and effort.

Combing the Consensus

The average horse fan would not only give his eyeteeth, but he'd probably throw in his wife, his business, home, automobile, if he has one, and very likely both his arms, if he could get a system that picked a winner whenever a selection was made. Well, the method described here selected 100% winners for the month of March, 1955, at Florida tracks. No bettor could expect more.

The method is detailed and not easily figured, but for 100% winners the most intricate method in existence is not too much for the serious-minded fan. The reasons for the many rules become more obvious upon close examination. Every rule was put in for a specific reason, so that when a selection is finally wrung through our wringer you can be sure that its chances are the best—*the very best*.

We started with the logical assumption of using the consensus to obtain winners because it is a known fact that approximately two-thirds of the horses that hit the finish line first are chosen as one of the three on the consensus of our racing paper. We used the *Morning Telegraph* for this purpose. With such a basis to start from it is possible to stretch and pound until a better average is obtained. For the month of March, 1955, this was accomplished, *and how!*

Now we know that depending on the consensus alone is not sufficient. It is necessary to gnaw away until we get the best possible consensus selection imaginable.

The first thing we did was to chalk off our three consensus horses in the past performances. Then we started analyzing these selections. Did our horse show 50% or better in the money efforts for the current and last year combined? Did it also show 50% or better in the money races currently, that is, in its present list of past performances?

If so, we felt we were on the right track for the possible winner. Since we were looking specifically for winners it was necessary to make sure that our animal won as often as, or more often than it placed or showed for the last two years combined. If not, the horse was knocked off our prospective list.

A horse with a high speed rating would render it capable of beating the best. With this thought in mind we searched for an animal that would show at least three races at speed ratings of 90 or more in its list of past performances. To make sure that the animal was not the kind that could go real bad we ascertained that none of its speed ratings showed 65 or less. Such a low speed rating in its list of past performances automatically disqualified the horse from further consideration.

In all races except the 5th, 6th, or 7th, in which the classier animals usually run, we wanted a field of eight or more horses. We felt that in these races a bigger field would give us a better chance of getting a decent price. In the more solid races, the field frequently was smaller anyway, and we often found a standout there, so that these races were listed as exceptions.

For purposes of simplicity all races were tabbed before scratches, so that if the field became smaller later on, the situation was ignored.

To obtain a horse that was in good condition, the animal had to show a race within seven days of today's event, or a workout not more than four days ago. Further, the animal had to show at least two wins during the last eight months.

From past experience, we knew that horses under three and over five were not in the best age group for successful racing. Three-, four- and five-year-olds are usually the best animals to wager on. They are young enough to have sufficient stamina, and not too old to be on the downgrade.

No horse that was picked twice (over a period of one month) was chosen for a third time. If an animal could win for us twice, we were not going to stretch our luck to see whether it could do it a third time. In this respect we felt that we were playing *with* the law of averages rather than against it.

With claiming races we ran up against a peculiar situation. Horses that were dropping in claiming price ordinarily should stand a better chance of winning. This logic, however, proved fallacious here. We soon discovered that most of these horses were being dropped because they were incapable of competing successfully at their previous level. Somehow they were either stalling off, developing infirmities, or their racing abilities were deteriorating.

However, horses raised in claiming price, or maintaining their same levels, were showing better results. The conclusion reached was that these horses were so good that a jump in price seemed negligible to their trainers. The horses that stayed at the same level were also racing in their proper class, and frequently were a lot better than their competition.

Not only does the system, therefore, refuse to accept a horse that is dropping in claiming price from its last event, but it even refrains from choosing an animal that dropped from its previous to last claiming price.

It is common knowledge that few horses repeat a winning effort more than once. To stick with the law of averages, no animal that won its last three races was eligible for selection.

Ties are inevitable, and to obtain a selection it is often necessary to resort to tie-breaking rules. Every effort was made to produce the best tie-breaking rules possible. The tie-breaking rules here are sound—they paid off in every instance.

RULES: *Combing the Consensus*

1. Limit your observations to races with eight or more horses shown in the list of past performances in your daily racing paper. *Exception:* When you come to the 5th, 6th, or 7th races, you may safely ignore the number of horses in the field.

2. Check off those listed in the Consensus. These animals are the ones designated by all the racing paper's handicappers to finish in the first three positions.

3. Now check these three horses to see that they show 50% or better in-the-money efforts for the current and last year combined. Also check to see that the horse shows the same in-the-money average in its current list of past performances. For example, let us say the horse shows ten races. In five races the animal finished 8th, 6th, 4th, 5th and 9th. The other five races show 1st, 2nd, 1st, 3rd, 2nd. Since the animal shows five out of ten in-the-money races, which is 50%, it qualifies on this score.

4. The horse must show at least three races anywhere at speed

ratings of 90 or more. All other speed ratings in its past performances must be *more* than 65.

4a. Horse's last race must not have been more than seven days ago, or, it must show a workout not more than four days ago.

5. Horse must show as many or more winning races as placing or show spots for the last two years combined.

6. Horse must have won at least two races within the last eight months.

7. Play only horses that are three, four, or five years old.

8. If today's race is a claimer, today's claiming price must not be lower than the animal's last claiming race (not necessarily its last race). Its last claiming race must not be lower than its previous claiming race. If no claiming races are shown in the past performances, or if only one appropriate claiming race appears, you may ignore the other rule or rules.

9. Play no horse more than twice during a month.

10. Play no horse that won its last three races.

11. *Play before scratches.*

12. Play no jumpers.

13. In case of tie, choose the horse with the highest speed rating of its most recent *winning* race at today's distance. If one or more horses does not have a winning race at today's distance, play the horse that shows such a win. If no horses tied show a win at today's distance, or if still tied, then—

a. If race is less than one mile eliminate any horse that does not show at least five races run for the current and last year combined. If all horses, or two, are still tied, or if no horses show the five-race prerequisite, select the horse with the best win consistency for the current and last year combined.

b. If race is a mile or more select the horse with the highest speed rating earned in any of its last seven races. Scan the horse's last seven races, pick out the highest speed rating and mark it down near the animal's name. If the horse shows less than seven races, just choose its highest speed rating earned. Then select the horse with the highest speed rating.

The 6th race at Gulfstream on March 18 is a good example to illustrate rule 8. The *Morning Telegraph* chose as its Consensus selections, All At Once, Charier and Good Tune in that order.

Good Tune was eliminated because it did not show sufficient 90 or
more speed ratings, nor did it have the necessary in-the-money
efforts of 50% or better in its chart.

All At Once showed more places than wins. It looked like Charier
might be the choice. Today's race was a claimer for $10,000.
Charier's last race was a starter's allowance for horses that had
run for $7,500. The horse's penultimate race was an allowance. It's
next race was at a $10,000 claiming price. This was the race we
were looking for. Since today's race was also a $10,000 claimer the
horse was still qualified. But we still had to look further for its next
claiming race.

This race showed a $12,000 claiming price. Since Charier had
dropped from a $12,000 claimer to a $10,000 one we could do
nothing more than pass it by. The reader must watch and remember
this rule, or he may select animals that are not qualified.

To make matters clearer it is imperative to take at least one case
and show how the selection was made. For an example, let's take
the 7th race at Hialeah on March 2, 1955. The Consensus picked
Social Outcast, Stan, and Maharajah. Since it was the 7th race,
there was no concern about the size of the field.

The best thing to do first was to make sure that the horses showed
at least three speed ratings of 90 or more. Maharajah was the
only horse that did not meet this prerequisite so he was eliminated.
All other races for Stan and Social Outcast showed speed ratings
greater than 65. So far both were good. Stan showed six in-the-
money efforts out of 11 in its chart, more than 50%. There were
ten races listed in its past performances, four winners and two
shows. Stan was okay so far. Social Outcast showed 13 in-the-
money efforts out of 16 in its charts, and out of ten races in its
past performances there were six wins, two 3rds and one place,
more than ample to meet our requirements.

Neither of the two horses had won their last three races. The
race today was an allowance, so there was no concern about the
claiming race rule. Both Stan and Social Outcast were five years
old, meeting our age requirement. Stan, although he raced last on
February 19, 1955, showed a workout on the day before the race.
Social Outcast won on February 25 and the 5th of February, 1955.

It also showed a workout on March 1, the day before the race.

WORKOUT: *Combing the Consensus*

(Hialeah-Gulfstream, March 1955)

Date		Race & Track	Horse	Win	Place	Show
March	1	6 Hia.	Simmy	7.10	6.20	4.50
		7 Hia.	Hickory Hill	8.00	4.00	3.20
	2	6 Hia.	Sailor	3.10	2.90	2.70
		7 Hia.	Stan	16.90	8.90	5.70
	5	4 Gulf.	Yock Tom	8.40	3.50	2.60
	9	7 Gulf.	Nance's Lad	11.80	5.70	4.40
	11	6 Gulf.	The Genius	2.90	2.70	2.50
	8	6 Gulf.	Gandharva	7.90	3.80	3.00
	12	7 Gulf.	Fly Wheel	4.60	2.70	2.50
	16	7 Gulf.	Nance's Lad	5.00	3.50	3.30
	19	6 Gulf.	Simmy	3.20	2.70	2.70
		Amount returned		$78.90	46.60	37.10
		Amount invested		22.00	22.00	22.00
		Profit on $2 wagers		$56.90	24.60	15.10

Both horses were tied. Today's distance was at 1½ miles. Neither of the animals showed such a distance (even though we were interested in a winning race) in their past performances, therefore, we had to use the tie-breaking rule. Out of its last seven races, Stan showed a high speed rating of 94, while Social Outcast produced 93. Stan was our choice.

Consensus Concurrence

Here's a system that's as simple as twiddling your thumbs, yet has possibilities that are almost amazing. The very simplicity of the system should make practically all system fans, as well as other species of race players, curious as to its possibilities. It is based on logical and sound deductions. However, longshot players will not find it appealing, because all play will fall on Best Bets, selections which must of necessity return small mutuel prices.

The beauty of the system lies in its simplicity, as well as ability to maintain a long winning streak. This is especially true in place or show betting. No knowledge of handicapping, or even ability to interpret a racing paper is necessary.

As the title of the method implies, the fundamental concept embodies the use of the consensus. Although I used the *Morning Telegraph* consensus to start with, any consensus in which five handicappers make their selections maybe used. Please note that at that time there were only five selectors. Now there are six, so that in using this method with the *Morning Telegraph* you would have to discard one selector and determine points as explained later.

Using the *Morning Telegraph,* I first scanned to see what horses had been rated with 30 points or more. In every case this horse will be the Consensus Best Bet at each particular track, but not necessarily the first choice of each selector. The *Morning Telegraph* determines points given to each of the horses listed in the consensus this way: Five points are given for each selector's first choice; 7 points if a horse is a selector's One Best (Best Bet) at the particular track; 2 points are given if the horse is a selector's second choice; and 1 point if it is chosen for third. It is possible for a horse to obtain the maximum of 35 points. This will occur when the animal is picked by all the selectors as their One Best Bet.

Rarely does it happen that a horse rated 30 points or more is not the first choice of all the selectors. If you will check closely, you will see that it *can* happen. For instance, if four of the selectors were to pick the horse as their One Best (Best Bet) the horse would get 28 points, and if the fifth selector only chose the animal for second, adding two more points to its total, the animal would receive exactly 30 points.

But 30 points or more is not the only prerequisite of our system. We must insist that the animal be chosen by all selectors as their first choice. In other words, we want 100% selector concurrence, not just a general agreement. To strengthen the method we will insist on still further evidence of unanimous approval by using another consensus. In fact it is not necessary to use the same consensuses employed by the writer. Any two different consensuses may be used.

We will not delve too much into the second consensus. With the second consensus all that will be necessary is that the animal selected in our first consensus be listed also as the first choice there, and that it have a total of 30 or more points. Both consensuses must show concurrence as to the first choice, and both must give the animal 30 or more points. In this way we will be backing the consensus choice of not only five experts but ten.

It would be of even further interest to make the exact stipulation of selector concurrence in the second consensus too, and see what happens. However, this system did not go so far. The *Morning Telegraph* also gives the *Daily Racing Form* consensus, and this is the second consensus that the writer used. If you can get a racing paper, or any newspaper for that matter, that gives more than one consensus viewpoint, it makes things very simple. But if you can't obtain such a paper, the consensus from any other source, such as a scratch sheet, is just as valid.

It is possible that the second consensus the reader intends to use does not give points to the consensus selections. That matter is easily solved by rating the horses exactly as in the *Daily Racing Form* or New York *Morning Telegraph:* seven points if the horse is a selector's Best Bet, five points for first choice, two points for second choice, and one point for third. It would be even more interesting if we could use two consensuses of ten selectors each, with a high point minimum qualification of 60 points. There are many possibilities for further variations, and the system fan should be encouraged to take time out and do some investigation of his own.

RULES: *Consensus Concurrence*

1. Selection must be the first choice of your first consensus with 30 or more points.

2. Must be the first choice of all the selectors in the first consensus.

3. In the second consensus the horse that is our possible selection must be listed as first with 30 or more points.

Although we are not suggesting its use, it is interesting to consider what a $2 *place* parlay on all 15 horses in the workout would return. Betting a minimum of $2 as our initial wager, and disregarding all change, since this cannot be bet at the track, a $2 parlay would have returned $115. A $10 parlay would have netted $575. Of course this type of parlay seems utterly ridiculous, and probably few would have the fortitude to do this. But after all, should the animal fail to place anywhere before the fifteenth bet, the player would have lost only the initial $2, or whatever the starting wager may have been.

There are other elements in this type of play which deserve further investigation. We would like to go into this thing a lot deeper. For instance, what if we were to extend our field of investigation to five or six or even more different consensuses? Would our winning percentage drop or get higher? Would place or show benefit or be harmed by the concurrence of so many selectors? What would be the effect on price? If so many different handicappers, experts in the horse racing business, agree, surely there must be a sound reason. It is when disagreement occurs among the experts that betting becomes haphazard and the race is classified as wide open.

But then the human element has to be considered too. How can we make sure that the animal will be sent to win today? Some stables don't like to win when the odds are very low. These are the stables that usually bet on their own horses. Frequently the selectors are familiar with the situation and for this reason many of them will not choose the horse as their first selections, surely not their Best Bets. However, humans are subject to error, and it may happen that all the selectors will back a horse that is not well meant.

The element of pure luck has to be considered also. The horse may be jostled or may fail to break quickly enough and then find it difficult to get through. This can happen more easily in races with a large number of entries.

Often a good way to make sure our horse is trying is to check the jockey who is riding the animal. If the jockey is the kind that is always trying your risk decreases. If a top-notch jockey is on the animal it is also often a good sign.

In the bigger races, where considerable money is to be won, all horses are usually trying. Of course there are exceptions here too. There are times when a horse is put in over its head so that it will show a poor performance, and then in the next race, or the one after, is entered where it can win, and often does, at a nice price. In many of the big money races the stable has to put up a substantial amount of money as an entry fee. It would be foolish to throw away this money in such a race. So if the race is one where the stable must deposit a substantial entry fee, it is obviously a good bet that the horse will be sent to win.

We've often wondered whether the number of horses in the field would have an effect on winning percentages. Decreasing the number of contestants seems to augur well for any system, as far as winning percentages are concerned. It seems logical to conclude that a horse should stand a better chance of winning in a field of six than in a field of twelve. But then again how would the smaller field affect price? In a small field a solid favorite usually goes off at very low odds.

Statistics show that the majority of winners come from among the horses that have shown good performances recently. Also more horses that have raced recently are returned winners. Condition seems to be an important factor. Animals that are capable of keeping up with the pace also have better chances. Workouts are important too. Many trainers use the workout as a final test to see whether the animal is ready. Horses showing several workouts before a race should be watched carefully. And then finally there is consistency—the innate ability and desire of an animal to win. An animal with consistency is always to be considered with respect as a possible winner.

There are many angles, all to insure that our horse is well meant and has the best possible chance, that can be incorporated into a system such as the one presented here. Will these additions make the system better? Will they make it worse? Or are the rules sufficiently adequate to maintain a steady profit? Our workout seems to point to profitable returns on the basis of the present system rules alone.

The Selectors' Spot Play System

Of course we all know that to merely follow a selector's or even a consensus' choices, would leave us in the red. But by analyzing the selections better results can be obtained.

Taking into consideration only those horses that were listed as one of the three choices of all selectors in the consensus the feeling persisted that something worthwhile could materialize. After all, if this horse was picked to come in on top, among the first three, by all five selectors, there must be something to the animal.

These selectors are experts in the racing game, and years of con-

WORKOUT: *Consensus Concurrence*

(May 1952)

Date	Horse	Race & Track	Win	Place	Show
1	Seaward	7 C.D.	3.20	2.80	2.40
2	Real Delight	7 C.D.	3.00	2.80	2.60
3	Squared Away	7 Bel.	3.70	2.90	2.60
	Pictus	7 Suf.	2.40	2.60	2.20
8	Occupatic	6 Suf.	3.80	2.60	2.40
10	Spartan Valor	7 G.S.	2.60	2.40	Out
14	Suggested	6 Pim.	....	2.20	2.20
15	Thasian Hero	7 Pim.	5.20	3.80	2.40
20	Porter's Broom	5 L.F.	3.60	2.80	2.40
23	Eddie Sue	5 Suf.	3.00	2.40	2.20
24	Real Delight	6 Bel.	2.60	2.50	2.30
27	Larry Ellis	7 Suf.	3.80	2.40	2.20
28	Tahitian King	6 Bel.	2.70	2.20	2.10
30	Basis	4 Suf.	5.60	3.60	2.60
	Suggested	6 Del.	....	2.70	2.30

15 selections win and place—14 selections show
13 won—86⅔%
15 placed—100%
14 showed—100%

Amount Returned	$45.20	$40.70	$32.90
Amount Invested	30.00	30.00	28.00
Profit	$15.20	$10.70	$ 4.90
Profit Across the Board	$30.80		
Profit Across the Board $10 Flat Bets $154.00			

Note the strange coincidence—7 out of the 15 selections were found in the seventh race. All 7 won.

Ed. Note: Note also that the 7th race in most instances was the feature race catering to better grade horses. Possibly this presents another "angle" for Consensus concurrence.

stantly working at this particular task has given them the experience that qualifies them as advisors of specialist capacity. But their capacity as advisors is not sufficient to provide for profitable selection, for were we to choose the horses only on the basis that all the experts have listed them as one of the three top contenders, we would find ourselves losing money.

As a basic starting point, however, these selections are worthwhile. It is absolutely essential for us to do a little investigating of our own. Incorporated with our own efforts the results are sure to be favorable.

First of all, there are certain races which are to be eliminated. Races for maidens, two-year-olds or jumpers are never to be considered.

From past experience, it has been found that horses showing recent workouts are often really being prepared for a win. One of our rules, therefore, will stipulate that the horse we are to select must show a recent workout; in this case within five days of today's race.

We will not risk our money on an animal that has not been racing recently. It is better to choose a horse that shows evidence of condition with a fairly recent race under its belt.

To make sure that today's distance is suitable to the animal, we will require as evidence a win or place at such a distance, as shown anywhere in today's list of past performances of the horse.

The animal must show a speed rating of more than 75 in the particular race in which it placed or won. If the horse does not show a speed rating in this qualifying effort, the animal cannot be chosen.

The reason for the speed rating is to prevent the selection of an animal which may have won because of the exceptionally poor quality of the contenders, or perhaps through some strange condition which slowed up the other animals, or merely because the track at that particular time may have been exceedingly slow. We do not want to depend upon an animal that needs certain specific track conditions in order to win a race.

At any rate, we must have a really good animal, and a horse that has demonstrated its ability to win or place at a speed rating over 75 can be considered more confidently than a slower horse, especially when our selections are made only from highly consistent animals.

All our selections must show a win consistency of 20% or better for the current and last year combined. To further insure the success of our prospective wager and to prevent lack of form, we will in addition insist that our horse show a winning and placing effort within two weeks of today's race.

All these factors should make for a sound, logical selection method. Although permitting the selection of horses that have already repeated a winning effort, we cannot take any further chances. Therefore, a horse that has won its last three races is to be ignored and cannot possibly become a play. There are rare times when an animal will win four, five or six successive races, but this is the exception rather than the rule. Play safe by avoiding such extra risks.

RULES: *Selectors' Spot Play System*

Now let us assemble our rules so that we can see exactly what we have:

1. Look for those horses that are listed as either first, second, or third choices of all the selectors in the consensus.

2. The horse must show a workout within five days of today's race.

3. The horse's last race must have been not more than eight days ago.

4. The horse must show a win consistency for the current and last year combined of 20% or better.

5. The animal must show a win or place at today's distance somewhere in today's list of past performances. The speed rating of this race must be more than 75. If there is no speed rating, the qualifying race is not to be considered.

6. The animal must have won or finished second in a race at any distance not more than two weeks ago (fourteen days).

7. Do not play any horse that has already won its last three races.

8. Play no maidens, two-year-olds or jumpers.

9. In case of tie choose the horse with the highest last speed rating. (Speed rating earned in the horse's last race where one is shown—not necessarily the last race run.)

Although the workout was based on the selections in the *Daily Racing Form,* any consensus can be used. The consensus in the *Morning Telegraph* or even a newspaper is sufficiently valid as a basic selecting point. Remember, however, that you do need a racing paper in order to check the other rules.

The rules in themselves are fairly simple, and it should be an easy task to ferret out the plays for the day. The selections are few and ideal for the bettor who likes to make an occasional wager.

For those horse fans who prefer more action, it is advisable to put together a number of similarly easy systems and in this way compile the number of plays they would like to make. As a rule, good things do not occur too frequently and so to those people who have the necessary patience often go the greater rewards.

If the reader will examine the rules carefully, he will notice that they are sound and logical and have been prudently thought out.

Some system fans may look at the nine rules and feel that they are being kidded about the system's simplicity. They might even suggest that it is no simpler than other systems that are based on selectors' choices.

However, let me point out the main reason for determining that this method is unquestionably easy to work, with comparatively very little time for calculation needed. Remember that only those horses chosen as one of their first three by all the selectors are ever examined. The other horses in the race are not consulted at all. The time consumed in examining every single horse in the race is what makes the average system so arduous. To demonstrate further, let's take a specific example and see how the selection was made.

On July 6, 1951, we opened our *Daily Racing Form* to the Consensus page. By checking the Graded Handicaps we find that the third race at Aqueduct is a Hurdle event. This race is crossed out on the Consensus page.

The fourth is for two-year-olds and the eighth has been prepared for maidens. We cross these races out too.

At Monmouth the first and second races are for maidens and the fourth is for two-year-olds. (The first is also for two-year-olds.) These races are therefore crossed out.

Only the third at Narragansett is eliminated, since it is a two-year-old race.

At Charles Town we find the first race to be for two-year-olds and it is eliminated.

The second and third races at Arlington Park are for two-year-olds. (The second is also for maidens.) Both are crossed off.

Of course if there were no graded handicaps we could still determine the type of race by looking at the past performances.

We now get set to start our selecting. The first selection that we come across is Keep Watch in the fifth at Aqueduct. Trackman,

Phar Lap and Sweep pick it as their first choice; Handicap and Analyst choose the horse as their second selection. No other horse qualifies in the race.

Turning to the past performances we find that the mare shows a workout on July 3, three days from today's race. She therefore qualifies on this score, but her last race was on June 21, fifteen days ago, much longer than our time lapse of eight days permits. Keep Watch is disqualified from further consideration and we go on to the next race looking for a play.

In the sixth race we find three possibilities as far as our initial rule is concerned. All of them meet the workout prerequisite, but only Thwarted qualifies under the lapse rule, having run his last race on June 30th, six days ago. The gelding also qualifies for consistency with ten wins out of 38 for both years. Since today's race is at $1\frac{1}{16}$ the animal is tripped up, for it shows no win or place at today's distance in its past performances.

In this way we go on checking and eliminating horses until we reach the sixth at Arlington Park, where our only selection for the day is made in Miss Highbrow.

The horse was picked by all but one selector for second. Phar

WORKOUT: *Selectors' Spot Play System*

Date	Horse	Race & Track	Win	Place	Show
July 3	Flushing Sam	6 Mth.	7.80	3.80	3.00
4	Tarport Kid	4 Mth.	7.60	3.40	2.80
	Volcanic	7 A.P.	....	4.20	3.40
6	Miss Highbrow	6 A.P.	11.60	6.20	4.20
7	Riverlane	7 Aqu.	....	....	3.10
	Sagittarius	7 Nar.	7.20	4.20	2.60
10	Shadow's Start	6 Nar.	3.40	2.60	2.20
13	Directoire	6 Mth.	4.60	3.40	2.60
14	Navy Flash	2 Aqu.	....	4.60	3.40
18	Eagle Eye	5 Mth.	....	....	....
20	Ballydam	6 A.P.	5.60	3.20	2.60
27	Joey Boy	7 Mth.	6.00	2.80	2.80
31	Riverlane	7 Sar.	5.20	2.60	2.20

69% Won—85% Placed—92% Showed

Amount Returned	$59.00	$41.00	$34.90
Amount Invested	$26.00	$26.00	$26.00
Profit	$33.00	$15.00	$8.90

Lap selected the animal as his first choice. No other horse qualified on Rule 1 for this race. Miss Highbrow showed a workout on the previous day; had raced last six days ago; had won seven of its twenty-two races for the current and last year combined for a percentage of better than .31; and had won at today's distance on February 14, 1951, as shown in her today's list of past performances, with a speed rating of 89. The filly had also won on June 25, eleven days ago.

The animal met requirements of both rules five and six. The horse had lost its last race and therefore it was not necessary to be concerned with the seventh rule. A definite selection, Miss Highbrow went on to win the race paying $11.60; $6.20; $4.20 across the board.

2.
MAKING PROFITS
FROM CONSISTENT HORSES

"Money makes money!" "Success breeds success!" These two classic expressions have been worn threadbare with use but they remain as true today as when coined by some ancient philosopher.

"Like begets like," could be added, and the formula for breeding the thoroughbred horse would be brought into the discussion. Breeders have believed in this for so long that it has advanced from theory to theorem.

Isn't there a simple pattern that bettors might follow?

There is: *Winners beget winners.*

Horses that have shown by past efforts that they can win are the same ones that win in the future. Horses that have consistently been in the money in the past are the betting implements of the days to come.

It is difficult to find a reasonable argument for betting on any horse that has not already shown ability and inclination to produce. It is true that about one-fourth of all the horses win 60% of all the races. Why then should any player bother with the unsuccessful, the inconsistent, and the disappointers?

Thus argue the advocates of consistency. Here are two systems that prove this point.

Playing Reliable Runners

Every method of playing the races is developed on the premise that events of the past will be substantially duplicated in the future. It is impossible to predict when a horse that has won once in fifty starts will win again and it is fallacious to wager on any such animal. But a horse that has established a record of many wins and money efforts is a sound animal to tie to.

Therefore, to be eligible for system play a horse must boast a record that shows frequent wins, backed up by a good percentage of times in the money.

A horse of this type which has been racing well in the recent past is always worth consideration. A system which brings up such horses for play is founded on logic.

The method described herein requires the horse to be a proven winner as well as one that gets into the money notches with considerable frequency.

If the horse is home first 20% of the time, it is getting something more than its share of the purses. That's the consistency requirement.

Also it must have raced recently and have shown a good race among its late starts.

RULES: *Playing Reliable Runners*

1. Horse must have won 20% or more of its races during the current and last year combined.

2. Horse must show at least two wins, current and last year combined.

3. Horse must have raced within eight days of today's event.

4. Horse must have finished first, second or third in either (or both) of its last two races.

5. In case of tie, play the horse with the highest percentage of wins, current and last year combined. If still tied, play the horse which won by the greatest number of lengths last time out, or, if neither horse being considered won, the horse which finished nearest to the winner in number of lengths. In the latter case finish position does not count. The number of lengths behind the winner is the determining factor. Thus, a horse which finished third by one length would be the play over a horse that finished second by two lengths.

6. Play no horse coming from a minor track and racing its first time on a major oval.

7. Play no jumpers or two-year-olds.

8. Selections are made after scratches are known.

Play the Best Horse

When a player handicaps a race and selects his choice to win, it is in his opinion the best horse in the race. His conclusion is often erroneous because his method of handicapping is not sound, or perhaps he is playing a race where three or more horses have equal chances of winning. Your method of selection must be sound and logical in order to make wagering profitable.

But what is sound or logical?

If we could pick the best horse in the race every time, discounting racing luck, our percentage of winners would be high and our profits enormous. But the question again arises, "How can we tell whether or not a horse is best?" Well, suppose our horse raced only very recently, say not more than six days ago, and it won that race or came in second? Today the horse is running at the same distance as its last race and its *Daily Racing Form* speed rating is at least two points higher than that of any other contender in its most recent race at today's distance. The speed ratings in the *Daily Racing Form* are excellent estimate of a horse's speed. The vast majority of winners come from among the horses carrying one of the top five speed rates. If a horse shows a two point higher speed rating, it is equivalent to being able to finish two lengths ahead. To further vindicate our trust in this animal, it must show by its past performances that it consistently runs "in-the-money." About 50% in-the-money consistency for the current and previous year combined is a good average.

Now do you see how our animal is shaping up? It is fresh and ready, having run not more than six days ago in a race where it won or came in second. Today it is running back at the same distance and the horse shows that it is faster currently than any other competitor in the race. Our animal also has a record for consistently being "in-the-money."

Here are the condensed rules formulated into a method of selection. Follow them without deviation.

RULES: *Play the Best Horse*

1. First eliminate all horses that do not show at least one race at the present distance within 90 days of today's event. Such horses are considered as if they were not running in the race at all.

2. Of all the horses left our horse must show:

a. its last race not more than six days ago at the present distance;

b. a first or second in its last race;

c. a 50% in-the-money consistency for the current and last year combined with one race leeway if ten or more races were run during this period. (For example, if the horse had run 13 races for the current and last year combined and came in-the-money only six times, it would still qualify, since one more in-the-money effort would yield the 50% necessary consistency.)

d. a speed rating at least two points higher in its last race than any other horse (that has not been eliminated under rule 1) made in its most recent race at today's distance.

3. Play no maidens, jumpers, or two-year-olds.

When you select an animal with all these qualifications, you can feel safe in assuming that you are backing the best horse. Of course, due to racing luck and other vicissitudes that flesh and blood creatures are subject to, our animal may not always win. Following these rules, however, will give you a best bet more reliable and consistent in winning power than any given by professional selectors. At the same time you will get a much better average price.

3.
WHEN TO PLAY A PLATER DROPPED DOWN IN PRICE

When a horse is placed against opposition inferior to that which it has recently been facing, it is reasonable to conclude that the animal will perform more productively. Serious bettors look for such situations and take advantage of them.

The problem remains, however, to determine with accuracy when a horse is actually being dropped in class.

In claiming races, the entered price is a fairly reliable guide. If the horse has raced fairly successfully at one price level and is then asked to compete at a lower scale, apparently it is being dropped in class.

It is no new idea to build a method of play around horses that are "moving down," but it is an idea based on the soundest of logic. When certain restrictions of performance are added, a useful and profitable plan may result.

With these facts as a basis of work, the following systems were devised.

Class Drop Method

When only claiming races are played, and if the past performances of the horse show that it is being entered at a price at least $500 lower than its last two races, we can usually conclude that the animal is being dropped in class. Frequently a trainer will move his horse up in a race or two and then drop it back to the correct level. If he has an animal with a good in-the-money consistency record, he will frequently succeed in winning a race, and perhaps a bet.

The selection method to be presented here is based on just such an animal.

Several important factors must first be considered in order for the method to be worthwhile. When an animal shows at least 33⅓% win plus place consistency for the current and last year combined it is a reliable betting tool. However, the animal must not be a maiden, a horse that engages in jumping races of any kind, and not a two-year-old, since a juvenile could not have raced last year. Also we must discard any horse that has not won a race either this year or last because, for our purposes, such an animal is not much better than a maiden.

We are now almost ready to start our method rolling, but we must provide for one further restriction to make sure that our selection is well placed. This one can quickly and easily be found by looking over the past performances.

If a horse qualifying for consistency shows definitely that its claiming price is at least $500 or more lower today than in its last two races, he is retained for play. If one of the animal's last two races was an allowance race or a handicap or anything else but a claimer at a price at least $500 more than it is being entered for today, eliminate it.

This method will pick selections at all kinds of prices, and every so often a big-priced one will come along. Profits, in the workout checked, came along steadily because of this factor.

Most good systems in which the losing streaks are not too long must pick some horses at good prices, since more win at shorter mutuels than at long ones. The longshots come along with sufficient regularity here to keep the game interesting.

I checked this method last year with scattered racing forms ranging from May through September, and also some in December. Results were excellent. From what they showed, together with the workout presented herewith, it seems reasonable to assume that this method has great possibilities.

Not only is a profit from win betting shown, but place betting also proved profitable. The workout, therefore, includes the place mutuel to demonstrate what can be expected from this play.

RULES: *Class Drop Method*

1. Play claiming races only.

2. The horse must have raced within ten days.

3. The horse must show a drop in claiming price of $500 or more from its last two races. The last two races must be claimers or the horse cannot be considered.

4. The horse must show either 33⅓% win plus place consistency or 40% in-the-money consistency for the current and last year combined.

5. Play no maidens, jump horses, two-year-olds, or horses that have not won a race last year or this year.

6. In case more than one qualify, play the horse with the best in-the-money consistency for the current and last year combined.

WORKOUT: *Class Drop Method*

(July 1948)

Date	Horse	Track and Race	Win	Place
July 1	Happy All	2 Aqu.	8.70	3.80
	Speed Bird	7 Mth.	—	—
	I Did	8 Mth.	—	3.60
	Impenetrable	8 Nar.	10.20	5.80
	Vinita Sickle	1 A.P.	—	—
July 2	Oatmeal	7 Aqu.	—	—
	Chrys-Doll	2 Mth.	15.80	9.80
	Bullsel	5 A.P.	—	—
July 3	Layaway	1 Del.	—	—
	Cinch	4 Del.	—	—
	Gerham	4 Nar.	—	—
	Big Casino	1 A.P.	26.00	7.60
July 5	Thor	8 Aqu.	10.00	5.40
	Black Tempest	1 Mth.	—	—
	Glory Girl	2 Mth.	10.60	5.80
	Busyridge	2 Nar.	—	—
	Daffydine	8 Nar.	—	—
	Command	9 A.P.	—	—
July 6	Happy West	4 Aqu.	—	—
	Vinita Ed	4 Mth.	—	—
	Sala Lou	5 A.P.	—	—
	Rose Light	6 A.P.	—	—
	Royal Risk	8 A.P.	4.00	3.20

Date	Horse	Track and Race	Win	Place
July 7	Cuban Bill	2 HdG.	—	—
	Don O'Sullivan	8 HdG.	—	—
July 8	Sudden Scare	4 Aqu.	4.40	3.60
	Sweepstake	7 Aqu.	—	—
	Empty Noose	8 Aqu.	—	—
	Plane Shadow	6 Mth.	—	4.80
	Palist	8 Mth.	—	—
	Tick Tack	7 Nar.	—	—
	Aldridge	8 Nar.	—	6.40
July 9	Quelle Belle	2 Aqu.	6.60	3.40
	Roman Runner	3 Aqu.	—	14.10
	Sweet Pegotty	8 Aqu.	—	—
	Soma Lad	2 HdG.	—	—
	Brevrome	7 HdG.	—	3.60
	Arthoa	5 Nar.	—	9.60
	Apropiado	7 Nar.	—	—
July 10	Greek Hero	1 Aqu.	—	3.10
	Kazbek	8 Aqu.	—	—
	Heaven Hill	1 HdG.	—	—
	Salford II	8 Mth.	—	12.40
	War Delegate	4 Nar.	—	3.00
July 12	Flaminian Way	8 Aqu.	—	—
	Cock Feather	5 HdG.	8.00	4.00
	Flag O' Peace	3 Mth.	—	—
	Kid Caution	4 Mth.	—	—
	Highway Fifty	1 Suf.	—	—
	Lunch Date	3 Suf.	—	—
	Big Party	4 Suf.	—	—
	War Atlas	8 A.P.	—	—
July 13	Bellclapper	1 HdG.	—	—
	Night Strike	4 HdG.	—	4.00
	Grey Hood	6 HdG.	5.40	3.80
	Head Show	1 Mth.	8.80	4.80
	Kenplay	2 Mth.	—	—
	Apropiado	5 Suf.	11.60	6.00
	Granizo	7 Suf.	—	8.40
July 14	Lucky Hit	8 Aqu.	—	5.30
	Flash Up	7 HdG.	—	—
	Subdue	8 Mth.	—	—
	Sly Tigress	1 A.P.	—	—
	Command	2 A.P.	—	—
	Sunnip	4 A.P.	7.20	3.60
July 15	Hi Pi	1 HdG.	6.80	4.20
	Lady Pam	7 HdG.	9.80	5.00
	Rough Ordy	8 HdG.	7.20	4.40

Date	Horse	Track and Race	Win	Place
	Vinita Ed	6 Mth.	—	—
	Blenweed	2 Suf.	5.20	3.20
	Equate	8 A.P.	6.20	3.40
July 16	Reno Ultimate	7 HdG.	22.20	8.40
	Frisk	1 Mth.	—	5.00
	Night Bomber	8 Suf.	—	—
	Poppa George	2 A.P.	—	—
July 17	Buck Ash	7 Mth.	—	—
	Broadway Daylight	8 Mth.	—	—
	Know How	1 Suf.	9.20	3.80
	Mary Like	1 A.P.	—	—
	Duckberry	2 A.P.	—	—
July 19	Gary Leslie	2 Sar.	5.50	2.80
	Maidez	3 Sar.	12.60	5.60
	Mighty Master	6 Sar.	—	4.60
	Alpine Astarte	7 Sar.	63.90	19.10
	Expendable	2 Mth.	—	—
	Hiya Pop	7 Mth.	—	—
	Speedee Bozo	3 Suf.	—	—
	Gus G.	2 A.P.	7.20	3.80
	Fighting Pete	8 A.P.	—	—
July 20	Isigny	7 Sar.	—	—
	Shaffie	1 Suf.	14.60	8.80
	Camolino	2 Suf.	—	—
	Farfalina	8 Suf.	—	—
	Vesuvio	4 A.P.	74.20	24.60
July 21	Dauntless Gal	1 Sar.	7.50	5.00
	Flying Tartar	3 Sar.	—	—
	Brest	7 Mth.	—	—
	Broad Daylight	8 Mth.	—	—
	Daffydine	8 Suf.	—	—
	Duckberry	1 A.P.	—	—
	Beneva	2 A.P.	—	—
	Bolus	8 A.P.	—	3.80
July 22	Dusty Days	7 Mth.	—	—
	Gremlin	8 Mth.	—	—
	Valdina Greedy	2 Suf.	—	—
	J. J. Lynch	7 Suf.	8.40	5.00
	Happy Joan	1 A.P.	—	—
July 23	Perhaps	1 Suf.	—	—
	Jimjoe	8 Suf.	—	—
July 24	Parhelion	2 Sar.	—	—
	Sason	2 Suf.	—	—
	Longhorn	1 A.P.	—	3.40

Date	Horse	Track and Race	Win	Place
July 26	Hiya Pop	1 Mth.	—	—
	Hadawin	4 Mth.	—	—
	Larry D.	8 Mth.	—	6.20
	Marksman	3 Suf.	—	—
	Sandslinger	8 A.P.	—	—
July 27	No Selections			
July 28	Friendly Don	2 Sar.	—	5.60
	Attendant	6 Mth.	5.80	4.00
	Cid Play	4 A.P.	—	—
	Quilt	8 A.P.	—	5.40
July 29	Impenetrable	8 Mth.	—	7.80
	Staters	4 A.P.	—	—
	Kelspride	8 Suf.	—	—
July 30	Ventolino	3 Sar.	8.30	3.70
	Isigny	7 Sar.	4.50	3.00
	Dusty Days	7 Mth.	7.40	4.00
	Thunder Hoof	5 A.P.	—	—
July 31	Copacabana	4 Sar.	—	7.40
	Chanteuse	7 Sar.	—	—
	Even Break	4 Mth.	4.20	3.60
	Silver Kite	3 Suf.	—	—

SUMMARY

Number of Win Selections ..	132	Return—$2 flat bets	$428.00
Number Won	34	Invested—$2 flat bets	264.00
Win percentage	26%	Profit	$164.00
Number of Place Selection ..	132	Return—$2 flat bets	$323.50
Number placed	55	Invested—$2 flat bets	264.00
Place Percentage	42%	Profit	$ 59.50

Double Drop-Downs

There is nothing more reliable than a properly dropped-down horse that is really being sent to win. Especially is this true when the animal can demonstrate an excellent race at a claiming price higher than the one it is entered for today. By "excellent" is meant a winning or at least a placing effort.

Horses that show they have been in contention with higher grade animals, and have either placed or won in these events should be watched carefully.

When such an animal not only shows a drop from its last race, but is being entered at a price lower than its last two races, the wary bettor stops for further investigation. This animal may be either a prospective winner or a horse that has gone bad.

When a horse becomes incapacitated through illness or accident, it often cannot recover sufficiently to cope with animals of its usual class. This frequently can be seen by the exceptionally bad races run at claiming prices at which ordinarily the animal would perform well.

Unfortunately, this type of animal raises serious questions in the trainer's mind. Either the animal must be lowered in class to try to obtain a win, or an attempt must be made to get rid of it. The trainer watches carefully, and if he sees a good spot he "lowers the boom." Who will be hurt by this depends on the animal's physical shape at the moment. If dropped in class sufficiently and if the animal's health is not impaired too much, the horse stands a good chance of winning. But if the animal is beyond repair, the trainer can only hope, pray, and anticipate that the horse will be claimed.

Now there are other spots where deliberate efforts have been made to place the animal among horses it figures to handle. These spots are usually found after a week or two of racing at the present track. At the beginning of the meet it is more difficult to classify an animal. A $3000 claimer at Saratoga may not be equivalent to a $3000 claimer at Rockingham.

The trainer has to probe carefully into this class element.

Only after seeing the horses run for a time can he even consider the claiming price at which his animal can be favorably spotted. When the trainer discovers that he can win without risking the loss of his horse by dropping his animal in claiming price, he will send the animal out trying.

Most of the danger surrounding dropped down horses lies in the question of legitimacy. Is the horse really being dropped in class? Often a horse will be raised in class and then dropped down where it really belongs. It is easier to determine that the animal is actually being dropped if it is lowered off its last two races, rather than the last one only. Then again if the horse shows a win or place at a higher claiming price than today's race, we can figure that the animal is definitely being dropped.

When working with class in claimers it is difficult to apply any other types of races for evaluation. It is best to stick to claiming races only in determining whether the animal is being dropped, or whether the qualifying winning or placing race is of higher denomination. So if the horse shows even one of its last two races at an allowance or handicap, or any race other than a claimer, it cannot be considered.

In the workout at Rockingham Park play was started some time after the meet was under way. Only on the 12th and 21st were there no winners. If the reader will check the workout he will notice that only with the exception of these two dates winners occurred day after day. Such results cannot help but make anyone playing the method feel chipper.

Although it is probably best to make a stringent rule concerning the qualifying win or place race, it is difficult to designate such a dogmatic prerequisite when the distance of today's race is not a popular one. The ¾-mile, $1\frac{1}{16}$-, and 1⅛-mile races predominate.

If the race today was at ⅞, one mile, one mile and 70 yards, or any other similar odd distance not run too frequently, it would be extremely hard to discover a winning or placing qualifying race at exactly this distance. It would seem logical, therefore, to make an exception with these distances. For ¾, $1\frac{1}{16}$ and 1⅛ miles we will be strict and demand a win or place qualifying race at exactly today's distance. For all other distances, a win or place at a distance within ⅛ of a mile (furlong) will be permissible to determine qualification.

If this rule were not inserted, we would rarely get a selection in the odd-distance races, and such events would usually be passed over without a play. For purposes of getting sufficient action, it is necessary to deviate from strict rules and make an exception where these unpopular distances appear.

RULES: *Double Drop-Downs*

1. Play claiming races only.
2. The horse's last race must not have been more than two months ago.
3. The horse must be dropping in claiming price from its last two races. The last two races must be listed at a higher price than

the horse is entered for today. The horse's last two races must have been claimers.

4. If today's race is at ¾, 1¹⁄₁₆, or 1⅛, the horse must show a win or place at exactly the same distance as today's race and at a claiming price higher than the amount entered for today. If today's race is at any other distance, the winning or placing race at a higher price than entered for today, must be within ⅛ of a mile (one furlong) of today's distance.

5. In case of tie choose the horse with the highest qualifying winning or placing race. If still tied, play the best win consistency for the current and last year combined. If there is still a tie, play the horse that raced most recently.

6. Play after scratches are known.

7. Play no maidens, two-year-olds or jumpers.

This method of play is comparatively easy to follow. The rules are not too complicated. There are only seven rules including the tie-breaker, the suggestion to play after scratches, and the elimination of jumpers, maidens and two-year-olds. Actually there are only four important rules to be concerned with.

4.
BEATING 'EM
WITH BEST BETS

Nearly all horse bettors would like to obtain a high percentage of winners. Many refuse to back chalk, while others play nothing else but. It's tough to buck the mutuels and try to get all decent payoffs, at the same time clicking with frequent winners. Playing the Best Bets as given in the Consensus of a racing paper will certainly return a significant percentage of horses that reach the finish line first, but the prices will be so small that no profit is made. Of course if you know how to sort these Best Bets you may manage to increase your percentage. This is one way of beating the races with Best Bets.

Another, and necessarily more difficult, method is to produce your own Best Bets. If you can do this and come up with horses that are not mentioned in the racing papers as Best Bets, or Consensus first choices, you're bound to obtain a substantial return. Especially is this true if you can meet the percentage of winners returned by Consensus Best Bets like those chosen by the *Daily Racing Form* or the *Morning Telegraph*. These papers have displayed about a 40% winning average for their Best Bet selections, year in, year out.

If you can beat this 40% average, using the racing papers' selections, you're guaranteed to stay ahead. Making your own Best Bets at a similar or better percentage should do even better.

The two methods that follow will show you how.

Best Bet Standout System

In the August, 1948, issue of *American Turf Monthly* I contributed an article called "The Consensus Standout System," which was based on using the top consensus rating (32 points) in the *National Racing Program,* a New York scratch sheet. A few weeks after that issue hit the stands, the *National Racing Program* stopped giving its top consensus horses 32 points, lowering it to 30. I was not aware of this until I started receiving mail which either accused me of malice aforethought or bluntly pointed out what had actually occurred. If the reader will check he will see clearly that the rating of 32 points top was being used up to the latter part of July, 1948. *American Turf* had its August issue on the stands during the early part of July.

Since a thing like this could happen, I determined to try to develop a best bet system that would have about the same terrifically high percentage (77% won, 87% placed, 97% showed in the Consensus Standout System workout) and would not depend on the whims of scratch sheets that are subject to revision.

The *Daily Racing Form* has been using its present method of computing its speed ratings for a long time now and I do not think they will suddenly revise it. However, even if this should happen, you could still play the method to be presented here because it depends on factors which can only be changed if the *Racing Form's* speed ratings are dropped entirely.

The best bets in the Consensus of the *Daily Racing Form* have maintained year in and year out approximately 40% winners. Recognizing this fact, I determined to use this as my starting point. With some tightening rules added, making provisions that will show our horse to be in form and easily the fastest horse currently at today's distance, we should increase the winning percentage. Also, we do not want a horse that is excessively weighted, especially if it is not accustomed to carrying high weight. With these restrictions, the method should ring up a high percentage of winners.

RULES: *Best Bet Standout System*

1. The horse must be a Consensus Best Bet of the *Daily Racing Form.*

2. The horse's last race must have been run not more than eight days ago.

3. The horse must have won or placed in its last race, which must have been at exactly the same distance as today's race.

4. The horse may carry weight as high as 115 pounds today, but if it is carrying 116 pounds or more, this weight must not exceed the weight carried in its last race by more than five pounds. For example, suppose the horse is carrying 117 pounds today. This weight is over our 115 pound limit, therefore we would have to see how much the horse carried in its last race. If it carried 112 or more, it would qualify. However, if it carried 111 or less last time out, the horse would not be considered. Our weight limit, if the horse is carrying 116 pounds or more today, is five pounds more than the weight carried in its last race.

5. The horse's speed rating in its last race must be at least two points higher than any other horse's latest speed rating at today's distance.

To clarify the rules we'll take a couple of plays and see how they were chosen or eliminated. Refer to the Workout of Results on page 41.

On July 15, 1948, Flicka Foot in the 4th at Havre de Grace was a consensus best bet. Her last race was run eight days ago at exactly the same distance, 5½ furlongs, and she won that race. Her weight today was not excessive, only 114 pounds. (Since this weight was under 115 pounds it was not necessary to see how much the horse carried in its last race). Her speed rating last time out was 79, two points higher than any most recent speed rating at 5½ furlongs of any horse in the race. Flicka Foot qualified completely and became Best Bet Standout selection. She won and paid $4.80, $3.00, $2.60.

Landlord was a consensus best bet in the 7th at Saratoga on July 21, 1948. He had finished second in his last race at the same distance as today, five days ago. Landlord was easily the best as far as most recent speed rating at today's distance was concerned, with 86. Pharalus was closest to Landlord with a speed rating of 82. However, the final test was the weight carried in this race by Landlord. He was carrying 121 pounds, and since this was much over our weight limit of 115 pounds, we had to ascertain whether it was excessive by looking at the poundage Landlord carried last time out. Landlord had lugged only 114 pounds in his last race, and since today's weight of 121 was seven pounds more, he was eliminated as a selection. Landlord lost the race, finishing 3rd.

When I checked the month of July, 1948, I became more and more enthusiastic, as winner after winner popped in. At the end of July, I looked at the results with gratification: 75% had won, 91% had placed, 100% had shown. This is nothing to sneeze at even though they paid low prices. There is a feeling of inner security when you lay down your bet and know that your chances of winning are so great. A guy like Tommy Meade, the well-known plunger, must bet thousands to show on a standout of the type presented here.

I continued to check my *Racing Forms* until at the end of August I ran out of them. There were only three qualified plays in August, but all three of them won, making a percentage total of 100% across the board.

Combining both months, the method showed 80% win, 93% place, 100% show. We had doubled the winning percentage of the *Daily Racing Form* consensus best bet, and that is something.

Luckily, these plays do not come along very often, for if they did, sooner or later many bettors would recognize them. Eventually they would be out-of-line odds-on favorites and even with the high percentage of winners, wagers on them would not be profitable.

WORKOUT: *Best Bet Standout System*

(July and August, 1948)

Date		Horse	Race	Win	Place	Show
July	2	Thwarted	6 Nar.	2.60	2.40	2.20
	3	Bellclapper	8 Del.	...	2.80	2.40
	10	Ample Reward	8 Nar.	...	2.80	2.20
	12	V. P. I. Clef	1 Mth.	5.40	2.60	2.20
	14	Perfect Bahram	6 Suf.	3.20	2.40	2.20
	15	Coronet Star	2 Aqu.	4.60	3.00	2.50
		Flicka Foot	4 HdG.	4.80	3.00	2.60
	20	Cordon	2 Mth.	4.00	3.00	2.40
	21	May First	3 Mth.	3.60	2.40	2.40
	22	Bullish	6 A.P.	3.80	2.60	2.20
	24	Lextown	3 A.P.	3.00	3.00	2.20
	27	Agilant	3 Mth.	...	...	2.20
Aug.	18	Pipette	7 Sar.	4.20	2.90	2.60
	23	Generator	8 Nar.	3.80	2.80	2.80
	25	Fort Mifflin	4 Atl.	3.60	3.00	2.40

15 plays, 12 winners (80%); 14 finished first or second (93%); 15 finished in the money (100%). Net profit on $10 wagers to win only, $83.00; place only, $43.50; show only, $27.50; across-the-board, $154.00.

Super-Fine Bests

It is a known fact that the average bettor suffers needless losses because he places too many wagers. Not all races can be figured to come up with an obvious choice. Most of the cheap races are usually wide open and to handicap such events becomes more a matter of intuition than observation.

If you are willing to listen to most professional advisors on turf betting, you will make as few bets as possible every day. One or two bets a day is often the way of the successful plunger or pro.

The problem of choosing the race on which to place your bet is often difficult to decide. In the method presented here the decision rested on the size of the purse. It is known fact that the races with offerings of large enough purses get the best horses stationed at that particular track. With a good-sized purse to run for, the danger that an animal may not do its best is definitely diminished.

Since we play just the highest purse race of the day, you might think only the short-priced or odds-on-horses would be our choices. Look at the workout and see for yourself.

The fact that the method managed to yield so many excellent prices, and also obtained such a terrific percentage of winners is sufficient to make anyone pause and reflect. Now we do not say that this percentage will be maintained month after month, but any system that can do this even for one month deserves attention.

However, since nothing, it is said, is sure but "death and taxes," our advice to the system fan is to give the method an intense check. The rules are extremely complicated and there is always the danger that the player may omit one of them. To play this method a meticulous mind is an obvious asset.

After some investigation it was discovered that races offering less than a $7500 purse were not as good to wager on as the higher ones. This led to only one conclusion—to play only races carrying a minimum purse of $7500. Races run by two-year-olds, maidens or jumpers were disqualified, since the type of horse running in these races is not so reliable.

Often more than one race qualifies, since they both may be offering the same size purse. In such an event separation rules have been set up to obtain the best type of race to wager on. Only once did we have to play two races on one day. This happened on the 30th, as you can see in the workout below.

There are certain factors that all good handicappers pay attention to when figuring the better races. Speed rates are always important. If a horse consistently earns high speed rates it is a good sign that the animal is not ordinary horseflesh. Just check off the three highest speed rates for all horses, earned in the last race, and see how many winners will come from this group.

Another important attribute is consistency. It may be more advantageous to harp on the win element here alone, but the animals that come in-the-money frequently and are not maidens should certainly not be discounted. A combination of better-than-average wins and in-the-money consistency is ideal.

Money earnings reveal the real quality of the horse. If an animal can produce above ordinary expectations, it is reasonable to assume that it has, to say the least, a bit of class. Watching out for those horses that show ability to cash in on the larger purses is a sound approach to successful wagering.

Recent races show signs that the horse has received the benefits of conditioning through actual competition. Workouts may also be employed for the same reason the workout also points out the trainer's efforts to determine the fitness of the animal.

An animal that has been made the favorite often should also be watched. More frequently than not the public choice will lose. However, the fact that the favorite does win about a third of the time, should be sufficient to mark the animal for observation. When a horse is consistently being made the favorite, chances are that the public knows what it is doing.

If a horse demonstrates that it has come in-the-money in at least two of its last three races it can be assumed that the animal is still capable of making a good try. When a horse stales off, it starts finishing way back. Should the animal suddenly develop infirmities this would also be shown in its past performances.

Trainers will often manipulate to obtain weight advantages. Although the element of weight still remains a comparatively moot question, it should not be ignored. After all, weight is the factor employed by every track handicapper in his effort to bring all the horses to the finish line in a dead-heat.

A good horse ridden by a top jock is always an excellent combination. Of course the jockey can't run for the animal, but a capable boy can do a lot to help it. Some horses will perform better under one jockey than another. It is therefore sound logic to examine the horse's rider.

We all know about horses that are rated Best Bets. The handicapper that selects an animal as his Best Bet for the day does so for good reasons. As a rule, an animal receiving such a rating has superior ability. If the horse should be chosen as a best bet in the consensus this rating means even more.

The analysis of the various factors to determine selection was made primarily because our method is largely based on the points each animal can rack up if it shows qualifications as designated.

RULES: Super-Fine Bests

A. *Selecting the race*

1. Play only the highest purse race of the day (considering all tracks listed in your racing paper today).

2. Purse value of the race must be $7500 or more.

3. Claiming races are not considered, unless the race is an optional claimer and no horses are entered for a claiming price. (It's rare anyway for a claimer to offer a purse of $7500.)

4. If the race turns out to be for two-year-olds, maidens, or jumpers, go to the next highest purse race. If conditions are still the same, go on to the next highest purse race, etc. Remember that the race we finally choose must have a minimum purse value of $7500.

5. If two races or more tie, choose the race with the most horses after scratches. *Exception*—If one race has more than 12 horses and the other less, choose the race with the fewer horses. Never play any race with more than 14 horses running after scratches. If such a race should be the one with the highest purse, go on to the next highest purse race (at least $7500). If still tied, play all races tied.

B. *Qualifying*

1. Select the speed rates earned by each horse in its last race. Put this speed rate next to the horse's name. The three horses with the highest speed rates qualify. If there is a tie for third highest speed rate, look for the horse's most recent winning race and check off the speed rate earned here. The horse with the highest speed rate qualifies. If a horse does not show any winning races in its past performances, eliminate it, provided, of course, that one or more of the other tied horses shows at least one win. If still tied, all such horses are placed on the qualifying list.

2. Horse may also qualify if it shows an average speed rate of 95 or more in its last five races. When qualifying this way the horse must also show at least 33⅓% win consistency for the current and last year combined.

3. Horse may also qualify if at least 80% of its races in today's

list of past performances show speed rates of 90 or over. This is not an average. For example, if a horse shows ten races in its past performances and eight of them are at speed rates of 90 or higher, the horse qualifies, since eight such speed rates out of ten equals 80%. To qualify here, the horse must also show at least 33⅓% win consistency for the current and last year combined.

C. *Point ratings—only for horses that have qualified*

1. Give the horse two points if it shows 20% or more win consistency for the current and last year combined.

2. The horse receives two points if it shows 50% or better in-the-money consistency for the current and last year combined.

3. Give the horse two points if it shows either the largest or second largest earnings for the current and last year combined of all the horses in the race.

4. If the horse has earned $50,000 or more for the current and last year combined, give it one point. Do not give it one point if the animal has already received two points for earning the highest or second highest amount of money of all the horses in the race.

5. Horse gets one point if 80% of its races show speed rates of 90 or higher. Do not give the horse the one point if it qualified under B (2 or 3).

6. Give one point to the qualified horse that shows the most stake races out of its last eight races. Compare only qualified horses for this. In case of tie give all tied one point.

7. If none of the qualifying horses show stake races, select the highest of the horse's three most recent claiming prices. If a horse shows only one or two claiming prices, select the highest. After the highest claiming prices have been determined, choose the horse that showed the highest claiming price. Give it one point. If such an occasion does arise, eliminate the horse or horses that do not show claiming prices. (This is rare.) If a tie still occurs give one point to all tied.

8. Horse gets one point if two of its last three races were in-the-money.

9. Of all horses qualified, give one point to the animal carrying the lowest weight. If tied, give one point to all tied.

10. Of all horses qualified, give one point to the horse that was favorite most often in the last six races. In case of tie, give all tied one point.

11. Of all horses qualified, give one point to the horse that raced most recently. In case of tie, give one point to all tied.

12. Of all horses qualified, give one point to the animal showing the most recent workout. In case of tie, give all horses tied one point.

13. Using today's jockey, scan the races of all qualified horses for a period of not more than four months from today's race. For every race that today's jockey won with the animal during this four-month period, give the horse one point. For every race the jockey placed or showed with the animal give the horse one-half point.

14. Give any qualified horse one point if it was chosen as a Best Bet by any handicapper. Give the horse that was chosen Best Bet in the Consensus two points. (A horse can receive either one or two points here, not both. If it was chosen Best Bet by more than one handicapper, it still can get only one point if it was not a Consensus Best Bet.)

15. Add points. Choose the horse with most points. If still tied, select the horse with the lowest weight, unless all tied are carrying 120 pounds or more. In that case, choose the horse with the best win consistency for the current and last year combined.

D. *Eliminations—If a horse is eliminated, the second-best or third-best, etc., becomes the selection.*

1. Eliminate any horse whose last three speed rates (in last three races) do not total 240 or more, unless the horse won its last race within a month of today's event at the same type of distance (either sprint or route) as today's race. Horse must also have been the favorite in its last race and earned a speed rate of more than 90. Also, weight carried today must not be more than three pounds greater than the weight horse lugged in its last race. *Or* horse must have won its last race more than six days ago at the same track as today and earned a speed rate of 90 or more in its last race. Also jockey today must be the same as in its last race.

2. Eliminate horse if it won its last four races. (A disqualification does not count as a win.)

3. Eliminate any horse that finished more than ten lengths behind the leader in its last race.

4. If at least 80% of Best Times are shown (*Daily Racing Form,* Chicago edition) at today's distance, eliminate the horse that does not show one of the three best times for the distance. If horse is tied for third best it still qualifies. (After scratches.) Ignore this rule if Best Time of our selection was made on a sloppy or muddy track. If, however, our horse is still one of three best even though the time was earned in mud or slop, the best time still counts.

WORKOUT: *Super-Fine Bests*

(All tracks—July 1955)

Date	Horse	Race and Track	Win	Place	Show
1	Alspal	6 A.P.	10.20	5.20	3.40
2	Parlo	6 Del.	4.00	3.00	2.60
4	Bobby Brocato	6 Aqu.	39.40	23.40	14.40
5	Illusionist	6 Aqu.	12.70	4.00	3.30
6	Ballydonnell	7 A.P.	11.80	7.20	5.20
8	Searching	6 Aqu.	4.50	2.60	2.10
9	High Gun	6 Aqu.	3.00	2.40	OUT
11	Insouciant	6 A.P.	18.40	11.20	8.20
12	Mr. Al L	6 Jam.	17.90	5.30	3.20
13	Montenegrin	7 A.P.	13.40	5.60	2.80
16	Nashua	7 A.P.	2.60	2.20	OUT
20	Gandharva	6 Mth.	....	3.60	2.60
21	Deux-Moulins	8 A.P.	5.00	3.00	2.20
23	Helioscope	6 Mth.	5.20	OUT	OUT
25	Summer Solstice	6 A.P.	6.40	3.80	2.80
27	Royal Battle	7 Mth.	5.80	3.40	2.80
28	Deux-Moulins	6 A.P.	7.80	3.60	2.20
30	First Aid	6 Jam.	5.80	2.70	2.10
	Nance's Lad	6 Mth.	....	....	2.20

Amount Returned	$173.90	$92.20	$62.10
Amount Invested	$ 38.00	$36.00	$34.00
Profit	$135.90	$56.20	$28.10

19 Selections—17 won	89%
18 Selections—17 placed	94%
16 Selections—16 showed	100%

5.
HOW TO BEAT
THE HALF-MILE OVALS

Playing the bush tracks has its distinct advantages. The bettor becomes familiar with the select group of animals stationed there and can more easily separate contenders.

Some horses move from one half-mile oval to another with such frequency that they become a little harder to classify. It is these animals that make play difficult at the opening of any of the small tracks.

No matter what the conditions or circumstances, there is a select group of people who get to know the horses stationed there so well that they can pick the winner in certain races more often than not.

The racing papers may not publish their selections at the bush tracks, but as a rule the scratch sheets will. The men who make the selections get to know the horses so well that they hang up a high percentage of winners. Certain types of races are more applicable. With this knowledge the author worked out a method way back in 1947 that beat the bush tracks using the selections given by the *National Racing Program*.

Beating 'Em in the Bushes

There is no need to go into voluminous detail when presenting a method of selection. The system player, as a rule, is not interested in the why's and wherefore's; all he asks is a set of straight rules to follow. Most likely he will start checking to see whether the method has any merit. He makes what he feels is a sufficient check, and if the method seems to hold water, he then may start playing it.

Men who write system articles frequently indulge in extraneous detail, while at the same time they try to make what they are saying sound interesting. In this respect they always succeed because, since most readers of turf magazines are hungry for any news that may make horse betting profitable, they devour every word.

However, I detest meaningless words. Action is what I like, and that is exactly what I intend to give.

There are certain half-mile bush tracks which start operating in May. Their activities end in the latter part of September. There are just about four months of racing and that is all. Favorites are more likely to win here than at the major tracks. Especially is this true in allowance races. They have few Handicap or Stake affairs. Profits can be made here. This is how I did it.

I used the *Nationl Racing Program,* (a New York scratch sheet) in order to get my morning line odds. Any good scratch sheet may be used if this one is not available to you. The tracks played in order of appearance are: 1. Charles‧ Town; 2. Bel Air; 3. Hagerstown; 4. Cumberland; 5. Timonium; 6. Marlboro.

RULES: *Beating 'Em in the Bushes*

1. Play allowance races only at the above tracks.

2. The play goes on any horse quoted at 8-to-5 or less on the scratch sheet.

3. If there is more than one in the race at 8-to-5 or less, play the one at the higher odds. (This also does not happen often.)

4. If there are two at exactly the same odds, play the one listed first in the *National Racing Program* graded handicap selections. (This also does not happen often.)

5. If a horse is listed as part of an "entry" and one is scratched before post time, odds are still considered as is.

Let us take each rule now and illustrate the play so that everything will be perfectly clear. I am omitting Rule 1 because it is obvious that all races must be allowance races.

Rule 2: In the 4th race at Charles Town on July 12, 1947, Your Majesty was listed in an allowance race at 7-5. There were no other horses listed at 8-5 or less. He was therefore our selection.

Rule 3: In the 6th race at Bel Air on July 24, 1947, Dr. Johnson was entered in an allowance race at 8-5. Also entered in the same race was Cy Dart, who was listed on the scratch sheet at 7-5. Our selection, therefore, was Dr. Johnson, since he carried the higher odds of the two. Dr. Johnson won and paid $9.00, $2.80, $2.40.

Rule 4: Boston Man and Comedy Player were both listed at 8-5 in the 7th race at Charles Town on June 20, 1947. The *National Racing Program* listed Boston Man on top and Comedy Player next in line for their graded handicap selections. Our choice was Boston Man, since he was preferred in the graded handicap. He won and paid $3.20, $2.40, $2.40.

Rule 5: At Charles Town on June 23, 1947, Annie's Dream and Gallant were listed as an "entry" in the 5th race, at odds of 4-5. Gallant was scratched. Although this may have changed the odds, we disregarded this situation. Annie's Dream was still our choice since the odds, as far as we were concerned, remained as is. She won and paid $2.60, $2.60, $2.20.

The Workout of Results included here covers the entire 1947 period of activity—from May 29, 1947 to September 24, 1947. It shows 100 selections, 62 winners (62%). Place mutuels were sold on 99 of these plays, of which 77 finished first or second (78%). Show mutuels were sold on 96 of these plays, of which 84 finished in the money (88%).

Net profit on flat bets of $10 to win only on each play was $289.00; on flat bets of $10 to place only, $144.00; on show bets, $73.00. That's a grand total of $506.00, or an average of $5.06 profit on each selection played.

Special Note: There is racing at Charles Town during the first three weeks of December each year, but I do not advise play at this time. The meeting is short, and it takes that long for the selectors to determine with any considerable degree of accuracy which horses are true favorites. If the reader will study the Workout of Results, he will notice that the first three weeks of play were unprofitable. My advise is to wait three weeks before starting play. Doing this will increase the winning percentage greatly. *(See Workout on page 59.)*

6.
FRONT RUNNERS

When a horse is capable of pushing out front and staying there until the finish you've got to give this animal more than a thought before making your play. All race-goers have seen these front runners needle out to head the pack and wind up with the winning laurels.

Not every animal can set a pace and keep it. You've seen many a horse strut out front, put up a little pressure, and then collapse. Naturally this is not the kind of horse we want to back. Only sucker money rides on the back of a proved quitter.

How then can we detect the real thing from the "phoney"? Let's settle down and look the situation over.

Front Runner Formulae

In order to discover whether a horse is really fit, many trainers will order the jockey to try to keep the animal out in front from the very start of the race. If the animal can stay ahead of the pack or close on the heels of the leader for at least one or two calls *(Daily Racing Form)*, the trainer may feel that the opportune time has arrived to send the horse out to win.

The objective of the trainer is then to find a race in which the horse's chances of winning will be increased. He looks for a spot in which the horse will be entered wtih a specific advantage.

Sometimes the trainer cannot find an obvious spot, but is determined to try with the horse in its next race anyway. Even though the spot may not be ideal, the bettor can still be reassured in backing the animal, because the horse is evidently fit and well-meant.

The trainer will often tip his hand to the observant horse player by doing at least one of three things which will signal that the horse will be trying today:

The animal may be dropped in claiming price, or it may be maneuvered into a spot where it is getting at least five pounds less weight than in its last race.

If neither of the conditions prevail then the bettor will have to look for a very recent workout. The workout is often the deciding factor for the trainer in determining whether his charge is ready. When the bettor sees such a workout, he can usually assume that the trainer has given the horse its pre-race test.

Sometimes the horse will show all three factors: drop in claiming price, drop in weight, and workout within five days of today's race. In that case the horse may be considered as a Best Bet. These occasions do not occur frequently.

In the workout presented here (covering May, 1949) seven such opportunities arose. Four won, and one of them—Painted Arrow—paid the fancy price of $33.60, $13.60, $6.60, across the board.

Even though we cannot determine whether the horse is in at an advantage, a recent workout (within five days of today's race) is sufficient evidence to permit the backing of the animal. We will have to place a little confidence in the trainer.

However, as previously shown, the horse is probably well-meant, is in good form and condition, and stands an excellent chance of taking the purse.

Such trainer manipulations occur mostly in claiming races. Therefore, in order to avoid confusion, it is best to stick to claiming races when backing this type of play. To determine clearly that a horse is being dropped in claiming price, it is obvious that the previous race must have been a claimer. The horse's last race may have been an allowance race or even a handicap, which may appear conclusively to be events of higher class.

This is not always true, and since it is confusing as well as difficult to ascertain, the provision in the system presented here was made to bind the play only to horses showing a claiming price in their last race. This claiming price must be higher than the price at which the animal is entered today.

Horses finishing ten lengths or more behind the winner in their last race, even though they showed our required early foot, are to hazardous a proposition to wager on. Such a dismal finish counteracts its good showing in the early part of the race. Such a horse probably is just a confirmed quitter, but whether or not this is true, it is preferable, as well as more profitable, to play horses that can show better finishes.

The workout encompasses 192 selections, out of which 47 were returned winners. The place and show positions shape up well too. Often when first position betting produced a loss, place and show betting brought a profit.

Those animals that have been racing at a minor oval and are now, for the first time, venturing to compete at a major course, must be avoided until they have demonstrated that they are capable of standing up against this better company.

There are some horses that do well under such circumstances, but as a rule they are to be avoided. The performance at a minor oval cannot be construed as sufficient evidence of what they can do against the superior horses at the major oval.

As a rule most major courses are ovals of a mile or more; races at the half-mile ovals are not given speed ratings by the *Daily Racing Form*. To simplify things so that the follower of this method may distinguish major ovals from minor, a rule has been established designating major ovals as those where the races are allotted speed ratings by the *Daily Racing Form*.

To make reasonably sure that the horse is in condition, it is necessary to provide a time lapse from the horse's last race to the present race. Ten days was chosen as the most appropriate time. Although an eleven- or twelve-day time lapse might be just as good, a system has to have arbitrary rules and from investigation the ten-day time rule seems to be best in most cases.

RULES: *Front Runner Formulae*

1. The horse's last race must not have been more than ten days ago.

2. The horse must have lost its last race.

3. The horse must have been first or within ½ length of the leader at the first or second calls *(Racing Form)*.

4. The horse must show at least one of the following three conditions. If it shows all three, consider it as a Best Bet.

a. The horse must be dropping in weight—at least five pounds less than the weight it carried in its last race.

b. The horse must be dropping in claiming price off its last race. Its last race must have been a claimer.

c. The horse must show a workout within five days of today's race.

5. Play claiming races only.

6. Play no maidens, two-year-olds or jumpers.

7. Do not play any horse that lost its last race by ten lengths or more.

8. Do not play horses that raced in their last race at a minor oval and are racing today at a major oval. All tracks at which no speed ratings are given are to be considered minor tracks. Those ovals showing races with speed ratings are considered major ovals.

Note: A particular race at a track may not show a speed rating because it was run over a turf course. Do not confuse this with a minor track. If speed ratings are given for the other races not made on the turf, the track is to be considered as a major oval.

9. In case of tie, prefer the horse if it has all three selection bases. If still tied, choose the horse with the best win consistency for the current and last year combined.

This system's merit lies in its ability to obtain above average prices frequently. It can be expected to get such prices because it backs all kinds of horses showing good as well as apparently bad finishes. The workout, although not too large, is of sufficient size to give it the stamp of approval.

WORKOUT: *Front Runner Formulae*
(May, 1949)

Date	Horse	Race & Trk.	Win	Place	Show	Basis
2	Helaneius	7 Jam.	10.30	5.50	4.20	c
	Mary Ann	2 Hdg.	....	....	....	wo
	Putitthere	1 L.D.	....	4.20	3.20	w
	Little Bits	4 L.D.	....	....	....	w
3	Shifty Mae	7 Jam.	....	....	5.80	w; wo
	Gay Love	8 Jam.	....	....	....	w
	Decoy	8 G.S.	14.60	7.00	5.80	c
	Honeybug	3 Hdg.	....	....	....	c; wo
	Monstrance	2 L.D.	16.20	7.00	5.00	c
4	Combine	1 Jam.	....	3.10	2.90	c; wo

Date	Horse	Race & Trk.	Win	Place	Show	Basis
	Tomsive	3 Jam.	....	3.90	3.20	c
	Acondale	3 G.S.	10.20	6.80	4.00	c; w
	Best Go	4 G.S.	....	6.00	3.00	wo
	Reade Castle	7 G.S.	....	....	....	w; wo
	Sam Bernard	3 Hdg.	....	3.40	2.60	c; wo
	Electron	8 Hdg.	110.20	30.20	14.40	wo
	Sea Bees	3 Suf.	14.20	7.60	4.60	w; wo
	Andrea Kay	1 L.D.	....	3.80	3.00	w
	Trident	2 L.D.	....	5.20	3.40	c
	Carysfort	3 L.D.	81.20	33.20	19.80	w
	True Pilate	7 L.D.	....	....	3.20	c; wo
	Vinita Toney	1 C.D.	....	....	3.00	w
5	Speeding Home	1 Jam.	....	....	....	wo
	Mike Lowy	5 Jam.	....	....	....	wo
	Lord Pathmate	7 Jam.	4.70	3.10	2.10	c; wo
	Guylark	8 Jam.	....	....	....	wo
	Western Front	2 C.D.	....	3.00	2.80	w; c
	Fair Arab†	8 C.D.	....	....	....	w; c; wo
6	Jhansi	1 Bel.	....	....	3.20	c; wo
	Harmony Hope†	1 Pim.	6.60	3.80	3.20	w; c; wo
	Take Ten	7 Pim.	....	....	....	w; wo
	Geronimo	8 Suf.	....	....	....	wo
	Chicalmo	8 C.D.	....	....	....	wo
7	Mayes Riley	2 Bel.	....	....	3.10	wo
	Tick Out	8 Bel.	....	....	....	wo
	Panacea	1 G.S.	....	....	....	wo
	Romancer	7 G.S.	....	....	....	wo
	Wye Care	2 Pim.	....	....	....	w
	Eddie Leonard	5 Pim.	....	....	....	c
	Blue Falcon	8 Pim.	7.80	4.60	3.60	c; wo
	Iced Over	1 Suf.	....	3.80	2.40	wo
	Lt. Bill	2 Suf.	5.40	3.20	2.80	c
	McCosh	1 C.D.	....	3.00	2.40	c; w
	Tintina	6 C.D.	....	....	....	c
	Thunder Hoof	8 C.D.	9.60	....	3.80	wo
9	Azure	4 Bel.	....	....	....	w
	Wassermatter	8 Bel.	....	....	4.20	w; wo
	Coquinet	7 C.D.	....	3.80	2.40	wo
	Uncle Mac	8 C.D.	....	4.80	3.40	wo
	Mattie Girl	8 G.S.	6.60	3.80	3.00	w
10	Deep Fen	4 G.S.	....	....	....	wo
	Markability	1 Pim.	....	6.00	3.80	wo
	Thin Dime	4 Pim.	12.80	7.00	4.80	c
	Gay Gino	3 Suf.	....	....	....	wo
	Painted Arrow†	7 Suf.	33.60	13.60	6.60	c; w; wo
	Pal Cross	8 Suf.	....	....	....	wo
	Sister Cora	5 C.D.	4.80	3.40	2.60	w; wo
	Blue Seal	7 C.D.	....	....	3.20	c
11	Count J L	2 Bel.	....	....	....	c

Date	Horse	Race & Trk.	Win	Place	Show	Basis
	All In Fun†	5 G.S.	....	....	....	c; w; wo
	Rockwood Argo	7 G.S.	....	6.00	4.80	wo
	Hefty	4 Pim.	....	....	....	c; wo
12	Blunt Remark	2 Bel.	....	....	....	wo
	Minneapolis	3 Bel.	18.90	8.00	4.10	w; wo
	Escrow	7 Bel.	....	....	2.50	c; wo
	Leadership†	1 G.S.	5.20	3.60	3.40	c; w; wo
	On The River	6 G.S.	....	....	....	c
	Cessation	7 Pim.	....	9.20	5.40	c
	Quatrefoil	7 Suf.	....	7.00	5.00	c
	Foxey Rose	5 C.D.	....	....	2.80	c; wo
	Old Iron	7 C.D.	4.60	2.80	2.60	wo
	Deliver	8 C.D.	....	....	....	c; wo
13	Mike Lowry	2 Bel.	19.10	8.80	5.30	c; wo
	Cutest Trick	3 G.S.	....	....	....	wo
	Discovert	5 Pim.	....	....	....	c; wo
	Kingrosa	8 Pim.	7.20	4.00	3.20	w
	Good Fun	2 Suf.	....	....	....	w; wo
	Time Eternal	2 C.D.	....	....	3.20	c
	Mountain Roar	6 C.D.	....	....	4.80	wo
14	Rita Dugan	8 C.D.	....	....	4.20	c
	Hornpipe	2 Bel.	20.90	8.20	3.50	c; wo
	Final Touch	8 Bel.	6.60	3.40	2.70	wo
	Gasparilla	7 G.S.	....	....	....	wo
	Henry Payne	1 Suf.	19.20	10.00	6.20	wo
	Irish Count	2 Suf.	....	....	....	wo
	Ground Fog	4 Suf.	11.60	4.60	3.40	wo
16	Nifty†	2 G.S.	....	3.60	2.80	c; w; wo
	Houlgate	7 G.S.	18.20	6.80	5.20	c; wo
	Bold Mate	8 G.S.	7.80	4.80	3.20	c; wo
	Two Deuce	1 Suf.	....	....	....	wo
	Ellehcor	2 Suf.	....	....	....	c; w
17	The Street	2 Bel.	....	....	....	wo
	Rockwood Argo	2 G.S.	....	....	....	c
	On The River	7 G.S.	....	....	....	c
	Royal Foot	8 G.S.	....	....	....	c; wo
	Dragertown	1 Suf.	....	....	....	c
	Top Foot	3 Suf.	....	4.80	3.00	wo
18	Spicebush	7 Bel.	....	....	....	w
	Golf Club	8 Bel.	....	....	....	wo
	Lady Pam	4 G.S.	8.60	4.40	3.20	wo
	Shako	5 Suf.	....	....	2.20	c
	Alanay	7 Suf.	....	....	....	c; w
	Disdoma	1 Det.	....	....	....	c; w
	Pussy Willow	8 Det.	....	....	....	c
	Little Tony	2 L.F.	....	....	4.00	c
	Be Brief	4 L.F.	5.00	3.60	3.00	c
19	Damson	4 G.S.	18.40	7.60	5.20	wo
	Decoy	8 G.S.	....	10.40	7.00	wo

Date	Horse	Race & Trk.	Win	Place	Show	Basis
	Respire	3 Suf.	7.00	3.60	3.00	c; wo
	Night Crawler	4 Suf.	....	....	....	wo
	Warrior Prince	5 Suf.	....	....	2.60	wo
	Dime	7 Suf.	....	8.60	5.40	w; wo
	Johnnie C	8 Suf.	....	....	....	c
	Uncle Mac	7 L.F.	....	....	....	wo
	Sir Monte	1 Det.	....	....	....	c; w
	Jimmie	2 Det.	4.00	2.80	2.20	w
	Spring Folly	5 Det.	....	....	....	c
20	Braggadocio	8 Bel.	6.70	3.90	3.30	w; wo
	Ocean Play	1 G.S.	....	5.00	2.80	c
	King Chico	4 G.S.	....	....	....	w
	Opening Day	7 G.S.	....	6.20	3.60	wo
	Palist	8 G.S.	....	....	4.00	wo
	Myshirley	3 Suf.	....	....	....	wo
	Monstrance	7 Suf.	....	....	....	c
	Flares Durbar	8 Suf.	5.60	3.80	3.00	c
	Susie C	2 L.F.	....	....	....	wo
	Glider Pilot	3 Det.	....	....	4.60	w
21	Rustle Broom	7 Bel.	.....	3.70	2.60	c; wo
	Ghazala	2 G.S.	....	....	5.40	w
	Fantom Venture†	1 Suf.	7.20	4.80	3.00	c; w; wo
	Magic Chief	8 Suf.	....	....	....	wo
	Jessica B*	1 Det.	5.00	4.60	3.40	w
23	Sickle Sue	1 Bel.	....	8.70	7.10	w
	Balinakill	4 G.S.	....	....	....	wo
	Herbie G	2 L.F.	5.80	3.60	2.80	c; wo
	Big Reward	2 Suf.	7.60	3.00	2.60	c; w
	Ruddy Glow§	8 Suf.	....	....	5.80	c
24	Guylark	2 Bel.	....	....	....	wo
	Peacelaw	7 Bel.	....	....	....	c; wo
	Ever Message	1 G.S.	6.80	4.40	3.20	c
	Red Sonnet	4 G.S.	....	....	....	wo
	Cresson Miss	8 G.S.	....	4.20	3.40	c
	Survey	4 Suf.	....	....	....	wo
	Questuary	5 Suf.	....	....	....	c; w
	Avoca Message	4 L.F.	....	....	....	c; wo
25	Bronze Medal	3 G.S.	....	....	6.00	w; wo
	Bad Light	4 G.S.	....	14.20	7.20	c
	Royal Foot	8 G.S.	12.60	6.60	4.80	w
	U. S. Bound	4 Suf.	....	....	2.20	wo
	Two Day Air	8 Suf.	....	....	....	wo
	Gold Proxy	4 L.F.	....	4.60	2.80	wo
	Dr. Roche	2 Det.	4.00	3.00	2.80	c
	Santa Claus	7 Det.	....	....	7.00	w
	Hi Neighbor	8 Det.	....	....	....	c
26	Rustle Broom	5 Bel.	....	....	2.70	w
	Bombcase	8 Bel.	....	4.80	3.30	c; wo
	Fresh Breeze	6 G.S.	....	....	....	c; wo

Date	Horse	Race & Track	Win	Place	Show	Basis
	Opening Day	7 G.S.	....	....	....	wo
	Spotty	1 L.F.	....	....	4.80	c
	Sgt. Brown	7 L.F.	....	6.60	5.60	c; w
	Royalong	8 L.F.	31.60	10.80	7.80	wo
	Doc Stearn	2 Det.	....	....	....	c
27	Spicebush	2 Bel.	....	....	....	c
	Croesus	7 Bel.	....	12.30	7.00	c
	Tascosa	1 Suf.	....	....	....	c
	Evening Flight	5 Suf.	....	3.80	2.40	c; wo
	Blue Nobleman	8 Suf.	....	....	....	wo
	Galla Babe	4 L.F.	....	....	....	c; wo
	Sue's Special	1 Det.	....	2.80	2.80	c
	Himmelee	3 Det.	....	....	....	w
	Dear Boots	5 Det.	5.00	2.80	2.20	c
	The Problem	7 Det.	....	....	....	c
28	Azure	1 Bel.	....	18.90	12.30	c
	Jolly Gremlin	8 Suf.	....	....	....	w
	Karakorum	1 L.F.	....	....	2.60	c
	Bonrilla	3 L.F.	....	....	....	w
	Sir Bim	4 L.F.	....	....	....	wo
	No Leddie	2 Det.	....	....	4.60	c
30	Sir Galavan	5 Bel.	68.40	22.00	11.00	c
	Devotedly	3 Suf.	....	....	....	w
	One Atom	1 L.F.	....	6.00	4.20	c
	Rocky Sir	2 L.F.	....	....	....	w
	Chance Bea	8 L.F.	....	....	....	wo
	Royal Chance	4 Det.	....	....	....	c
	Soma Lad	7 Det.	....	....	....	c
31	Sandy Alan	4 Bel.	....	....	....	wo
	Withastar	4 Del.	5.00	3.50	2.50	c
	Cresson Miss	7 Del.	12.40	5.50	3.40	c
	Foxy Scott	8 Suf.	....	....	....	wo
	Lerner's Girl	5 L.F.	....	....	....	c
	Jessica B	2 Det.	....	....	....	w
	Lucky Josie	7 Det.	8.20	4.20	3.20	c

† Best Bet
* Field won
§ Won dead heat—disqualified and placed third
w—Weight.
wo—Work Out.
c—Class.

192 Win Selections — 47 won — 24%
192 Place Selections — 80 placed — 42%
192 Show Seleceions — 107 Showed — 56%

Amount Returned $723.00	$518.70	$450.40
Amount Invested $384.00	$384.00	$384.00
Profit $339.00	$134.70	$66.40

Profit $2 flat bets across the board $540.10

WORKOUT: *Beating 'Em in the Bushes*

			Win	Place	Show
5/29	Inez M.	5C.T.	...	...	...
	Annie's Dream	6C.T.	4.20	2.80	2.20
5/30	The Shah	6C.T.	...	...	...
5/31	Spikery	6C.T.	...	2.80	2.20
6/2	Sunday Knight	6C.T.	3.20	2.80	2.20
6/6	Equinow	1C.T.	...	...	2.60
	Bulrushes	4C.T.	...	...	...
6/9	Comedy Player	7C.T.	...	3.20	2.80
6/10	Hot Pole	5C.T.	...	4.80	3.20
	Remolee	6C.T.	...	2.80	2.80
6/11	Sure Footed	2C.T.	...	3.00	2.60
	Alarosa	3C.T.	...	...	...
6/12	Your Majesty	4C.T.	5.20	2.80	2.40
	*Comedy Player	6C.T.	4.00	2.60	2.20
6/13	Heaven Hill	1C.T.	...	2.40	2.20
	Road Scraper	5C.T.	...	...	2.40
6/17	War Chain	6C.T.	...	...	...
6/18	Scotsun	4C.T.	7.00	3.40	2.20
	Boston Man	5C.T.	4.40	2.60	2.20
6/19	Slam Bid	5C.T.	...	2.60	2.40
6/20	Lady Romery	6C.T.	...	...	...
	Boston Man	7C.T.	3.20	2.40	2.40
6/21	Rise To Follow	5C.T.	...	...	...
6/23	Annie's Dream	5C.T.	2.60	2.60	2.20
6/26	Annie's Dream	4C.T.	2.60	2.40	2.20
6/27	Double Reward	4C.T.	5.60	3.40	2.80
6/28	Carib Song	2C.T.	...	...	...
	Slam Bid	4C.T.	5.20	3.60	2.80
	Aldridge	7C.T.	...	4.20	3.40
	Honoured	8C.T.	3.60	2.80	2.40
6/30	Lawless Miss	6C.T.	2.60	2.40	2.20
7/1	Double Duty	5C.T.	3.40	2.60	2.60
	Rebline	6C.T.	3.20	2.40	2.20
	Louis L.	8C.T.	7.00	4.00	2.80
7/2	Your Majesty	5C.T.	4.40	2.80	2.40
7/4	Talcum Spray	2C.T.	4.60	3.60	2.60
	*Boston Broom	7C.T.	...	...	2.20
7/8	Heaven Hill	1C.T.	...	3.20	2.20
	Asaider	6C.T.	...	...	2.80
	Double Duty	7C.T.	3.20	2.60	2.20
	Whipped Cream	8C.T.	...	4.60	2.60
7/10	*Fall Guy	6C.T.	...	2.20	2.20
7/11	Tintrell	6C.T.	7.00	2.60	2.40
	*Scotsun	8C.T.	...	3.40	2.40
7/12	*Flamare	2C.T.	4.40	3.00	2.20
	Comedy Player	7C.T.	5.20	3.00	2.40

			Win	Place	Show
7/14	Bardy	7C.T.	10.40	3.60	2.80
7/15	Heaven Hill	1C.T.	5.40	2.60	2.20
7/17	Halogi	6C.T.	...	...	...
7/18	Blue Nobleman	1C.T.	3.20	3.00	2.20
	Sincon	5C.T.	...	...	...
7/19	How Happy	4C.T.	7.40	3.20	2.80
7/22	White Easter	5C.T.	3.00	2.80	2.20
	Beau Wynn	8C.T.	3.40	3.20	2.80
7/23	*Tres Chic	4Blr.	3.40	2.40	Out
7/24	Dr. Johnson	6Blr.	9.00	2.80	2.40
7/25	Spain's Armada	3Blr.	4.00	3.00	2.60
	Annie's Dream	6Blr.	4.00	2.60	2.20
7/26	*Ginargie	6Blr.	2.80	2.40	2.20
	Army Belle	8Blr.	...	3.00	2.40
8/2	Annie's Dream	6Blr.	3.40	2.60	2.20
8/5	Army Belle	5Hag.	...	...	2.60
	Annie's Dream	6Hag.	2.40	2.20	2.20
8/7	Comedy Player	5Hag.	...	4.20	3.40
8/15	Valley Poise	4Hag.	3.00	2.20	Out
8/16	*Our Damsel	5Hag.	3.00	2.80	Out
8/19	*Louray O'Neill	5Cum.	4.40	3.00	3.60
8/20	Coral Water	5Cum.	...	...	2.60
8/21	Annie's Dream	5Cum.	2.40	Out	Out
8/22	Beau Wynn	6Cum.	4.00	4.40	3.20
8/23	Tandis	5Cum.	7.60	3.20	2.80
8/26	*Army Belle	5Cum.	3.40	4.20	2.60
8/27	Annie's Dream	6Cum.	Won but disqualified—Placed last		
8/28	Tandis	3Cum.	4.00	2.60	2.20
	Army Belle	6Cum.	...	3.40	2.20
8/30	Let 'Em Wander	3Cum.	3.00	3.00	2.60
	Kitty Kilts	4Cum.	3.40	3.00	2.20
9/1	Porto Jr.	3Tim.	...	...	2.60
	Dainger Girl	4Tim.	...	...	3.60
	Meetmenow	5Tim.	3.00	2.80	2.20
9/3	Lawless Miss	5Tim.	2.20	2.20	2.20
9/4	Beau Wynn	5Tim.	5.80	3.00	2.40
9/5	Ginargie	5Tim.	...	...	2.20
9/6	Lawless Miss	5Tim.	4.20	2.80	2.20
9/8	Louray O'Neill	4Tim.	2.80	2.60	2.20
9/9	Mythman	3Tim.	3.60	3.00	3.00
	Lawless Miss	5Tim.	...	2.40	2.20
9/10	Porto Jr.	4Tim.	4.80	3.60	2.60
	*Louray O'Neill	5Tim.	2.40	2.20	2.20
9/11	Tumble Boy	7Tim.	2.80	2.80	2.40
9/13	Sand Rose	3Mar.	...	...	...
	Meetmenow	6Mar.	2.80	2.40	2.20
9/18	In Debt	4Mar.	4.60	3.20	2.20
	Army Belle	7Mar.	6.00	2.80	2.40

			Win	Place	Show
9/20	Love My Gal	3Mar.	3.60	2.80	2.20
	*Glory Girl	4Mar.		2.80	2.40
9/22	Kitty Kilts	7Mar.	...	...	2.20
9/23	Chrys Doll	5Mar.	3.00	2.80	2.20
9/24	Tres Chic	3Mar.	4.20	2.60	2.20
	Louray O'Neill	6Mar.	3.40	2.80	2.20

* Entry

100 plays, 62 winners (62%); 77 first or second (78%); 84 first, second or third (88%). NET PROFIT, $10 wagers win only, $289.00; $10 wagers place only, $144.00; $10 wagers show only, $73.00; $10 wagers across-the-board, $506.00.

7.
PLAYING THE LONGSHOTS

Longshots! Longshots! Longshots! The never-ending quest of so many players, the word "longshot" has become almost synonymous with riches in racing talk.

Some people may think a longshot seeker is a complete idiot. The average horse player does not confine himself to such utter specifics. He may refuse to accept a price below a certain set figure, but he does not grope for really big ones. This attitude is correct if price is the only criterion.

Not every longshot player is working in the dark. There are quite a few successful players who aim only at the "longies." Of course they don't back any horse that's going off at extraordinary odds. They look for certain points, bearing in mind the fact that they will not hit on a winner every time they place a bet. They recognize the fact that one big payoff will act as a bulwark against many losers. This way you don't need many winners to roll up a substantial profit.

Take a gander at the two systems that follow. Maybe they'll turn you into a longshot player.

Double Five Longshot System

The winter season is supposed to be a time for hardship. The snow, the sleet, the bitter cold tested the mettle of our pioneer predecessors. It took a hardy man to survive these rigors and carve out a home for himself and his family.

We who bet on the horses find the winter season arduous too. This is the time when we can rack our brains, be as patient as Job, take every necessary precaution, and still fail to come up with a winner.

What makes it so much simpler to pick a winner during the summertime? Those punters who have made a study of horse racing know the answers. First of all it is a difficult task to determine a horse's class during the winter months. Horses are being shipped from all over the country. These horses are unknown to the bettors at the tracks. After all, the people wagering at the tracks are the ones that determine the odds on each animal.

Then again, the past performances are not a true criterion of each animal's actual ability. Especially is this true with claimers. A horse that has been racing in $3500 claimers in New York is certainly not to be classed with $3500 platers in Florida.

Winter is not a season for form. It is not a time when horses run as they are expected to. It is getting close to the end of the year, the horses are growing older, the feed bills have to be paid. This is the time when the trainer has to come up with a win to carry him through until the next year. The trainer and his stable will need enough money to rebuild.

Some animals may have ceased to be satisfactory racing tools. They may have developed injuries or sickness, or may have gone the way of all flesh. Just as in any other business, a man must constantly replenish his stock with new merchandise. So he uses the animals that he can rely on to build up his bankroll. He sharpens them surreptitiously and then bides his time, waiting, like a lion stalking his prey, for the opportune moment to make his kill.

Since it is so difficult to determine class, as well as condition and form, during the winter, the trainer searching for a spot to make a coup will find his task a little easier.

But what type of animal is ready to win? The trainer knows from experience and from scientific data that a five-year-old is at its peak of maturity. It is obvious that a mature animal is stronger, faster, hardier than a younger or older animal. Of course if the older or younger animal is of higher class, this does not hold true.

However, when we consider horses on about equal class levels, the more mature animal is to be preferred. Since five years is the age when a horse is usually at its best, the trainer will search his barns for such an animal. If he finds a horse that is sound and fit, the trainer will prepare to condition the animal for a planned coup.

Of course this premeditated plot is not always successful. This should be no concern to us. What we are interested in is catching enough of these longshots to build a nice, cozy nest egg. We need only a few of these bankroll-building longshot winners to keep us way out in front.

The trainer may also have a horse in his barn that he feels is sharp as a tack. He will send this animal into a race without any attempt at winning. The horse may wind up trailing the other animals, or it may put in a fair effort.

Usually if the trainer is out for a real watermelon-cutting the animal will finish up the creek, far behind the others. Then the trainer, rubbing his hands gleefully, will get ready "to bring home the bacon." He will rush the animal back into competition as quickly as possible, because he does not want the animal to lose its form.

When such a situation occurs the wary bettor can be in on the coup. Of course, please remember that you'll get more than your share of losers, for "the best-laid plans of mice and men aft gang a-gley." For the hardy longshot bettor such a situation holds no qualms. He understands that trying to catch real longshots also entails a necessary evil—long strings of losers. Yet he also knows that a few winners at box-car mutuels can build a bankroll up fast. After all, it is not the number of winners but the profits that any bettor is out for.

So if you're interested in putting on the feed bag at the same trough with these tough, desperate, but astute trainers, you've got to expect a lot of losers with your few winners. If you want to turn your meat and potatoes into caviar and champagne, then you've got to keep at least one eye on the tote board. The system to be presented here cannot be played just any time. It is strictly a winter system and can only operate successfully during this season.

More than one trainer, of course, will have the same idea. It is not an original trainer manipulation to use a five-year-old or a sharp horse for a planned coup. It is an old stand-by method used successfully by trainers "way back when." You will, therefore, usually find more than one qualified selection in each race.

What can you do about it? Well, if you've a lot of time and patience you can carefully devise a practical and sound method of separation. Probably with sufficient research this can be done. In the workout presented here our choices were based on the odds only. The qualified selection going off at the highest odds became our choice. In this way many winners were lost, but we did collect on those with the longest payoffs.

Let's rehash a few plays to see what we are up against. On December 20th, 2nd race at Tropical Park in a field of eight horses, seven were possibilities. We checked off all the qualified selections and then looked to the tote board for our final choice. Bob's Ace, a five-year-old gelding, was listed at the highest odds, 15-to-1, so he was our selection. Running at second highest odds, at 11-to-1, was Tiny Admiral, a five-year-old horse. Brown Brutus, another five-year-old gelding, went off at odds of 10-to-1. Brown Brutus was the winner. Perhaps the real winner could have been determined by analysis of the past performances of each horse. Maybe yes and maybe no.

Another example of a similar situation was produced on the same day. In the 7th race at Tropical there were three qualified selections, Suleiman, Starecase, and Dominave. Suleiman went off at 20-to-1. Dominave showed odds of 13-to-1, and Starecase left the post at 15-to-1. We had to choose Suleiman at 20-to-1, since he was the horse with the highest odds. In this way we lost a $33.40 winner.

This situation, however, worked in reverse on December 15th, when separation of qualified selections at the highest odds gave us Gaby H. at a magnificent $182.80 payoff. So you can settle for picking them at the highest odds, or do some research and develop your own separation method. But please don't forget that the separation device used here brought a profit for one month of $534.40. Remember also that the success of this method depends on catching real longshots.

RULES: *Double Five Longshot System*

1. First check off all five-year-olds. Make sure they are not maidens.
2. Then check off all horses that have raced not more than five days ago.
3. Play no maidens or jumping races.
4. Play after scratches are known.
5. There will usually be ties. Play that qualified horse going off at the highest odds.

This system gets a lot of action at the track. At Tropical Park there were 197 selections during the month of December, 1952. (See workout.) In all cases the odds were rather clear and specific, and there was no doubt as to what horse was the selection to be wagered on. It may happen in the future that the tote board will not be so specific. In this eventuality it is advisable to play two horses, provided that the odds are sufficiently high to be worthwhile. The player who does not care to do this might make an arbitrary rule to avoid play unless the selection is perfectly obvious. As we have already said, this was not necessary for play at Tropical during the month of December, 1952.

Only the win mutuel is shown in the workout, although many horses finished second or third. There were some good place prices. For example, on December 11, in the 7th race at Tropical, Didapper finished second and paid $30.20. Chombro paid $17.30 for place on December 17, also in the 7th race. In spite of the good place prices only win is recommended for play. In the long run you will find that when you depend on price to produce profit, the only way to wager is right on the nose.

All attempts at handicapping or analyzing the past performances of each individual horse were deliberately left out. This makes the system very simple. However, there were certain observations made while compiling the workout which leads this writer to believe that tightening the rules might prove fruitful. It would certainly tend to increase the winning percentage.

For one thing, take Gaby H., The four-year-old gelding that won for us in a six-furlong, $2500 claiming race, on December 15th at the box-car mutuel of $182.80. If you examine the horse's past performances you will notice that the animal won a race at the same distance on the 21st of October, less than two months ago.

This win was made at an Eastern Oval, Rockingham Park, and at a claiming price of $2000. The past performances show good and fair tries up to the point of its last race. Previous to the animal's last race the horse was never further than 7¼ lengths from the winner at the finish of any of the races listed in today's past performances. When the horse won its race at Rockingham it turned in a fast .22 for the first one-fourth in the six-furlong race. This was the best one-fourth the animal ever made in the seven races listed. In this winning race at Rockingham the animal beat Little Harp and Time Roll, a couple of good horses.

The question now arises: Was this $2000 claiming race of a higher class level than today's $2500 claimer? The difficulty in properly evaluating class levels in claimers now asserts itself. On December 4, 1952, Gaby H. made his first appearance at Tropical Park. The horse was entered in a $2500 claimer.

Entered in an eleven-horse field Gaby H. managed to finish 6th, beaten by 6¼ lengths. This was not too bad. Six days later the horse was entered in similar company and showed a poor race all the way. With twelve horses in the race, Gaby H. finished 10th, beaten by 12 lengths. This smelled fishy and even smelled fishier when the animal was rushed back to competition five days later. The wary bettor must have raised an eyebrow when he saw this in the past performances.

But there were other horses in the same race using the same maneuver. For example Ula, a six-year-old mare, had won a race at six furlongs on October 24, 1952, in a Garden State Park $3500 claimer, and at odds of 43.20-to-1. In this race Ula had beaten Agrarian-U, an aging yet good horse. Obviously Ula was considered a classier animal, even though the mare had also raced twice at Tropical Park at $2500. Ula had finished 10th in its last race, four days ago, beaten by 5¼ lengths in a field of 12. This horse, also a qualified selection, went off at $11.05-to-1, and finished second to Gaby H.

Six of the other horses entered in today's race with Gaby H. showed in-the-money efforts in their last performances. Two of them had won their last race. However, one of the last out winners, Birdie Lullie, scratched and was not a contending factor.

The Gaby H. race is a good example of trainer manipulation for a price. A sharp animal is made to appear bad, and then when everyone is looking out of the window, it comes home at a whopping mutuel payoff. Examining the past performances, therefore, seems to augur well for the person who wishes to operate on the system as it stands at present. The system fan might insert a rule stipulating that the animal must show a fairly recent win at today's distance in its present list of past performances.

Sometimes the system will hit upon a selection that is definitely not being manipulated by the trainer. There may be another qualified selection in the race, or this horse may be the only one. Usually this animal will be outstanding in some respect, either because of an excellent last performance or its obvious superiority in class. This horse will naturally go off at comparatively short odds. The reader may or may not accept this type of animal for play. You will find that when you have such an isolated selection, at low odds, the horse will be well-meant, and will very often win. Most of the system selections, however, were horses that went off at longshot odds.

The Longshot Play

If you're looking for a big bundle—to make a lot out of a little—you've got to be a longshot player. There's no way of getting away from it. If you can collect enough box-car playoffs, you're bound to come out ahead. And you don't need the high percentage of winners that the chalk bettor relies on.

I used to know a guy who was a consistent chalk eater. "Look," he would say, "you think I'm hanging around here for my health?

WORKOUT: Double Five Longshot System

(1952)

Date	Horse	Race	Mutuel
Dec. 1	Intercept	1	....
	Lady Locks	2	....
	Double Blush	4	....
	Roman Jean	6	7.50
	Ignition	7	....
	Dooly	8	....
	Many Gifts	9	....
2	Whiskey John	1	....
	Flying Weather	2	6.90
	Trust	3	....
	Locks	4	....
	Best Host	5	87.60
	Mr. Willie	6	19.50
	Chicle II	7	....
	Beirut	8	72.90
	Broken Arches	9	....
3	Woodside	1	....
	Still Unsolved	2	....
	Bucky C.	3	....
	Spanish Armada	5	....
	Sun Rene	7	....
	Lesliefay	8	....
	Jump For Joy	9	....
4	Stop and Think	1	....
	Nate Herzfeld	2	....
	Connie Jo	3	....
	Hot Rock	5	....
	Empty Pockets	6	6.40
	Rollicking Lad	7	....
	Excise Tax	9	....
5	By Your Leave	1	....
	Didapper	4	....
	Red Comet	5	....
	Kinsman	6	....
	Miss Place	8	....
	Gloam	9	....
6	Kenwood	1	....
	Madam Cross	2	....
	Visional	4	131.70
	Flight Captain	5	....
	Marie Eileen	6	5.70
	Golden Gloves	7	....
	Orphean	8	....
	Fulton Market	9	....
8	After You	1	....
	French Quarter	2	....
	Bucky C.	3	....
	Swan Dive	4	....
	Kings Daisy	5	....
	Wolf Cry	6	....
	Sir Strome	7	....
	Hindi	8	....
	Selector	9	7.70
9	I'm O. K.	2	55.40
	Party Request	4	....
	Heredity	6	7.60
	Jane's Gal	7	....
	Betsy Marie	8	....
	Little Captain	9	....
10	By Your Leave	1	....
	Sand paper	2	....
	Barths-Belle	4	5.40
	Silver K.	5	....
	Chombro	7	....
	Chureo	8	....
	Attentive	9	....
11	Hyprocrisy	1	95.50
	Huddle	2	....
	Hopeful Sam	4	....
	Flight Captain	5	....
	Col. Kimble	6	....
	Didapper	7	....
	Tel-Aviv	8	....
	Hoplite	9	....
12	Rugged Boy	2	5.70
	Bowditch	3	....
	Flapnot	5	....
	Pucketeer	6	....
	Saddle Bags	9	....
13	Lead All	1	....
	After You	2	....
	By Your Leave	3	....
	Fondest	4	....
	Feud	5	....
	Dominave	6	....
	Wolf Cry	7	....
	Salaise	8	....
	Caboose	9	34.10
15	Gaby H.	2	182.80
	Always Home	3	....
	Brown Brutus	4	....
	Harrimont	5	....
	Old Tom	6	....
	Rusty	7	....
	Bonnie Hill	8	....
	Bashful Son	9	....
16	Pakistan	2	....
	Blue Thistle	3	....
	Feint	5	....
	Little Captain	7	....
	Mucho Mas	8	....
	Trespass	9	....

Date	Horse	Race	Mutuel	Date	Horse	Race	Mutuel	Date	Horse	Race	Mutuel
17	Don't Wait	1	……	23	Trinacria	5	……		Giggle	7	……
	Hopeful Sam	2	……		Mr. Smug	6	……		Great Parham	8	……
	Crohessian	3	29.50		Fourdees	7	……		Inezmuch	9	……
	March Brat	4	……		Wise Market	8	……	27	Hollowbrook	1	……
	Trinacria	5	……		King Freedoms	9	……		Bickett	2	……
	Father Link	6	……	24	Thunderjet	1	……		Witch Doctor	3	……
	Chombro	7	……		Great Admiral	4	……		Rechecked	4	……
	Trumpet Call	8	……		Lesliefay	6	……		Goya's Pass	5	22.60
	Kanza	9	……		Cellini	7	……		Abbezac	6	……
18	Honey Jar	1	……		Sneak Easy	8	……		Oil Capital	7	……
	Quick Mission	2	……		Tel-Aviv	9	……		Fighting Fair	8	……
	Lesliefay	6	……	25	Preacher	1	……		Visional	9	……
	Lead Pad	7	……		Liberty Luck	2	……	29	Daughter C.	1	……
	Trumpet King	8	……		John Peel	3	……		Lot O Luck	2	……
	Larry D.	9	51.30		Petite Lassie	4	……		Spring Khal	7	……
19	Fiery	1	……		Lucky Harp	5	……		Swoop	8	……
	Free On	4	……		Flight Captain	6	……		Patty's Day	9	……
	Top Command	5	……		Dead Duck	7	……	30	Thendara	1	……
	Colonel Zeder	6	……		Daughter C.	8	……		Swan Dive	2	……
	Be Swayed	7	……		Winging Along	9	……		O'Reigh	4	……
	Milo	8	……	26	Let's Think	1	……		Rough Cookie	6	……
	Look Here	9	……		Look Here	2	……		Lucky Codine	7	……
20	Bashaw	1	……		Great Admiral	4	……		Triograph	8	……
	Bob's Ace	2	……		Polly's Delay	5	……		Sun Cross	9	……
	Brunswick	3	……		Marta	6	……	31	Winstay	3	……
	Is There	4	……		Villager	7	……		Even Later	4	……
	Whitleather	6	……		Salaise	8	……		Infaith	5	……
	Suleiman	7	……		Peter Vinegar	9	……		Seventy-Seven	8	……
	Sir Strome	8	……		Sedulous	1	73.70		Brother Ghost	9	……
	Dooly	9	……		Pakistan	2	13.50				
22	In Faith	1	……		Winning Prince	3	……				
	Watch Union	2	……		Reinforce	5	……				
	High Back	4	11.10		Didapper	6	……				

Amount Returned $928.40
Amount Invested $394.00
Profit on $2 wagers $534.40

You think it feels good every time I make a bet and pick a loser. What am I here for, to support the bookie?"

There was no need to tell me how he felt. I was human too. I had suffered the agony of backing the wrong horse, the sting of figuring a wrong angle. I too had groped for a horse that would bring that happy smile to my face when it passed the finish line first and I went up to collect.

Well to get back to this chalk player—a worrier if I ever saw one. This guy played the short-priced ones and he landed on plenty of winners. Once I ventured to ask him whether he was ahead of the game. That bloke looked at me as though I had just come out of the screwball factory. "Are you kidding?" he asked.

This guy was a loser. He was bound to be. Of course if he had had a really worthwhile method, his play might have shown a profit. But he didn't. He'd back the favorite, or some consensus selection, or some short-priced horse his favorite newspaper selector had picked as his choice for the day.

Then there was a character we called "Longshot Larry." Here was a guy with a different emotional and mental setup altogether. His specialty was longies, and when some of them stepped down for him there was no happier man in the house. You probably could run your car a whole week on the current of anger that ran through the bookie when he had to pay off on one of Longshot Larry's winners.

At that time the bookies were paying 50-1. This guy didn't seem to be faring badly. Not at all. He always sported a new car, flashed a nice bankroll and dressed sharp as a tack.

Losers? He got plenty of them, but one of his winners took care of lots of losers. There was many a day when he didn't even see the faintest light of a winner. Whether or not he had a system I don't know, but he was making hay while the others burnt theirs up.

So of course you're now saying, "Okay, okay, I'm for the longshot play! But how do I do it? How can I get longshots that will keep me rolling in the long green?"

First of all, the bettor must confine his play to claiming races only. If a trainer is contemplating a maneuver to obtain a price, he will probably use the common plater rather than any superior animal. The better horses usually run in races where the purses are large enough to arouse the stables' appetites. Why risk a superior animal for a price that may not materialize? Purses in most claiming races are so small that it is only through trainers' manipulations that the horse can be made to pay for its feed.

From time to time a plater will show a good performance, either winning or coming in the money. When the trainer hustles the horse back to competition he often finds plenty of money backing it. The odds naturally seems to drop to a low level.

If the trainer is interested in obtaining a good price, it will not do well in its next race. In fact, the animal's performance will prove to be a dismal failure. It will finish the race far behind the winner. A lot of bettors seeing such a bad showing, will conclude that the animal has already run its good race and is now staling off.

Of course, many times it is just that, and the public is right, but frequently enough this bad performance is merely a planned maneuver. In one way or another the horse was deliberately forced into a bad race with the object of obtaining a much better price in its next try. If the horse is one that is improving instead of going downgrade, the animal will often pay off at a juicy price in the race following the bad one.

Naturally, not even the trainer can predict the outcome of the race to his complete satisfaction. However, so many of them do win that it makes the probability worth watching.

Similarly, a horse that lost its last race by ten lengths or more may not have finished in the money in its penultimate event, but is still being maneuvered for a price.

On scanning its list of past performances, you will note that this animal has already won a race at exactly today's distance. If in today's race the horse is being dropped in claiming price, $500 or more, there is a good possibility that the animal is out of the money as well as an extra bundle derived from the mutuel machines. Should the animal be dropping $1000 or more in price from its last race, then, if you can find a winning race in its past performances, within $\frac{1}{16}$ (a half-furlong) of today's distance, you may still expect to get a good payoff on a planned maneuver.

Don't back just any horse, however. Make sure that the animal is a winner by seeing that it has won at least two races for the current and last year combined. Maidens often pay off in the high brackets, but since these animals have not as yet shown that they can win, why take chances and back them with your hard-earned money? A large percentage of horses running every year never win a race.

RULES: *The Longshot Play*

1. Play claiming races only.
2. The horse's last race must not have been more than 15 days ago.
3. The horse must have lost its last race by 10 lengths or more.
4. The horse must have finished in the money in its next to last race, which must not have been more than two months ago.
5. If no selection is made on the basis of Rule 4, then selection can be processed if the horse lost its last race by ten lengths or more, shows a win anywhere in today's list of past performances at exactly today's distance, and is dropping in claiming price $500 or more from its last race.
6. If selection is still not made, the horse can be chosen if it lost its last race by ten lengths or more, won a race anywhere in today's list of performances within ⅛₆ (a half-furlong) of today's distance, and is dropping $1000 or more in claiming price from its last race.
7. The horse must have won at least two races for the current and last year combined.
8. Play no maidens or jumpers.
9. In case of tie, play the horse with best win consistency for the current and last year combined.

To prove that longshots can be selected at tracks other than that on which the workout is based, the following example is presented:

On August 10, 1955, in the fifth at Hazel Park, Equilla's past performances showed that it had lost its last race by 12 lengths. This last event occurred on July 26, exactly 15 days ago. On July 18, 1955, the five-year-old mare had won the race.

It so happened the distance was exactly the same as today's. As you can see, this win was made a little over a month prior to today's race at Hazel Park. The race won was at Rockingham Park. The July 26th race was also at Rockingham Park, but at the higher claiming price of $3000. The distance was still the same (1¹⁄₁₆). Since the horse had lost this race by 12 lengths, apparently it was assumed to be running out of its class.

The last racing day for the present meeting at Rockingham Park was August 6, and Equilla four days later showed up at Hazel Park in a $2500 claimer. It was a drop in claiming price of $500 from its last race, but it was exactly the same price at which the animal had been entered in its penultimate race at Rockingham Park, where it had won at odds of about 8-1. Was this a maneuver for a price or simply a natural drop into the horse's class? Apparently the bettors at Hazel Park were of the latter opinion.

The horse had won four of 46 races for the current and last year combined. There was a tie with another horse, Deliberate, a four-year-old gelding, that showed a win consistency of two out of 29 races for both years. Deliberate had not won a single race out of its eight run in 1955, but it had finished second twice and third once. Equilla had won two out of 20 races for the current year.

Equilla's better win consistency would have made it our selection. Equilla won and paid $41.80, $12.80, $7.20 across the board. Equilla was the better horse of the two for other reasons which it is not necessary to discuss here. If the reader is curious he may check the past performances in the Chicago *Daily Racing Form* of August 10, 1955. I have seen many other longshot winners at various tracks, which could have been selected with the rules shown here.

In the fifth at Rockingham Park on July 15, 1955, there was a claiming race at a distance of 1⅛ miles. The field consisted of only eight horses. The past performances of each horse were scanned. Since our primary purpose was to find an animal that had lost its last race by ten lengths or more, it was quite easy to run down the list of horses and cancel out those that did not meet our requirements.

Only one horse, Roundhouse, had lost its last race by ten lengths or more. The six-year-old gelding had finished 10th, beaten by 13 lengths, in its last race on July 11, four days ago. Since no horse could be selected if it raced last more than 15 days ago, our horse met the time requirement also.

Our inital search was for an animal that had come in the money in its next to the last race. Roundhouse had finished 6th in its penultimate race, and, therefore, did not qualify on that score. But it still could become our selection if it showed a win anywhere in its list of past performances, at exactly today's distance. The horse must also have won at least two races for the current and last year combined.

On the bottom of its list of past performances, on March 23, 1954, the animal showed a win at 1⅛ miles, today's distance. The horse had won two out of its 15 races for current and last year combined and qualified on these grounds too. Since no other animal could possibly become a selection on the basis of our primary prerequisite after determining that the horse had lost its last race by 10 lengths or more, within 15 days of today's event, Roundhouse was our selection.

The horse won and paid $42.80, $13.80, and $5.80 across the board. Remember, however, that if there was an animal in this race that met all the other requirements, and finished in-the-money in its next to last race, at a time no further away than two months from today's event, we would have to stick to this horse and Roundhouse could not be considered.

Research really has shown that longshots can be obtained in the manner described. Whether or not a substantial profit on such a method can be maintained over a long period of time is hard to say. I feel certain, however, that if a good longshot system can be devised, backing the type of horse mentioned here, it can readily fit into the picture. The player intending to back this method should make a thorough check before putting up his cash. However, past experiences seem to augur well for this type of play. Bet these longies, if you're not afraid of long strings of losers.

WORKOUT: *The Longshot Play*

(Rockingham, July 4—August 6, 1955)

Date	Horse	Race	Win	Date	Horse	Race	Win
July					Jimparo	9	....
6	Kum-on-in	4	....	21	Chano	5	....
	Collision	8	35.20		Tony's Gem	8	....
	Lee's Highpep	9	....	22	Isayolboy	8	....
7	Angel Slipper	9	....		Golden Choice	9	23.40
8	Insomnia	8	....	23	Changeling	4	....
9	Happy Bound	1	13.20		Collision	8	....
	Bob O'Boy	2	....	25	Gala Morn	5	....
	Mike's Money	9	....	26	Yearn	2	....
11	The Pheasant	2	....	27	Sickle Sue	2	....
	Rosa G	5	....		Mr. August	5	13.80
	Mr. August	8	....	28	Nothing Yet	2	....
	Arletod	9	35.00		Mr. Cumberland	5	....
12	Neversink	8	....		Roundhouse	8	....
13	Lady Priam	2	....	30	Command Me	4	....
	Shannon Gal	8	....				
14	Royal Viking	3	....	*August*			
	Olympic Queen	5	18.60	1	Uncle Don	8	....
	Insomnia	8	....	3	The Claw	6	....
	Deb's Devil	9	....		Finchhaven	9	....
15	Roundhouse	5	42.80	4	Indian Lad	6	....
	Full Brother	8	....	5	Fillequine	6	....
16	Lady Dil	8	....				
18	Tiger Mel	2	39.40	Amount Returned $277.00			
	Pleasant Time	4	10.80	Amount Invested ....$ 94.00			
19	John Peel	2	28.20				
	Cablet	8	....	Profit $183.00			
20	Moi et Toi	4	16.80	47 Selections—11 Won—23%			

8.
HOW BACKING FIVE-YEAR-OLDS
GIVES YOU AN EDGE

The scene is a Roman amphi-theatre. Three men are being pitted against one another in a trial of strength—possibly to the death, if the people witnessing the bout desire it.

One is a youth, lithe and slender. The second is husky and mature, in the prime of manhood, while the third seems close to middle age, waning in virility.

The contest begins. The mature man strikes the youth fiercely with ironclad fists and smashes him to the ground. Then he turns to meet his older adversary. They slug and parry, then suddenly the older man is down and the contest is over. The crowd roars.

Nothing unusual, however, has occurred. The best fitted has won over the immature and the one of declining physical powers.

A mature, fully-developed man will almost always defeat a younger or older man of approximately equal strength. If the younger or older had been greatly superior physically then of course things might have been different.

Racing fans may learn a lesson from this situation. A horse when five years of age is at the height of its development, in the prime of its physical prowess. Thus horses at this age figure to have a little the better of it when meeting rivals of comparable ability.

Playing Five-Year-Olds

With these facts in mind, we set about devising a method of selection based upon five-year-olds. Past performances show that five-year-olds win a greater percentage of their races than other age groups.

Since most horses are raced into condition we will require an initial tightening race as a prerequisite for a system selection. This will serve to eliminate horses that have been out of competition for a considerable length of time and are not really expected to win, even by their stables.

RULES: *Playing Five-Year-Olds*

1. The horse must be a five-year-old, and must have raced within eight days.
2. Must have won at least one race this year or last.
3. If there is but one five-year-old in the race and it meets two

other requirements, it is a play without further qualification. Consider horses that show 50% in the money or better for both years in preference to other five-year-olds.

4. If more than one horse qualifies up to this point procedure is as follows:

a. In claiming races, take the horse whose claiming price in its last race was $500 (or more) higher than the last-out claiming tag of the others under consideration.

If no horse ran its last race at a claiming price $500 higher than others under consideration, or, if the last out for one or more was not in a claiming event, play the horse with the best in-the-money percentage for this year and last.

b. In events other than claiming, play the horse with the highest in-the-money record.

If more than three were in the money 50% of the time, pass the race.

c. In *all* races, if there are more than three five-year-olds in a race and no one of them shows a 50% in-the-money record, pass the race.

5. Selections must be made after scratches are known.

6. Play no steeplechase or hurdle races.

New Thoughts on Five-Year-Olds

I contributed an article to *Turf and Sport Digest* entitled "Playing Five-Year-Olds." The basis of the method demonstrated was the fact that a five-year-old thoroughbred is at its peak and therefore should be capable of defeating contenders of equal class younger or older. A study conducted by the late Edgar G. Horn showed the winning percentage of five-year-olds to be somewhat greater over an extended period than horses of other age groups. The workout presented in the system covered the month of August, 1948, in which 320 horses qualified as system selections. The large number of selections operating at a considerable profit, $222 for win alone, based on a two-dollar flat bet, stamped the method as meritorious.

In order to ward off as many risky bets as possible on animals which had not raced recently, we had provided a tightening provision, requiring that the horse must have raced within eight days of today's race. Checking the previous month, July, 1948, I discovered that many five-year-olds were successful in reaching the winner's circle when they had raced within 16 days of today's race, twice the previous allotted time. The eight-day rule was still good, but the method was missing out on quite a few long-priced horses that would have enhanced the profits. I determined not to change the eight-day rule but to add the stipulation of a last race within 16 days when no selection could be chosen from the eight-day last-race requirement. Another discovery I made was that five-year-olds which showed at least 50% in-the-money consistency for the current and last year combined were more likely to win than their less consistent brethren. Of course, this type was not as numerous and playing them alone limited the action. However, for the person who is not averse to lesser action, playing these will produce a higher winning percentage.

These 50%-or-better horses were preferred in the workout. Wherever an animal showed such performance the other five-year-olds were disregarded. Providing the horse did not scratch, it became our selection. This type of animal was chosen regardless of whether it had raced last within 16 or eight days of today's race, even if another animal without this consistency had raced last within our preferred time limit (eight days). If one 50%-or-better in-the-money horse was selected, the horse that raced within the eight-day time lapse was preferred to the one that raced within the 16-day period if two or more were in the same time limit they were separated exactly as horses that did not show this consistency.

In all cases selections were made after scratches were known. This is of obvious importance, for you may have two qualified selections, choose one after using the separation rule only to have the horse scratch. The other horse which would then be the selection would have been by-passed.

Rules 1 to 4 bring up selections from among the preferred 50%-or-better horses. These are covered in Workout A. Rules 5 to 7 supplement the first four to give broader play.

RULES: 50%-Or-Better Selections

1. Play only five-year-olds. No maidens or jumpers.
All selections made after scratches.

2. Horse with a two-year in-the-money record of 50% or better is a play if:

a. It raced within eight days.

b. No horse with 50% in-the-money record raced within eight days, a horse which meets the consistency requirements and has raced within 16 days is acceptable.

3. If more then three come up for consideration (after scratches) under Rule 2, pass the race.

4. If two or three qualify under Rule 2, separate as follows:

a. If in a claiming race, take horse which raced against highest claiming price last time.

b. If still a tie, or if one or more of the horses did not race in a claimer last time, take the horse with the best in-the-money percentage. (See explanatory note after rules.)

The broader method, which gives many more plays and might be preferred by those seeking "action" is developed by adding the following rules to those already given. It is understood that horses selected under the first four rules are given preference over those brought up by Rules 5, 6, and 7.

5. If there is but one five-year-old in the race and it raced within eight days, it is a play. If there are more than three five-year-olds in the race (after scratches), pass the race.

6. If none qualify under the eight-day rule, play any five-year-old which raced within 16 days, if it is the only five-year-old in the race. If there are more than three after scratches, pass the race.

7. If two or three horses tie under Rule 5 or 6, make selection as outlined under Rule 4.

Rule 4 may need some clarification. To explain we will set up a hypothetical tie among three horse, five-year-olds, each of which raced within eight days. Horse A raced last at a claiming tag of $5,000; horse B's claiming price last out was $4500, while horse C raced last in an allowance event. Horse B would eliminated, since horse A had raced at a higher claiming tag.

The unknown quanity is horse C, since it had raced in an allowance event in its last race. We cannot pin this type of race down to a claiming price, therefore we will have to resort to our consistency rule for separating horse A and horse C. We will choose as our selection that horse which shows the highest percentage of in-the-money performances for the current and last year combined.

I have spot-checked this system throughout the year and can truthfully say that it can be relied on to produce longshot winners at any month of the year. This is because the system does not specifically concern itself with horses that have shown recent good form.

9.
HOW TO MAKE MONEY BETTING PLACE

This is the question before the house: Is it possible for the player to "cinch" a profit by playing odds-on horses to place?

I have done some research on the subject at the request of readers of my articles. I offer no conclusions, preferring that you draw your own.

To begin with, let us examine the reasoning of those who advocate this form of betting. It goes something like this:

"Most of the time it is foolish to put your cash anywhere but straight on the nose. The reasons for this are: first, that the winning pool goes entirely to the holders of one ticket, whereas the place pool has to be divided in two, and the show pool, naturally, is cut up three ways; and secondly, that the breakage is only deducted once from the win pool, while for place and show the extra pennies are taken out twice and thrice, respectively.

"If you are playing horses at good odds, wagering for win only is to be preferred. The place price on such horses can often be half or even a third of the win price. But when you wager on odds-on horses this cannot possibly happen, since the smallest payoff, according to track law, cannot be less than five cents on a dollar. So that if an odds-on horse paid as high as $3.90 to win, the place price could never be one-half or less of the win price. The smallest possible return for place is $2.10.

"This condition puts place betting on horses going off at less than even money at a distinct advantage when compared to the possible place odds on longshots or even ordinary good odds. Frequently, because the odds on the horse are so low to win, comparatively smaller play is made for place, resulting in an overlay in the second position, should the horse win or place."

So much for the backers of "cinch" play. What are our findings?

Progressive Place Betting

Now it stands to reason that the average horse player—the "two-buck Benny"—cannot afford to bet on odds-on horses. You can't make much money if your net return is 80 cents or perhaps even a dollar. However, the fascinating part about playing odds-on horses lies in the winning frequency of the second spot. Such continuous winning tends to make a player feel good.

Feeling good, unfortunately, is not the objective of the average horse player. For the man who can afford it, ample bets should bring favorable results, neat and tidy profits. But what is the fellow going to do who cannot afford large bets but certainly would enjoy the prospects of cashing mutuel tickets with extreme frequency? Well, if he must insist on two-buck bets, then it becomes hopeless. You simply cannot make money on odds-on horses to place with two-dollar flat bets.

However, for the player who can afford to risk $20, $40, or perhaps as high as $60, the method to be demonstrated here might prove interesting.

Recommended for play with the method are two sliding progressions. You can start with a two-dollar bet and progress upward to $20, $40 and if necessary $60, should losers occur, and slide downward, $60, $50, $40, $30, $20, and two dollars when winners occur at the $60 level. There will rarely be an occasion for betting higher than $60, since the type of horses played does not seem to produce more than two losers in a row.

If you can afford to start with a twenty-dollar bill and work your way up with a loser—for example, $20, $40, $60 and down with winners, $60, $50, $40, $30, $20—your chances for a bigger profit are much better.

This sliding progression works beautifully in any method with a winning percentage of 70% or better, because under such circumstances strings of successive winners are bound to occur, whereas consecutive losing streaks are much smaller in number. In all cases (see workout) at Rockingham and Keeneland, there were never more than two losers in a row. In fact, at Keeneland there were never two losers in succession. Later on in this article the actual play will be demonstrated, using one of the workouts so that the method of progression will be as clear as possible.

The progression that starts with two dollars obviously is less risky, but yields smaller profits. With the odds-on horses, also recommended for play, are entries going off at odds of 2-to-1 or less. Wagering on these entries has been inserted into this method for two reasons:

Firstly, profits can be enhanced by connecting with a winner going off at odds higher than our mainstay odds-on horses would show. Should we lose, raise our ante, according to our progression, and hit a payoff of even money or more, our profits immediately swell to substantial proportions.

Secondly, should the entry finish 1-2 there is an excellent chance that our wager for place will return as good a price as win, sometimes even higher, or at least almost as much as that paid by the winner. This obviously is due to the fact that the entry pays off on the entire place pool, and does not share with any other animal as would be the usual situation when two different horses, not connected in the wagering, finish first and second.

For example, at the Rockingham meet, on October 25, in the 5th race (see workout) the "A" entry finished first and second, and the price for place was the same as for win ($3.40). Another example can be seen at the Keeneland meeting, where on April 10, in the 3rd race, the entry finished 1-to-2, paying $5.40 for win and $5.00 for place.

There are not really any specific rules, as such, for this is not a system that deals with the intricacies of form, condition, pace, or other usual relative factors. But since we must remember to look for certain kinds of odds-on horses, let's work up a set of rules, regardless.

RULES: *Progressive Place Betting*

1. Play only horses running at odds-on prices (odds of less than even money) or entries (two or more horses running on one ticket —field horses are to be considered similar to an entry) going off at odds of 2-to-1 or less.

2. In case of tie, play the horse or horses running at the lowest odds.

To test this progressive place betting on the types of horses suggested, three workouts of entire meets at three separate tracks were compiled. In all cases flat bets for win showed a loss, while place betting produced a profit, even though the amount was very small.

As we all know, no wagering ever stays on a straight level. You have your winning streaks followed by losing slumps and vice versa. For example, the average winning percentage of favorites at all tracks combined is roughly about 33%, but there are individual track meetings where only 28% or even 20% of the favorites win. If you could wager consistently at a special track or tracks where our type of horses normally win an average share of the races then it seems that success can be assured. The tracks at which the workouts were made were chosen at random to give representative conditions during spring and fall.

The winning percentage of odds-on horses should normally be about 50%.

This percentage, naturally, is not conducive to profitable play. Since no profit can be earned on the win end, progressive play for win alone can only produce greater loss. Place betting on odds-on horses should produce from 70-75% winning returns, and it is not uncommon to have a higher winning percentage.

Inserting play on entries at 2-to-1 or less tends to reduce our winning percentages, and although we do obtain, at times, a good place return, which fattens our bankroll, this reduction may prove a hindrance.

Let's take the Keeneland meet for an actual demonstration of how the two progression methods work. We will use the progression that starts with the small wager of $2.00 first. (Please see workout to follow the play.) On April 9 we find the "A" entry, in the 4th race, going off at odds of ten cents to a dollar. Betting $2.00 to place on the entry we win 20 cents. We put this amount down in our win column.

In the fifth race we win 80 cents and we put this amount down in our win column too. On April 10th we win $3.00 on the 3rd race and put this amount down. In the 4th race we have a loser, so we put the $2.00 into our loss column.

Since we have encountered a losing bet, the next wager, according to our progression, must be $20. The horse wins at odds of ten cents to the dollar and we earn $2.00. Place this amount in the win column.

Now we regress, but at a lower rate, since we know that our winning percentage is so high that strings of consecutive winners are exceedingly likely, and we can recover more money by betting more. Hence the reason for not returning immediately to our initial bet. Betting $10, on the next selection we win $5.00 when our choice pays off at $3.00 for $2.00 to place.

We return to our initial bet of $2.00 and we win in succession: 60¢, 60¢, $1.20, 20¢, 80¢, and 40¢. On the 17th we hit a loser. We place the $2.00 lost in the lose column and prepare to wager $20.00 on the next selection.

In the 5th race our horse wins at $2.40 and we pocket a profit of $4.00. Our next bet will be $10.00. In the 6th race on April 18 there is an odds-on entry selection, but since no place betting is allowed, we cannot play. The 21st of April brings us a $2.40 return, and the 20¢ to a dollar payoff on our $10.00 bet yields a $2.00 profit. We revert to our initial $2.00 bet and collect 40¢ on the next play.

Unfortunately our final play is a loser, and we cannot recover our $2.00 loss, which we have placed in the loss column. If you intended to wager on the next Keeneland meeting, it would be advisable to use the progression and make your initial bet at the next meet $20.00. The final result in the 2-20-40 progression is a win of $21.20 and a loss of $6.00 for a net profit of $15.20.

With the 20-40-60 progression much more money can be earned.

Let's see what happens at Keeneland. Starting with $20.00 we win $2.00, $8.00, and $30.00 in succession. Our 4th bet is a loser, so we place the $20.00 in the loss column. Progressing to $40.00 on our next bet, we win $4.00. Regressing to a $30.00 wager, we win $15.00. Then coming back to our original wager, $20.00, we win $6.00, $6.00, $12.00, $2.00, $8.00 and $4.00, in swift succession.

Next comes a loser, so we are again out $20.00. Betting $40.00 on our next selection we get back $8.00 in winnings. Then, sliding back to $30.00, we click with a $6.00 profit. Reverting to our original bet of $20.00 we win again, netting $4.00. Our last bet loses, so we again chalk up a $20.00 loss. The final results show $115.00 won and $60.00 lost, for a net profit of $55.00.

A similar check was made for the Jamaica spring meeting April 1 to May 5, 1953. This meeting was too long to reprint the workout but here are the results.

There were 47 plays, of which 37 placed. The flat bet profit on a $2.00 play was $3.70. The 2-20-40 progression produced a profit of $72.50 and the 20-40-60 progression a profit of $111.00.

We said we were going to draw no conclusions. We are not. However, we do ask you to consider the results before asking just one question.

At Keeneland, the 2-20-40 progression called for an investment of $86.00 to earn a profit of $15.20. At the same track the 20-40-60 progression needed $400 to earn $55.00.

At Rockingham, the 2-20-40 progression invested $232.00 to win $39.80 and the 20-40-60 plan $650.00 to win $51.00.

This is the question for your serious consideration: Is this type of betting for you?

WORKOUTS: *Progressive Place Betting*

A

(Keeneland Meet—April 2-23, 1953)

Date	Horse	Race	Win	Place	Show
9	A entry	4	2.60	2.20	2.20
	A entry	5	....	2.80	2.20
10	A entry	3	5.40	5.00	3.20
	Prince Mike	4	....	....	....
	Correspondent	5	3.00	2.20	Out

Date	Horse	Race	Win	Place	Show
11	Blaze	4	3.20	3.00	2.20
	Berseem	5	3.20	2.60	2.40
	Hill Gail	6	....	2.60	2.20
15	A entry	4	3.40	3.20	3.00
	A entry	6	....	2.20	2.20
16	Belle Nell	2	3.00	2.80	2.60
	Golly	5	2.80	2.40	2.20
17	A entry	2	....	....	2.20
	Correspondent	5	2.80	2.40	2.20
18	A entry	6	2.60	Out	Out
21	Air Mail	2	3.20	2.40	2.20
23	Straight Face	6	....	2.40	2.20
	Breakers	7	....	....	....

2-20-40 Progression Workout A

Wager	Profit	Loss
2	.20	..
2	.80	..
2	3.00	..
2	....	2
20	2.00	..
10	5.00	..
2	.60	..
2	.60	..
2	1.20	..
2	.20	..
2	.80	..
2	.40	..
2	....	2
20	4.00	..
10	2.00	..
2	.40	..
2	....	2
Return	$21.20	6
Lost	$ 6.00	
Profit	$15.20	

20-40-60 Progression Workout A

Wager	Profit	Loss
20	2.00	..
20	8.00	..
20	30.00	..
20	....	20
40	4.00	..
30	15.00	..
20	6.00	..
20	6.00	..
20	12.00	..
20	2.00	..
20	8.00	..
20	4.00	..
20	....	20
40	8.00	..
30	6.00	..
20	4.00	..
20	....	20
Return	$115.00	60
Lost	$60.00	
Profit	$55.00	

B

(Rockingham Meet—September 22-October 25, 1952)

Date	Horse	Race	Win	Place	Show
Sept. 22	U. S. Navy	7	3.20	2.20	2.20
24	Mesmer	7	....	....	2.40
25	Main Strength	2	3.60	2.80	2.40
	Miss Ellaneous	9	....	2.40	2.20

Date	Horse	Race	Win	Place	Show
Sept. 29	B entry	5	....	....	....
	A entry	7	....	....	....
30	Warren's Gray	7	3.80	3.00	2.60
Oct. 1	B entry	7	....	2.60	2.20
3	Queen's Taste	4	....	2.20	2.20
6	A entry	7	....	2.40	2.60
7	Swamp Theatre	3	3.80	2.60	2.60
	Rose King	7	3.80	2.40	2.40
8	Tis Jose	6	....	2.80	2.40
9	L'Avion	1	....	....	2.40
14	Bar Dal	8	3.00	2.60	2.20
16	Wolf Cry	5	....	2.80	2.40
22	Warren's Gray	5	....	....	....
23	Nine Gees	1	3.40	2.80	2.20
	A entry	3	4.60	2.40	2.20
	Bold Bolo	5	3.40	2.60	2.40
25	A entry	5	3.40	3.40	2.80
	Larry Ellis	6	3.80	2.80	2.20

2-20-40 Progression Workout B			*20-40-60 Progression Workout* B		
Wager	*Profit*	*Loss*	*Wager*	*Profit*	*Loss*
2	.20	..	20	2.00	..
2	....	2	20	....	20
20	8.00	..	40	16.00	..
10	2.00	..	30	6.00	..
2	....	2	20	....	20
20	....	20	40	....	40
40	20.00	..	60	30.00	..
30	9.00	..	50	15.00	..
20	2.00	..	40	4.00	..
10	2.00	..	30	6.00	..
2	.60	..	20	6.00	..
2	.40	..	20	4.00	..
2	.80	..	20	8.00	..
2	....	2	20	....	20
20	6.00	..	40	12.00	..
10	4.00	..	30	12.00	..
2	....	2	20	....	20
20	8.00	..	40	16.00	..
10	2.00	..	30	6.00	..
2	.60	..	20	6.00	..
2	1.40	..	20	14.00	..
2	.80	..	20	8.00	..
Return	$67.80	28	Return	$171.00	120
Lost	$28.00		Lost	$120.00	
Profit	$39.80		Profit	$ 51.00	

10.
HOW TRAINERS
MANEUVER TO WIN

Books have been written about trainer's methods of procuring winners. There are so many angles, so many twists, that it would fill this entire book if we were to discuss them all.

The first method described here employs the "cover-up angle," whereas the second system uses the simple device of claiming a "hot horse." Now it is not easy to become a good halterman. It requires years of experience, and you will usually find the "older boys" meeting with the greater success. A trainer with a hot horse will try his best to "hide" it. It therefore becomes a battle of wits, with one trainer trying to keep his horse under wraps while the other pokes around to uncover it.

The angle used here by the man with the halter is a good one. Try it out for size. It might put some substantial U.S. currency in your pockets.

The Trainer's Cover-Up System

There are times when an observant horse player can find a horse which obviously figures to win on the basis of its last performance. This situation holds true when the animal is racing at a different distance today and has shown in its last performance that the present distance is suitable.

If a horse raced at a route in its last effort and was leading at the stretch or pre-stretch, it would seem that a shorter distance might have resulted in win. When the horse is re-entered in a sprint race we can surmise that the thought has also occurred to the trainer or that he deliberately raced the horse that way as a cover-up.

If today's race is not more than 15 days from the horse's

previous race, there seems to be little doubt that the horse is well-meant. Here we have an animal that is in excellent condition, in good form, and is well placed at a distance where it shows it can win. Add the ingredient of consistency to the recipe and we can assume that our horse has an excellent chance of taking the purse.

We will not be satisfied with anything much less than 20% win consistency, for our horse. (We will allow a one-race leeway, so at times the percentage will go down to a little over 19%.) The animal must not only show 20% win consistency (for the last year and this year combined) but we will not accept this percentage figure if it is based on only one win.

In other words we want to be convinced that our horse is capable of repeating a winning effort. An animal with such sound winning habits is certainly a good betting tool to start with. The method to be presented here does not confine itself to drops in distance to sprints from routes only. A horse that has raced at a route and was leading at the stretch can also be expected to win at a slightly shorter route distance.

When an animal wins a race and increases its lead from the stretch to finish, a longer distance in its next race would be appropriate, too. When the horse is stepped-up into such distances as just explained, and has definitely shown by its performance in its previous race that the distances are suitable, the bettor is again riding along with the trainer.

Although the trainer's intentions appear to be quite transparent when such conditions are shown by the horse's last performance, many bettors refuse to accept such an open and shut invitation to profits merely because the distances are different from one race to the other. Especially is this true when the animal is entered in a sprint race off a last effort at a route.

Although the method showed a 50% win percentage, the workout given here is not long enough to stamp it as conclusive evidence. Based on sound logic, however, and with a full month's workout to prove the point, the method seems to have possibilities.

To present an infallible system to the readers is always the ultimate objective of any honest system writer. Unfortunately, the most that can be done, is to present the idea and then back it up with sufficient data to prove it meritorious. In offering this system to the readers of *American Turf* monthly, I feel that this end has been accomplished.

Limiting the action to only one type of distance change would make the system distasteful to most fans. There was an attempt, therefore, to harness more than one kind around basically the same idea. The three angles herein combined give the player of this system triple action on sound, solid, well-meant horses.

RULES: *Trainer's Cover-Up System*

1. The horse's last race must not have been more than 15 days from today's race.

2. If the horse's last race was at a route and the animal was leading at the stretch, consider it for selection if it is dropping in distance (today's race) ⅛ of a mile or less.

3. If the horse raced at a route last out, consider it for selection if it meets the following requirements and today's race is a sprint.

a. If today's race is at ¾ of a mile or less, the horse must have been first at the pre-stretch (second call, *Daily Racing Form*) of its last race.

b. If today's race is more than ¾ of a mile, consider it if the horse was first at pre-stretch (second call, *Daily Racing Form*) or stretch (third call, *Daily Racing Form*) of its last race.

4. Distance increase: Last race must have been at a route where the horse must show that it was first at the stretch call and won the race, gaining ground from stretch to finish. Today's distance must be less than ⅛ of a mile greater than the distance of its last race.

5. The horse must show 20% win consistency for the current and last year combined. The horse must show at least two wins for both years. A one-race leeway is allowed if the horse raced 21 or more times both years combined. Four wins out of 21 would be O.K., five wins out of 26, etc.

6. If horse lost last race, it must not have been by more than six lengths.

7. In case of tie, play the horse with the earliest last race (closest to today's date) providing this race was not more than ten days

from its last race. If still tied, choose the horse with the best win consistency for both years combined.

For those players who do not care to bet on longshots this method should prove ideal. Most of the time, as the workout shows, the bettor will get some good-priced winners. Only occasionally will he come up against a short price. When this occurs, it is the privilege of the player to accept the horse or reject the animal from consideration.

Although there were no longshots in the workout, the method still produced a profit of $72.70 on a $2.00 flat bet wager for the month of April, 1949. Knocking off the five highest prices in the workout would still show a flat bet profit of $17.00.

To make things clearer let us take one of each type of selection from the workout and show how it was chosen as a play.

On April 7th, in the fifth at Bowie, Dry, a four-year-old colt, was entered in a race at one mile and 70 yards. The horse's last race was at $1\frac{1}{16}$; this was a drop in distance of less than $\frac{1}{8}$ of a mile and since the horse showed that it had been first by two lengths in the stretch of its last race ten days ago, the horse was under consideration (see Rule 2). The horse's performance chart shows four wins out of 21 for the current and last year combined. The animal qualified with the consistency rule on the one-race-leeway basis. The horse had won its last race. It became our selection and won the race.

Bosmond, a horse that had won four out of its last 18 races, for better than 20% win consistency, was in the fifth race at Jamaica on April 9, 1949. The horse had been leading by one length at the pre-stretch of its last race at $1\frac{1}{16}$. Today's race was a sprint at $\frac{3}{4}$ of a mile. The horse had finished second, beaten four lengths in its last race seven days previously. It was a qualified selection (see Rule 3a).

The seventh at Lincoln Downs on April 9, 1949, produced another type of distance change selection in the horse Rakemup. The gelding had raced eight days ago at one mile and had been first at the stretch by a head, then pulled away to win by 1¼ lengths. Today's race was $1\frac{1}{16}$, an increase of $\frac{1}{16}$ of a mile. The horse showed a consistency record of three wins out of 15, for a per-

WORKOUT: *Trainers' Cover-Up System*

(April 1949)

Date	Horse	Race and Track	Mutuel	Type of Play†
April 1	None			
2	Brown Crackle	3 L.D.	4.40	DI
	Vinita Rev	5 G.P.	8.20	DD
4	None			
5	None			
6	None			
7	Dry	5 Bow.	13.60	DD
	Balbar	8 Bow.	....	DD
8	Ballast	6 Bow.	....	DI
9	Bosmond	5 Jam.	14.30	DS
	Rakemup	7 L.D.	13.20	DI
	Manna H	6 G.P.	9.00	DS
11	None			
12	True Pilate	4 L.D.	....	DS
	Brown Crackle	5 L.D.	....	DS
13	None			
14	Twilight Trail	4 Jam.	8.80	DS
	Flaming Lady	8 Jam.	11.20	DI
	Comet's Tail	7 L.D.	....	DD
15	Spicebush	7 Jam.	....	DS
16	First Reward	8 Hdg.	8.20	DI
18	None			
19	Turn Back	5 L.D.	6.80	DS
	Miss All Sweep	2 G.P.	....	DS
20	None			
21	None			
22	Bad Light	3 Hdg.	....	DS
23	None			
25	Sunny River	3 L.D.	13.40	DS
26	None			
27	Bannerday	7 Jam.	....	DS
	Retintin	7 Hdg.	....	DI
	Oom Paul	6 L.D.	3.40	DS
	Polo Highgood	8 Kee.	....	DI
28	Lictor	8 Hdg.	....	DD
29	None			
30	Boo Boo Shoo	5 Suf.	....	DS
	Suntos*	5 L.D.	10.20	DS

*Entry won

26 selections—13 won—50%

Amount Returned $124.70

Amount Invested 52.00

Profit 72.70

† DI—Distance increase

† DS—Drop Route to Sprint

† DD—Distance Drop Route to Route—⅛ of a mile or less

centage of 20. It met all requirements (see Rule 4) and become our selection.

Study the rules until you have them thoroughly fixed in your mind, then if you have a batch of current *Racing Forms* available, work with the system on paper. You will soon learn to spot the good plays, most of which will be from cover-up races used by trainers to get their horses primed for a winning effort.

Spotting Claimed Horses

When a trainer claims a horse, he has made an investment similar to purchasing a business. Since he has laid out a sum of money, it is only natural that he is eager to regain it and try to make a profit. Some people who know little about a business, will put their money into it haphazardly, practically ensuring its loss. However, the man with business acumen will invest only when he is reasonably sure that his money will return a profit.

Many horses are claimed which never see the winners' circle. They are usually bought by men who know little about racing. The clever trainer or owner, like the intelligent businessman, tries to make reasonably sure that the claimed animal is a sound business proposition.

As a rule, a highly consistent animal which has proved by past performances that it has the ability to win is worth being claimed. This kind of horse can usually be brought into condition to win a race within a short time after being claimed.

If the win does not occur after two months have passed, we can often assume that this time, unfortunately, our smart owner or trainer has been stuck with a lemon. It happens to the best of them, even in ordinary business, but not too often. It is very possible to pick up cripples in a claiming race; a trainer will often drop a horse in claiming price in an effort to get rid of it.

It is also true that such an attempt may be made solely to win a purse and it is not an easy task to determine the trainer's objective. That is one of the hazards of racing which the bettor as well as the trainer making the claim must accept.

The method to be presented here is so arranged that in most cases it avoids this risk. Of course the animal may win later on, but as a rule it is best to lay off the horse if it has not won for two months. It is also safer not to play the animal if it has not raced recently, since most platers have to be raced into condition. The necessity to handicap a claimed horse is eliminated; there is no need to second-guess the animal or the trainer's intentions. The chances are that the horse will be trying if it has not yet won for the new owner and has raced recently.

In confining himself to wagering only on consistent claimed horses the bettor will avoid a lot of headaches. There is no need for making sex or weight allowances, probing deeply into the past performances of all the horses entered in the race, examining class, speed, etc. This is a simplified method of obtaining winners, and from time to time it clicks on a real longie. Although in the workout given here the method did not produce many staggering payoffs, I know that this is true. For example: On September 14, 1949, Texas Brags, a horse that had been claimed two days before, won the 5th race at Aqueduct at a mutuel of $52.70. This is not a rare occurrence. If the reader will check several other months, he will see what I mean.

RULES: *Spotting Claimed Horses*

1. The horse's last race must have been run not more than ten days ago.

2. The horse must have been claimed within two months from today's race and as yet did not win for its new owner. A little "c" next to the horse's claiming price listed in its past performances shows that the horse was claimed in that race. For an example, refer to the reproduced past performance chart of Grandpa Max, who raced on April 13, 1949, in the 5th at Lincoln Downs. The circled area shows that on March 12, 1949, in the first race at Fair Grounds, Grandpa Max was claimed for $2500.

3. The horse must show a win consistency of 20% or better for the current and last year combined, with at least two wins for this period. If the horse has won only one race for both years, it cannot be considered. A one-race leeway is allowed if the animal has started at least 16 times for both years combined. For example:

three wins out of 16 tries would qualify; four wins out of 21 is O.K.; five wins out of 26, etc.

4. If a tie occurs, choose the horse with the best win consistency for both years.

5. Play no two-year-olds or jumpers.

If the reader will observe the rules closely, he will notice that of necessity he will often be playing against a horse that has already lost for him. In fact, it could happen that the horse may be backed several times, fail to win, and then be discarded. I am pointing this out because I wish to demonstrate that such a situation can exist without harming the system in the least.

From these plays I found that a best bet could be determined which would raise the win percentage without hurting the profits in the slightest. This was done by applying a revealed form rule to the horse's last race.

The Best Bet rule requires the horse to be either first, second, or within three lengths of the winner at the finish or first, second or within three lengths off the pace at any call.

The Best Bets, of course will limit the action somewhat, but since they stress revealed form in the horse's last race, they should ring up a higher percentage of winners. For those who desire safety in preference to action the Best Bets are recommended.

To make things a little clearer, I will take two horses to illustrate how one was selected and the other rejected.

On April 1, 1949, in the 8th at Bowie (see workout) we find only one horse (Wrightstown) that has been claimed within two months of today's race without winning for its new owner and has a win consistency of at least 20% for the current and last years combined. He had won four out of 17 races for both years. His last race was run on March 29, three days ago. He is, therefore, a qualified selection.

This horse also meets our qualifications as a best bet, since he shows revealed form in his last out, for he was up close to the pacemaker at the first three calls. The gelding was third by three lengths at the first call, second only by a length at the pre-stretch and third by a length and a half at the stretch.

Let us take just one more case. This one is important, because I know many system fans who will check this method may make the mistake which will be pointed out, thereby backing a horse that does not qualify, and then blame the method.

On April 14, 1949, Striker Pilot, running in the 6th at Gulfstream Park, looked like a qualified system selection. The colt's last race was on April 9, five days ago, where he had finished 6th, 2¾ lengths behind the winner. He was also within striking distance at the 1st call and the 3rd call where he was 1¾ lengths and 1½ lengths off the pace respectively.

The horse was claimed February 21, 1949 in his third from last race, definitely within the 2 months time limit. He looked like a spot play Best Bet, but, he had won the race following the one in which he was claimed. Since he had already won for his new owner, he could not be considered. If you are going to play this system, be careful here. This is the spot where you may make an error.

Ironically enough, Striker Pilot won that race, paying $12.50. However, don't let this influence you to ignore the rule which stipulates not having won for the new owner. You will certainly regret it.

Since many horses prefer certain distances it might be appropriate to insert a rule specifying a good showing, say a win or place, at today's distance somewhere in today's past performances. Also a horse that wins its last race by more than a length can be expected to go a further distance in its next race and probably win. So, we will add the following rules and see what happens:

1. The horse must show a win or place at today's distance in today's list of past performances. If *today's* race is at one mile and 70 yards, the horse may be considered if it shows a win or place at $1\frac{1}{16}$. There are not too many races at 1-70, so it would be very difficult to qualify a horse at this distance. However, if today's race is at $1\frac{1}{16}$ the horse must show a win or place at exactly the same distance somewhere in today's past performances.

2. If the horse has won its last race by more than one length, it is considered if today's race is at the same distance, or greater but in the same category. In other words, if the last race was at a route, there would be no question. But if the last race was won in a sprint, then today's race could be at a greater distance—but it must also be a sprint. If the last race was a sprint and today's race is a route, the horse in question cannot be considered. (A route is a race at a mile

or more.) The influence of these two rules is indicated on the workout by the horses shown in italics. It limited the selections to 16, of which seven won a percentage of .44. It increased the win profit on all plays to $112.10 and on Best Bets to $115.10.

Readers who wish to limit the number of their plays will find these additional rules a distinct advantage.

WORKOUT: *Spotting Claimed Horses*

(April 1949)

Date		Horse	Race and Track	Mutuel
April	1	*Wrightstown**	8 Bow.	$13.40
	4	Lord Caprice	8 L.D.	. . . .
		*Breakage**	1 G.P.	12.50
	5	*Lady Alice*	6 Bow.	5.00
	6	*Fleet Command*	8 Jam.	. . . .
		Grandpa Max*	6 L.D.	. . . .
		Gray Beard	4 G.P.	. . . .
		Kentucky Day	8 G.P.	. . . .
	8	Risky Betty	5 G.P.	. . . .
	9	Lord Caprice*	1 L.D.	. . . .
		*Freedom Ring**	2 L.D.	8.00
	11	*Magnus**	6 G.P.	. . . .
	12	*Viva Teddy**	8 Hdg.	5.00
	13	Grandpa Max*	5 L.D.	9.20
		Coronet Star	2 G.P.	. . . .
	15	*Split The Wind**	7 Hdg.	. . . .
	16	*Coronet Star**	2 G.P.	. . . .
	18	Monifieth	4 Hdg.	. . . .
	19	Lord Caprice*	8 L.D.	. . . .
		Elk Hills*	9 L.D.	. . . .
		*Magnus**	7 G.P.	. . . .
	20	March Chick*	8 Hdg.	. . . .
		Blue Agent	3 Kee.	. . . .
	23	*Expedite**	3 L.D.	10.00
	25	*Shifty Mae**	4 Jam.	. . . .
		*Magnet**	5 Hdg.	90.20
	26	Laurania	8 Jam.	11.60
	28	Lord Caprice*	4 L.D.	. . . .
	30	*Lord Caprice**	9 L.D.	. . . .

* Best Bets
29 selections—9 won—31%
* Best Bets—19 selections—7 won—37%

Amount Returned All Selections	$164.90	* Best Bets	$148.30
Amount Invested All Selections	58.00		38.00
NET PROFIT on $2 win wagers	$106.90		$110.30

11.
WHEN TO WATCH
THE JOCKEY

Playing jockeys is much easier than picking horses to win races. All you have to do is look for the name of your favorite jockey and place your bet on the horse he is riding. You don't have to worry about past performances, class, form, consistency, etc. Yes, it's a very simple way of playing the races. However, if you do this steadily, race in and race out, you will almost surely land in the local poorhouse. If you expect to take a profit out of racing, you must not bet on the jockey alone, disregarding the horse entirely. The jockey can't do the running for the horse, as everyone knows. But he can be mighty helpful if he knows his business. A good jockey and a fit horse always is an attractive combination.

Jockey System

Once a jockey has managed to make a name for himself, he attracts trainers who are out to win a purse. They naturally try to get a boy who will give the horse a good ride, so whenever a trainer thinks his horse is ready he will seek the services of the best jockey he can find. If he can get the best boy on the grounds, or second-best, he has a good chance to put over his horse.

Some of the more prominent jockeys ride under contract to certain stables, but in such a case you can bet they are winning stables or a prominent rider wouldn't have signed the contract in the first place. Even a topnotcher must be careful to assure himself good mounts, for reputations don't last long unless they're maintained, and this goes for jockeys as well as ball players and cookie salesmen. Of course, on occasion even the best jockey must ride a bad horse, but they get more than their share of horses that figure to win.

Now what is all this leading up to? Just this: If you pick out the one or two best jockeys riding at a particular circuit, and bet on their mounts only when the "signs" say the horse is fit-and-ready, then you stand a very good chance of making your wagering profitable over the long haul—which is all that counts.

When a horse finishes in the money, it is an indication that it is in form, or rounding to form, and perhaps is ready to win its next race. Now, if the stable puts a topnotch jockey in the saddle, and the horse gets sufficient support from the bettors to make it the favorite or close to it, that animal is a sound investment for the player.

In most instances, if the horse is not ready to win, the stable would not feel it necessary to obtain the aid of an ace booter, nor would the horse be likely to obtain strong support from the public, or the men who handicap 'em for the daily racing papers and newspapers. As it is now, the favorite comes home in front better than one-third of the time; with this angle added, we can expect the horse to romp home around half of the time. Of course, we won't always be playing the favorite, but we will always be playing a well-backed horse. And at the rate of 50% winners, we need only slightly better than even-money average price to come out with a profit.

Here are the system rules; study them carefully and follow them to the letter in making your selections.

RULES: *Jockey System*

1. Play only those horses ridden by the two leading riders at the circuit you are playing. (A "circuit" consists of all the tracks in a given area, such as the New York circuit, which comprises all the tracks in the New York area, namely Jamaica, Aqueduct, Belmont Park and Saratoga.) We suggest using two jockeys because if you use only one you will not get much action. And, as a rule, the two top jockeys are about on a par in skill anyway.

2. To qualify for play, the horse must—

a. Have finished in the money (first, second or third) last time out; and

b. Be listed at the lowest odds in the price line you are using (a scratch sheet price line, or any dependable price line that is made up after scratches). (If another horse in the same race has the same odds, the system horse still qualifies.)

3. In the event that two horses qualify for place in the same race, play the one listed highest on the scratch sheet or whatever set of graded selections you are using.

These are the only three rules. In order to prove that this system works, I have included here a workout of results covering the two-month period of August and September, 1947. In making up this workout I used Arcaro and Atkinson, beyond question two of the best jockeys then in action at the New York circuit. I used the *National Racing Program,* a leading New York scratch sheet, for my guide as to odds and graded selections. Another reason I used this scratch sheet is that it indicates when a horse finished in the money in its last race by placing a small numeral to the right of its name. For example, Gallorette[3] means that Gallorette finished third last time out. Using a scratch sheet which does this, or any other type of graded selections which tells where each horse finished last time out, obviates the need for a daily racing paper with past performances.

Now permit me to give a couple of illustrations to make the rules clear. On August 4, 1947, (see Workout of Results) in the 8th at Saratoga, Ted Atkinson rode Oatmeal, quoted at 2-to-1. The next shortest-priced horse with the lowest odds. Checking Oatmeal's performance last time out, we find a small 3 after his name on the scratch sheet, which tells us that Oatmeal finished third last time out. Therefore, he qualifies in all respects. He won, paying $6.10, $4.10, $3.00.

WORKOUT: *Jockey System*

				Win	Place	Show
Aug.	4	Gallorette	6 Sar.	4.90	3.10	Out — Arcaro
		Oatmeal	8 Sar.	6.10	4.10	3.00 — Atkinson
Aug.	5	Trapeze	5 Sar.	5.80	3.40	2.50 — Atkinson
		My Request	6 Sar.	...	3.00	2.60 — Arcaro
		Jeep	7 Sar.	...	...	... — Arcaro
Aug.	8	Chally Mally	2 Sar.	...	...	2.70 — Atkinson
		First Flight	6 Sar.	...	...	... — Arcaro
		Half Brother	7 Sar.	...	...	... — Arcaro
		Sweet Pegotty	8 Sar.	...	4.90	3.70 — Atkinson

				Win	Place	Show
Aug.	9	First Flight	1 Sar.	4.50	3.20	3.20 — Arcaro
		My Request	4 Sar.	3.60	2.40	2.40 — Arcaro
		Misleader	5 Sar.	...	...	... — Atkinson
		Trapeze	8 Sar.	...	3.10	2.50 — Atkinson
Aug.	11	Captain Andrew	2 Sar.	6.60	4.30	3.80 — Atkinson
		Relic	5 Sar.	3.60	3.40	3.00 — Arcaro
		Nomadic	6 Sar.	...	3.20	2.90 — Atkinson
		Salerno	7 Sar.	...	...	2.50 — Arcaro
		Haile	8 Sar.	6.90	4.70	4.20 — Atkinson
Aug.	13	Lady Marilyn	1 Sar.	6.90	4.60	3.60 — Arcaro
		Oatmeal	8 Sar.	...	...	... — Arcaro
Aug.	16	Upbeat	1 Sar.	...	...	... — Atkinson
		Better Self	4 Sar.	3.80	2.60	2.40 — Arcaro
Aug.	18	Sleigh Bells	7 Sar.	6.60	3.40	2.60 — Atkinson
Aug.	20	Humaya	7 Sar.	4.10	2.70	2.50 — Atkinson
Aug.	21	Khyber Pass	5 Sar.	...	...	Out — Arcaro
Aug.	22	Mighty Master	2 Sar.	...	5.60	4.10 — Arcaro
		Relic	4 Sar.	3.30	2.50	2.30 — Arcaro
Aug.	23	My Request	4 Sar.	3.10	2.40	Out — Arcaro
Aug.	25	Jackamine	6 Sar.	7.10	3.00	2.30 — Arcaro
Aug.	27	Captain Andrew	1 Sar.	...	3.70	3.00 — Atkinson
		Gretna Green	8 Sar.	4.70	3.50	2.60 — Atkinson
Aug.	28	Chief Barker	5 Sar.	...	...	2.40 — Arcaro
		Ace Admiral	6 Sar.	...	...	... — Arcaro
Aug.	30	Better Self	5 Sar.	...	...	... — Arcaro
Sept.	1	Mangohick	7 Aqu.	6.00	3.40	2.70 — Atkinson
		Haile	8 Aqu.	4.00	2.70	2.30 — Atkinson
Sept.	2	Salerno	6 Aqu.	...	3.20	2.30 — Arcaro
Sept.	3	Vinsfurlough	2 Aqu.	...	...	2.40 — Arcaro
		Poppa George	5 Aqu.	2.50	2.10	Out — Arcaro
		Best Dress	7 Aqu.	...	...	... — Arcaro
		Mae Agnes	8 Aqu.	7.30	3.70	3.10 — Atkinson
Sept.	4	Mama Fufu	1 Aqu.	5.60	3.80	3.00 — Arcaro
		Roman Jobe	5 Aqu.	3.40	2.60	2.50 — Arcaro
		Okeetee	7 Aqu.	5.00	3.70	2.90 — Atkinson
Sept.	5	Cencerro	4 Aqu.	...	2.40	2.10 — Atkinson
Sept.	6	Lucky Reward	5 Aqu.	...	...	... — Atkinson
Sept.	12	Indique	6 Aqu.	3.60	2.50	2.20 — Atkinson
Sept.	13	Mahlima	1 Aqu.	...	3.60	3.00 — Arcaro
		My Request	4 Aqu.	3.30	2.40	2.40 — Arcaro
Sept.	17	Oatmeal	8 Aqu.	5.20	3.60	2.60 — Atkinson
Sept.	18	Equinox	7 Aqu.	4.50	2.80	2.70 — Arcaro
Sept.	19	Solater	5 Aqu.	...	2.70	2.40 — Arcaro
Sept.	20	But Why Not	7 Aqu.	4.30	2.80	2.30 — Arcaro

				Win	Place	Show
Sept.	23	Quick Reward	6 Bel.	...	3.00	2.20 — Arcaro
		Haile	8 Bel.	4.20	3.20	2.80 — Atkinson
Sept.	24	Upbeat	4 Bel.	...	3.20	2.70 — Atkinson
Sept.	26	Bisby	8 Bel.	9.70	4.60	3.40 — Arcaro
Sept.	30	Sir Bim	2 Bel.	...	...	3.70 — Arcaro
		Athene	5 Bel.	...	4.20	3.30 — Arcaro
		Bright Sword	6 Bel.	...	...	... — Atkinson

60 plays, 30 winners (50%); 43 finished first or second (72%); 45 finished first, second or third (80%) (no show mutuels sold on four plays). Net profit on $10 flat bets to win only, $151.00; place only, $115.00; show only, $69.00; across-the-board, $335.00.

On August 11, Atkinson rode Captain Andrew in the second race at Saratoga. Captain Andrew was quoted at 5-to-2. There was another horse in the race quoted as 5-to-2, but that didn't eliminate Captain Andrew because there was no horse in the race at lower odds (see Rule 2, Section *a*). On the scratch sheet's graded selections Captain Andrew showed a small 1 after his name, which means he won his last race. Therefore, he was a qualified play, and he won, paying $6.60, $4.30, $3.80.

The accompanying Workout of Results is a complete, accurate and reliable report of all qualified plays for the months of August and September, 1947. There were no plays on the first three days of August: that is why the first play in the workout appears on August 4.

I do not think you can find a better method of playing jockeys than this one.

The Triple Threat

It is not unusual for a horse that really figures to win on the basis of class, condition, and form to wind up out of the money. Bewildered horse players feel like tearing up their racing papers along with their losing tickets when such incidents occur.

A horse may appear, on the basis of past performances, to be a mortal cinch; it may go off at ridiculously short odds and yet fail to come in among the first three. Such situations cause many to conclude that they might as well bet on wrestling matches and to feel constrained to cast aspersions on the fair name of the sport.

This is only the conclusion of those who are trying to fix the blame for their own failures on someone else. Nearly every loss can be explained, if a careful study is made of the result charts and past performances.

With the element of racing luck ever present and the normal fluctuations of form what they are, losses must be expected along with wins. The problem is to keep them at a minimum. To do this every reason why a horse may lose must be weighed.

Not the least important factor in a horse's winning is the ability of its rider. The greatest gamblers of all time have stressed that it is absolutely essential to have the proper jockey to ensure the safety of the wager.

It does not necessarily follow that the leading rider in percentage of wins, money earned, or in number of wins, is the best for any particular horse. An example of this was the case of Phalanx, a good horse that seemed to perform to the best of his ability under Ruperto Donoso.

Switching from Arcaro to anyone else ordinarily would seem a poor way to improve a horse, but experts agreed that Phalanx performed better for Ruperto than he did for even the redoubtable Eddie.

Trainers are constantly experimenting to get the riders best suited to their horses. But there are times when the preferred rider is not available. When he is, and the horse is favorably placed, its chances of winning are enhanced.

If a jockey who has already won with this horse, has the mount, well and good—the trainer need look no further. If not, and the previous booter has shown little with the animal, then a jockey change might be the answer. The trainer therefore searches for a boy he thinks would be more successful with his charge. When this jockey has been found, the animal becomes a triple threat, if it is in a spot where it can win, has had a recent race, and the jockey has been picked on the assumption that he can handle the horse properly. With a step like this, winners should not be hard to get.

The problem for the bettor is to ascertain when the horse is in the right spot. For this he must consult the past performances. If the horse shows that he has won a race at a higher claiming price than the top price of the race under consideration, then we can feel that he is probably capable of handling the present company. Since it is difficult to measure the class of horses running in allowances, stakes, and handicaps, only claiming races are considered.

Horses that finished 12 lengths or more behind the leader last time out should automatically be rejected. It is difficult to excuse such a race and it does not pay to risk money on horses that show poor performances.

RULES: *The Triple Threat*

1. Play claiming races only.
2. The horse's last race must have been within ten days of today's race.
3. Horse must show a win in today's past performances at a higher claiming price than the top claiming price of today's race. (Claiming price of the race, not of the individual horse.) A race in which the horse finished first but was disqualified is considered an actual win.
4. The horse must not have won its last race.
5. Eliminate any horse that lost its last race by 12 lengths or more.
6. Play no females.
7. The jockey riding the horse today must have won with this horse as shown somewhere in today's list of past performances, or must not be the jockey that rode the animal in its last race. (Either there must have been a switch in jockeys or the horse must be ridden by a jockey who shows he won with this horse somewhere in today's list of past performances.)
8. In case of tie, choose the horse that shows a workout within five days of today's race. If still tied, pass the race.
9. Play no two-year-olds, maidens, or jumpers.
10. Play after scratches are known.

From the two-month workout presented, we can assume that the results are not mere coincidence. There were 166 selections and 52 winners. Although not exactly conclusive, the check signifies that the method has merit.

Females were discarded from consideration because an extensive check shows them to be less reliable and more subject to disturbing influences. This is still a controversial subject among followers of thoroughbred racing, but there is ample evidence of the soundness of this conclusion. The rule robbed the method of quite a few winners, but it also eliminated many losers.

A check showed that horses which display a workout within five days of today's race are to be preferred over those which do not have such a recent workout to their credit. The separation rule, therefore, prefers the animal showing a workout within five days of today's race.

Out of 72 selections which showed such a recent workout, 26 were returned winners.

To clarify things somewhat, it might be advisable to demonstrate how the system works by choosing a selection from the workout and showing step by step the processes involved.

For this exercise the 8th race at Jamaica on April 6, 1949 will be used. The race is a claiming race. It therefore meets our primary qualifications. It is not a two-year-old affair or a jumping race. There are 12 horses after scratches and none of them are maidens. Each of the animals entered lost its last race.

The first thing we do is to check off all those horses with last races, not more than ten days ago. Maidens and horses that finished 12 lengths or more behind the winner in their last race are eliminated, if any such are in the race. All of the horses but one have raced within the required ten-day time limit. This animal, Lanky, lost its last race by 12 lengths and is a female, so she is out of the picture on three counts. Foxy Jack, Misabi, Rose Canyon and Sason also lost last time out by 12 lengths or more. This leaves only seven horses to be considered. Misabi, Esterita and Flight Nurse go out, as they are females.

Now there are only five horses left to probe. The claiming price of this race is $3000, so we con the past performances of the remaining five horses to see whether any of them won a race at a higher claiming price. Invitation shows a win at a $3500 claiming price. The Kicker won a $4000 claimer and Fleet Command won at $5000. These are the only three horses that show a winning claiming race at a higher price than today's race. All three seem to be spotted right and it appears that each trainer is anticipating a possible win.

The acid test remains. Has the right jockey been chosen? D. Dodson is riding The Kicker. The horse's past performances do not show that this jockey has scored with the horse previously, and he rode the animal in its last race. Therefore no switch has been made. Since the stable is going along with the same boy, no third threat in the horse's chances to win has been added.

The same situation holds true with Fleet Command. The jockey here is S. Boulmetis.

Although Invitation's past performances do not show that the jockey riding him today ever won with the animal, the element of switch is present. The stable has switches from R. Howell, who rode the horse in its last race, to C. Rogers. The triple threat is on.

Rogers, keeping the horse "in hand for the first half-mile," brought the animal into "command from the outside, leaving the backstretch"; the horse drew "out under mild urging rounding the second turn," and, "under a sustained drive through the stretch, stalled off "Quaker." Invitation paid $73.00, $24.80, $17.90 across the board.

When the horse player wagers on a horse that is such a triple threat, he has a solid play and very often gets an attractive price.

WORKOUT: *The Triple Threat*

(March-April 1949)

Date Horse	Race & Track	Win	Place	Show	Jockey Switched or Jockey who won with horse
Mar.					
1 Duquesne	9 F.G.				R. L. Baird
Big Head	6 O.P.	5.00	3.00	2.40	L. C. Cook
Town Hall	7 O.P.	10.90	5.80	6.00	H. Litz'n'r to G. South
Broker	3 S.A.	44.30	20.30	11.80	J. W. Martin
Elmo Vistic	4 S.A.				G. Glisson-W. Litz'bg
2 Viva Teddy	8 Hia			3.40	E. Nelson to V. Nodarse
Bill G.	5 F.G.	17.00	8.20	4.20	J. Delah'ye-J. West
Dagon	6 F.G.				H. Keene
Darmin	8 O.P.	12.20	5.20	3.40	A. J. Lind'y
3 F. B. Eye	8 F.G.	20.60	8.40	7.20	D. Madden-V. Ter'nova
Gold Boom	3 S.A.			3.20	G. Glisson
4 Jellico	8 F.G.	6.60	4.60	3.80	R. L. Baird
Tabosa	1 O.P.	5.10	3.80	2.90	F. Keene
Big Burly	6 O.P.				W. Hughs-P. Glidewell
Duffy	3 S.A.			4.50	J. West'pe-R. Summers

Date	Horse	Race & Track	Win	Place	Show	Jockey Switched or Jockey who won with horse
5	Big Buster	1 F.G.				P. Ten'glio-H. Keene
	Rodman Keenon	9 F.G.		5.80	3.80	C. Picou
	Little Geromo	8 O.P.				N. Cartw't-W. Eads
7	Hinkston	3 O.P.				L. C. Cook
8	All or Nothing	1 O.P.	8.20	3.70	3.40	N. Cartw't-W. Eads
9	High Mayor	2 F.G.			7.60	H. Keene
	Lucky Charles	1 O.P.				G. P. Ryan-W. Eads
	Melvin	5 O.P.	41.40	19.90	10.30	H. Litz'er-G. South
11	Fleet Command	4 G.P.				B. James-F. Pannell
	Gary Leslie	5 G.P.				H. Lind'g-B. Strange
12	Grandpa Max	1 F.G.	5.00	3.40	2.40	D. Madden-H. Keene*
	Chance Voyage	3 F.G.	5.20	3.60	2.20	R. L. Baird
	Goblin	5 F.G.		3.80	3.00	R. Lowery-J. West
	Rodman Keenon	8 F.G.				C. Picou
	Star Graduate	9 F.G.	4.80	3.40	2.60	J. Delah'ye
	Vinita Toney	3 O.P.		5.40	3.70	J. D. Jessop-L. Wickel
14	Jingle Jangle	7 G.P.			6.20	C. Pennock-E. Polk
	Thunder Hoof	4 O.P.				H. Feath'n
	Copper Pot	5 O.P.				N. Jemas
15	Leadership	4 G.P.				R. J. M'tin-D. Wagner
	Director	8 G.P.	10.00	5.30	3.10	A. D. Rivera-W. M. Cook
	Hinkston	6 O.P.	7.40	4.00	3.00	L. C. Cook
16	Accipitor	4 G.P.				G. Schreck-R. Howell
	Starry Cant	3 F.G.				G. Hettinger-W. Mann
17	St. Jock	7 G.P.				B. Civ'ello-R. Howell
	Maxmar	5 O.P.				J. D. Jessop-B. Fisk
	Big Head	6 O.P.				L. C. Cook
(March-April 1949)						
18	Top Score	7 G.P.				E. Nelson-L. Batch'ler
	Thunder Hoof	5 O.P.				H. Feath'on-L. Wickel
19	Jonathan D.	1 G.P.	11.90	6.50	3.60	L. Batch'ler-E. Nelson
	Nowadays	2 G.P.	8.80	4.70	3.10	A. D. Rivera-W. Saunders
	Santa Claus	7 G.P.	20.70	11.80	9.10	E. J. Knapp-J. Stewart
	Starry Cant	3 F.G.				W. Mann-J. Green
	Valdina Perion	9 F.G.				A. Skoronski-B. Bass
21	Vinita Toney	4 O.P.	7.50	3.70	2.70	L. Wickel-F. Keene
22	Concrete	5 G.P.				D. Wagner-L. Batch'ler
	Menever	8 G.P.				G. Schreck-E. Flutie
	Blob Jr.	5 F.G.				M. Danisi-E. Coffman
	Silent Max	2 O.P.			3.20	D. Ling'nf'r-A. J. Lind'y
23	Timboo	3 G.P.		3.20	3.10	L. Batcheller-P. Roberts
	Cabbagetown	5 F.G.	14.40	10.20	5.20	A. Gaith'r-H. Keene
	Big Wig	6 F.G.		6.80	4.00	J. Combest-H. Keene
	Duquesne	9 F.G.				J. West-R. L. Baird

Date	Horse	Race & Track	Win	Place	Show	Jockey Switched or Jockey who won with horse
24	Bolo Tie	2 G.P.	12.90	6.30	4.20	J. Choq'tte
	Curier	2 F.G.				M. Danisi-H. Keene
	Copper Pot	5 O.P.				N. Jemas
25	Chero-Kaid	2 F.G.				W. Mann-P. S. Boyle
26	King Gail	8 F.G.				E. Coffman-H. Keene
28	Segundo Sombra	8 G.P.		3.80	3.30	G. Schreck-W. M. Cook
31	Mason Dixon	7 Bow.				L. Olah-J. Lynch
	Grey Beard	4 G.P.				M. A. Bu'n-M. Corona

Apr.

Date	Horse	Race & Track	Win	Place	Show	Jockey Switched or Jockey who won with horse
1	Hemjohn	4 L.D.			2.60	F. Dodge-A. Licata
2	Shako	4 Bow	5.80	3.20	2.60	P. S. Boyle
	Cee Raf	3 L.D.				D. Brigley-L. Pafundi
	Elk Hills	8 L.D.			5.50	L. Pafundi-J. Baird
	River Flares	3 G.P.				J. Cowley-J. Stewart
	Ariel Sweep	4 G.P.	6.20	3.80	2.90	B. Strange-R. Nash
	Spanaqua	8 G.P.				H. Wallace
4	Camp's First	8 Jam.				J. Delah'ye
	Easy Homer	7 Bow.				L. Bauer-H. L. Pierson
	War Ballad	8 Bow.		11.60	5.40	H. Clagg't-R. Fitzgerald
	Tascosa	1 L.D.	5.60	3.80	3.20	G. Gleason-S. Chiap'tta
	Akbar	7 L.D.		6.20	5.00	M. Pena-A. Licata
	Eternal Way	1 G.P.				M. A. Buxton-C. Errico
	Banovina	5 G.P.				A. Skoronski-R. Nash
5	Gary Leslie	5 Bow.			2.80	J. Lynch-R. J. Martin
	Border Vintage	1 L.D.			2.40	M. Pena-A. Licata
	Dwight Harar	8 L.D.				G. Dodge-R. DeStasio
	Arrested	4 G.P.				G. Schreck-C. Pennock
	Darby Dimout	7 G.P.				E. Nelson-J. McCoy

April

Date	Horse	Race & Track	Win	Place	Show	Jockey Switched or Jockey who won with horse
6	Profano	7 Jam.	6.30	3.40	2.90	H. Woodhouse-E. Arcaro
	Invitation	8 Jam.	73.00	24.80	17.90	R. Howell-C. Rogers
	Last Show	4 G.P.		9.30	5.30	W. Zakoor-R. Nash
	Fighter Jack	8 G.P.	9.40	5.10	4.10	A. Skoronski- G. Schreck
7	Burt's Reward	8 Jam.				T. Atkinson
	Hemjohn	2 L.D.		4.00	3.20	A. Licata-R. Keane
	Know How	4 L.D.	3.80	3.40	2.80	A. Lind'y-S. Chia'tta
	Biloxi Bay	5 L.D.		3.60	3.60	B. Fisk-T. Spencer
	Mulligatawney	7 L.D.			3.80	B. Fisk-F. Keene
	Swimmin' Hole	1 G.P.				G. Schreck-F. Fernandez
	Respire	4 G.P.		5.40	3.20	J. Phillippi-R. Bauer
8	Helaneius	2 Jam.	5.20	3.50	2.60	J. D. Jessop-E. Arcaro
	Wary Flight	6 Bow.				R. Scott-C. Kirk
	Mason Dixon	8 Bow.	9.60	5.60	5.00	J. Lynch-N. Pariso
	Bolo Tie	2 G.P.	4.10	2.30	2.40	J. Coq'tte-F. Fernandez
	Vip	8 G.P.				J. Culmone-H. Ramirez

Date Horse	Race & Track	Win	Place	Show	Jockey Switched or Jockey who won with horse
9 Dwight Harar	7 L.D.		10.60	7.80	R. De Stasio-F. Dodge
Duck Berry	3 G.P.	11.80	6.60	3.80	T. Fico-J. McCoy
11 Gallalad	5 Jam.				E. Guerin-M. Danisi
Coolite	2 L.D.		4.40	3.00	W. Hawk'h-E. Danhauer*
Mulligatawney	7 L.D.				F. Keene-P. Keiper
Timboo	3 G.P.	14.40	6.00	4.10	G. Schreck-L. Batchel'r
12 Fighting Don	2 Jam.	6.20	3.40	2.80	T. Atkinson
Vim	1 Hdg.	4.00	2.80	2.20	R. M'Kenna
Viva Teddy	8 Hdg.	5.00	3.20	2.60	D. M'an'w-B. Hacker
Cee Raf	2 L.D.			4.20	D. Brigley-S. Chiap'ta
Magnetic Star	8 G.P.				W. Stag'r-C. Pennock
13 Dwight Harar	7 L.D.			4.80	F. Dodge
Shining Deed	2 G.P.	9.00	5.30	3.70	C. Pennock
We Hope	4 G.P.				J. Stew'rt-C. Pennock
Okamsel	7 G.P.	8.40	5.00	4.30	R. Nash-C. Pennock
14 Burt's Reward	8 Jam.			5.10	T. Atkinson-M. Danisi
Tascosa	4 L.D.	4.20	3.40	2.60	D. Brigley-S. Chiap'ta*
Marled	7 L.D.			2.20	A. Carvalho
Little Tony	4 G.P.	7.50	4.90	3.70	E. S. Wilson-L. Batchel'r
15 Maelstrom	2 Jam.				R. Bernh't- D. Dodson
American Wolf	7 Hdg.		3.80	2.80	L. Batchel'r-J. Stout
Bomb Command	2 G.P.				C. Pennock-C. Errico
Tree Land	8 G.P.			3.20	J. Chestn't-L. Batchel'r
16 Cound Did	1 Jam.	16.20	6.80	4.40	E. Guerin
Dime	8 Jam.				D. Gorman-A. Kirkland
Even Break	2 Hdg.			2.60	R. Kline-B. Strange
Prince Tread	3 Hdg.			2.80	L. Batchel'r-S. Brooks
V. P. I. Clef	7 Hdg.	30.80	10.80	4.60	R. Will'ms-C. Givens
Mightiest	1 L.D.	5.20	3.40	2.80	J. Baird-R. DeStasio
Cee Raf	2 L.D.				S. Chip'a-F. Keene
Respire	2 G.P.		4.00	2.70	R. Bauer-L. Batchel'r
Arrested	3 G.P.				J. Phillippi-G. Schreck
Hidden Ace	8 G.P.		3.80	3.50	T. Fico
18 Hy Spread	1 L.D.		7.40	5.00	D. Lamb
Kentucky Son	1 G.P.		5.10	3.60	F. Solim'a-F. Fernandez
Jay Forst	3 G.P.				E. J. Knapp-L. Batchel'r
19 The Kicker	1 Jam.				D. Dodson-L. Hansman
Deep Fen	2 Jam.				F. Lewis-N. Pariso
Mi Scandal	4 Jam.				F. Lewis-N. Pariso
Crystal Dodger	8 Hdg.				F. Zehr-D. Deason
20 Rush Act	1 Hdg.	6.40	3.60	2.80	C. Kirk-S. Brooks
21 War Fund	5 L.D.				A. Florio-L. Hulsl'der
22 American Wolf	8 Hdg.	4.80	2.80	2.40	J. Stout-C. Kirk
Dwight Harar	2 L.D.		4.00	3.20	F. Dodge
Jellico	8 L.D.				A. Car'lho-F. Keene
23 Little Gaucho	1 Hdg.	7.00	5.00	3.20	M. Basile-I. Hanford

Date	Horse	Race & Track	Win	Place	Show	Jockey Switched or Jockey who won with horse
25	Sir Harry x	4 Jam.	12.40	4.70	5.10	T. Atkinson-C. Rogers
	Camp Play	1 Hdg.			3.80	B. Vand'iff-S. Brooks
26	Diavolaw	7 Kee.				C. L. Martin-J. Richard
27	Tomsive	3 Jam.				M. Sor'no-B. James
	Viva Teddy	8 Hdg.				W. Downs-B. Hacker
	Hy Spread	1 L.D.	6.20	4.00	3.40	D. Lamb
	Play Pretty	3 L.D.		4.00	3.00	J. Baird
	Tascosa	5 L.D.				F. Keene-E. Zulker
	Blue Badge	4 Kee.	4.80	3.80	3.00	J. Combest-G. Gilsson
28	Happy West	1 Jam.		5.90	3.60	C. Rogers
	Combine	2 Jam.				M. Danisi
	Trier	8 Kee.	6.40	4.40	3.80	D. Scurlock-G. Glisson
29	Tomsive	8 Jam.			2.20	B. James-W. Rustia
	Gay Texan	1 L.D.	7.20	4.00	2.80	E. Danh'er-F. Keene
30	Freezout	1 Jam.				E. Arcaro-M. Danisi
	Golden Scotch	2 L.D.	4.20	3.40	2.60	R. DeStasio-W. Hughes
	Cabin Creek	4 L.D.			2.40	A. Mont'ro-A. Gaither

x Field won.
* Also won with horse.

164 Win Selections	52 won	31.7%
164 Place Selections	74 placed	46.3%
164 Show Selections	95 showed	58 %

Amount Returned	$591.00	$422.90	$377.00
Amount Invested	328.00	328.00	328.00
Profit	$263.00	$ 94.90	$ 49.00

12.
WINNING BY WATCHING SCRATCHED HORSES

Spotting his horse properly is a job that keeps a trainer constantly on his toes. Often the trainer will discover that he has pulled a boner and placed his charge in competition where it stands little chance of winning. Under such circumstances what does an intelligent trainer do? You're right! He scratches the horse, and then looks around for another race where the animal can be spotted more favorably.

Sometimes you will find the animal being scratched from one race after another. This doesn't always mean that the trainer has made an error in judgment. Sometimes the trainer loses out in the drawing for post positions because too many horses have been entered in the race. Then again, although the horse may have been previously entered with good intentions of running, expectedly at the time of the race, or even a day or two before, the animal may fall ill or become injured. Under such unforseen circumstances the trainer has no alternative but to scratch the horse. What we are interested in here primarily is the horse that is scratched because the trainer spotted it incorrectly and discovered his mistake in time. A horse that is maneuvered in such a manner should be watched carefully, for when the right spot has been found, you're fairly certain that the animal is well-meant, and stands a good chance of winning the race.

Starting From Scratch

Time and again players have discovered, often much to their disgust, that a certain good thing, they were prepared to back heavily was scratched. Then, when they have forgotten all about the animal, they will find its name in the winner's column of a racing chart, often at a price which will make them feel like kicking themselves.

That's just it! Don't let these winners get away from you. Stick with them for a while. In this Chapter, I will attempt to show you how.

Now a trainer does not usually go to all this trouble for a horse that he knows is "strictly for the birds." This does not mean that maidens are automatically eliminated. Many horses that have as yet to win a race are maneuvered into spots where they can cope successfully with the competition and reach the winner's circle first to earn the major share of the purse. But such a horse is not an ordinary maiden, and it is not too easy for an outsider to determine its possibilities for a successful effort.

There are systems that confine themselves totally to the search for such particular maidens. Certain arbitrary rules must be designated for such play.

Stress is laid here on consistency, for it will be found that a horse with a good past performance record is a lot safer to bet on than the mediocre in-and-out type. Of course trainers do win with inconsistent animals, but the far more numerous losers tend to make wagering on them precarious as well as unprofitable.

RULES: *Starting From Scratch*

1. List all horses that scratch today and meet the following requirements:

   a. Horse must show a win consistency of at least one out of six for the current and last year combined. If the horse shows only races for the current year, then an average of one win out of six for this year alone is permissible.

   b. All horses selected must show a last race run no more than one month from today's event.

   c. Play no horses that are late scratches, because they ran away or were injured at the post.

2. Play these scratched horses if they appear in the entries (at the same track as when they scratched) within three racing days of the day they were scratched, and meet the following requirements:

   a. The horse must show a last race run not more than three weeks (21 days) ago.

   b. The horse must not have finished more than seven lengths from the winner in its last race.

   c. The horse must be dropping in weight from its last race, *unless* the horse won its last race. If the horse won its last race, forget all about its weight.

3. If a tie occurs, play the horse running at the lowest odds.

   ADDENDA: All horses that do not show up within three racing days after they scratch, are to be allowed two more racing days to become selections. However, the three-day horses are considered first. If a five-day horse appears in the same race with a three-day horse, the three-day horse is always to be chosen. Play these horses if they appear within five racing days of today's event and meet the exact requirements for selection covering the horses that are found, at the same track as when scratched, within three racing days of the day the horse was scratched.

NOTE: The first day's past performance records, November 29, 1952, did not appear in the *Morning Telegraph*, from which the workout was made. Therefore, the workout starts with the first available date, December 2. Naturally we cannot possibly list December 1, because this was the first day from which our scratched horses were chosen. The Charles Town meet in this workout covers the period from December 1 to December 20, 1952, although the actual meeting ran November 29 to December 20. November 29 was a Saturday.

The extra time for selections in the initial set of rules (Rule 2*b*) is allowed so that we do not lose out on any good opportunities from horses that miss their first effort, but come right back immediately within two days. Such a horse is really well-meant and stands an excellent chance of winning its second attempt. However, we leave this to the discretion of the system fan. He may eliminate any of the two rules, or specifically designate only one time lapse. Why the scratched horses were not initally qualified on the basis of the provision under Rule 2 (21 days) rather than under Rule 1 (one month), needs further explanation. An added reason for this rule disparity is that a horse may run once after a scratch, with the race being primarily used as a conditioner, and then be ushered back in a day or two for a real try. We do not want to miss out on the second attempt of such an animal. Also a horse may just miss, and since the trainer feels that the animal will never be sharper, it may be sent back as quickly as the next day with a better than average chance of winning.

Here's how to go about making up your list of scratched horses. The process is fairly simple. First we scan the scratched list. Of course only the scratched horses can be eligible for play. The horses scratched today are now analyzed through their past performances to see whether they meet the requirements under Rule 1.

When we have found such an animal, we place it on our eligible list, noting the final date for possible selection, which of course will not be more than three racing days after the horse was scratched. Then we scan through the entries at Charles Town to see whether these horses appear in any of those three racing days.

For purposes of simplification you can use the alphabetical list of entries in your racing paper. In this way you can almost immediately spot the horse. Make certain, however, that the animal is entered at the same track where it scratched. If the animal is entered at another track, it cannot qualify. There is definitely an angle used by trainers in which the horse is moved to another track, and a lot of winners are obtained that way. But this system has not been designed for such play.

Should our horse fail to appear in the entries within the three days after scratch, as designated, the animal will still be given two more days to show up. Remember, however, that if two or more qualified horses appear in a race, and one of them showed up within three days, while the other (or others) appeared within five days, the animal that was sent back within three days is to be preferred.

We also note the two-day extension date on our list of eligible scratched horses. In this way we will know exactly what dates our horses may be chosen for selection.

WORKOUT: *Starting From Scratch*

PLAYS

Date	Race	Horse	Mutuel
12/2/52	9	Beech Hill	
12/3	7	Eatontown	
12/3	8	Sef's Bet	
12/11	8	Beech Hill	5.30
12/12	9	Semolina	
12/12	9	Perfect Power	
12/13	8	Prince Dandy	19.90
12/15	9	Some Lord	
12/19	1	Linda's Lady	
12/19	5	Sef's Bet (2)	
12/19	8	Thwarted	
12/20	6	Colonel Phil	
12/20	6	Semolina (2)	17.50
12/20	7	Suleiman	
12/20	7	Eatontown (2)	
12/20	8	Prize Ring	6.80
12/23	8	Some Lord (2)	12.30
12/24	1	Thwarted (2)	
12/27	7	Eatontown (3)	
12/30	4	Jantember	6.00

Date	Race	Horse	Mutuel
12/30	8	Thwarted (3)	6.50
12/31	9	Espedeco	15.50
1/1/53	5	Captain Gabe	
1/2	5	Great Parham	
1/2	9	Gulf Stream	
1/3	6	Suleiman	
1/3	7	Jet Fleet	
1/3	8	Perfect Power	
1/6	6	Abbezac	
1/6	9	Sef's Bet	
1/7	9	Tio Tito	
1/9	4	New Dream	9.60
1/9	9	Blue Danube	
1/10	8	Perfect Power	
1/12	4	Tio Tito	7.70
1/12	8	Boston Gray	
1/13	5	Linda's Lady	
1/13	7	Suleiman	4.90
1/13	8	Gulf Stream	13.30

		39 Plays	
		12 won—31%	
		Amount Returned	125.30
		Amount Invested	78.00
(2) Number of times played.		Profit	47.30

13.

HOW TO GET WINNERS
BY CONSULTING THE RESULT CHARTS

Digging into past performances is usually the logical way to produce successful plays. It is just as frequently a process for determining trainers' actions. There are very few trainers who do not digest daily the past performances listed in the racing papers. But these trainers also study the result charts, where they can often obtain information definitely not shown in the past performances.

The way the horse ran in its last race is often a determining factor for its near-future success or failure. From each performance the trainer tries to evaluate his animal's current ability. In the same way he studies his competitors' horses. On the basis of these observations he angles for a race where he feels his horse will be a contender. If the stable bets on its horses, the trainer may be searching for a spot where a good price can be obtained. Sometimes he will be unable to find such a race, and if his charge is really ready and fit he will have to content himself with the purse money and a comparatively short price rather than risk the animal's loss of form. Most horses have to be raced into form. After they reach their peak they will begin to taper off. The process of conditioning must be started all over again, with the loss of money and precious time. For this reason the player can usually feel safe in assuming that an attempt will be made, as quickly as possible, to maneuver a sharp horse into a spot where it can win. As a rule, if this animal does not win within a reasonable length of time after its sharp effort, it may be concluded that the animal has staled off and that its good race was the best it was capable of, even though it did not win.

Winners From the Charts

For the harried, tired working man who likes to bet on the horses, probing through the past performances often is a tedious chore.

But how else can he win?

By simply reading the result charts and preparing a list of those horses that have made sharp efforts in today's races, the bettor can obtain a plan of action that will produce many winners. He need not delve deeply into the running of the race. All that is necessary is to watch for certain remarks made by the chart caller concerning horses that finished in the second spot.

Why bother only with horses that finished second? Why can't horses that finished third or even fourth be considered? Well— a horse that was capable of finishing right behind the leader, and receives this favorable comment, seems to be an animal who might have been the winner under a little more favorable circumstances. That can't be said for an animal that permitted two or more horses to finish ahead of it. A horse that just missed winning must be sharp. With the added emphasis of the chart caller's favorable comment there are excellent chances that we are on the trail of a prospective winner.

When the chart says that the animal finishing second "was getting to the top one" or words to that effect, we can deduce that the horse is in form. Perhaps with a little added distance the horse might have won. In sprint qualifying races this logic looms as a pertinent factor. A horse that was literally breathing down the winner's neck has certainly advertised itself as a good prospect in its next effort. Should such a horse be rushed back to the races within a week or so, it will frequently wind up as the favorite. If the horse fails to win the race following its excellent effort, and perhaps does not perform nearly as well as expected, chances are that the following race will bring better odds. These are thoughts that must also be running through the trainer's mind. The crux of the problem lies in the length of time the horse can maintain its form.

Other comments which should evoke alertness on the bettor's part are: "closed with a rush," "closed strongest," "closed ground," "made up ground." Remarks of this kind obviously demonstrate an impressive race. If the chart caller felt disposed to comment so favorably, we can acknowledge the animal's fitness. Whether or not the animal can improve is another matter. Enough of these horses, however, will improve, or be spotted in a race where they can handle the competition, to make the method suggested here worth while. Nevertheless, it would be foolish to expect every qualified selection to win.

If the qualifying race was a sprint and today's distance is longer, the possibilities that the horse is well-meant become more apparent. This does not necessarily mean that if the animal is entered in another sprint (of equal distance or less), following the qualifying race, that it isn't really trying or can't win. Since the probabilities for success are more favorable when the animal is running at a greater distance, we will accept the horse for play only under such circumstances. Although we must take risks, it is only common sense to make our wagers with minimum hazards and under the most favorable conditions.

In a qualifying route race we are not concerned with the distance of the next race. Usually endurance is one of the main assets for routes. Horses racing in such events must be able to complete the distance under sufficient steam. An extended distance of a mile or more will test the animal's ability to last. If the chart caller has noticed something exceptional in the horse's move, it is sufficient evidence to prove that the animal qualifies on the basis of stamina and fitness. Such a horse is ready to win, and if it has a trainer worth his salt, the next distance need only be adequate for the animal to do its best. The trainer should know his animal's capabilities, and if he is interested in a winning effort, the horse will be spotted at a suitable distance.

The suggested actual betting method is unconventional, and is not used in the usual system. Since our qualifying animal is expected to win in the near future, and since we are not specifically sure when and where, we are compelled frequently to wager more than once. If the horse fails to win after our third bet on it, we must discard it from further consideration. But, of course, we will remember to give the horse three chances to come through. Should the horse win before the third bet then it will also not be played again.

In case our horse qualified in a sprint we must wait for it to be entered at a greater distance. If this type of horse should win a race at exactly the same distance (sprint) as the qualifying race, we refuse to consider the animal further. The same situation also holds true, of course, if the winning race was at a shorter distance than the qualifying race. The horse is crossed off our list. There is no such concern over horses that qualified in route races.

The following rules determine the list of qualifying horses.

1. Refer to comment in the racing result charts only to obtain qualified horses for future play.

2. List all horses that finished second, and received any of the following comments:

   a. "was getting to the leader" ("top one," etc.)
   b. "closed with a rush" ("good burst of speed")
   c. "closed strongest"
   d. "appeared to be the best of all"
   e. "made up ground"
   f. "closed ground"

(Obviously the remark "getting to the leader" is synonomous with "getting to the top one." Similarly "closed with a rush," and "closed with a good burst of speed" are sufficiently alike.)

3. Play horses listed three times. If the horse wins *on* or *before* the third try (bet) do not play it again. Discard it from your list. Watch the entry lists and play them when they appear.

4. If the horse's original qualifying race was in a sprint, the next three races in which you can wager on the animal must be at a *longer* distance (not necessarily a route). If the horse should win at the *same* distance or *less before your third bet,* eliminate horse from your list.

5. The chart caller's remarks do not have to be exactly the same as listed above. The essential thing is that the remarks have the same meaning.

6. Plays must be at the same track as qualifying races.

7. If a horse gets more than one qualifying race, but is still eligible for play on a previous effort do *not list it again.* There is no tie-breaking rule. When more than one horse shows up in a race all are to be played.

The reader will notice that the list of selections shows a horse picked on the last day of the meet. This was only done to make the list complete. Obviously the horse could never become a play if wagering is confined to the track at which the qualification occurred. The workout here was made for the Tropical Park meeting only. However, when this meeting ended, it would not be illogical to carry on the play at the next track on the same circuit, providing of course, that the wagering races did not occur at a time too remotely removed from the qualifying races.

The following paragraphs should help clear up any questions surrounding Rule 4, which really needs some explanation. For purposes of illustration the horses, Pampas Beauty and Espedeco were selected.

On December 6, 1952, Pampas Beauty finished second. The comment was "The latter [Pampas Beauty] rallied to be *making up ground* on the winner." The phrase, "making up ground" qualified the horse for our prospective winner list. Examining this chart, you will note that this horse was fourth at the quarter, two lengths behind the third horse, Sir Fay, and one-half length ahead of the fifth horse, Head For Home. At the half, Pampas Beauty was in the same position behind Sir Fay, but now two lengths ahead of Head For Home. At the stretch, Pampas Beauty was second, four lengths behind the leader and final winner, Marie Eileen, and 1½ lengths ahead of the third horse, Goya's Pass. Pampas Beauty finished only two lengths behind the winner and four lengths ahead of the third horse, Calicut. Such an excellent move surely would be stamped in the mind of any astute bettor for future reference. Yet the chart writer had already given us ample assurance of Pampas Beauty's future chances with his remark, "making up ground."

The bettors at the track did not think much of Pampas Beauty's chances in this race, for the horse went off at odds of 24.40-to-1, and paid $12.20 for place. This was a six-furlong race and the person intending to use our method would have had to wait for a race at a greater distance in order to bet on the animal. Pampas Beauty's next race was on December 22, where it went off at odds of 4.20-to-1, and won the race. Unfortunately this race was a sprint (six furlongs), exactly the same distance as Pampas Beauty's qualifying race, so according to our rules there would be no wager. The animal then would have to be discarded, since it had already won a race following the qualified one.

Even though a winner would have been obtained on this occasion if no such distance rule existed, you will find that many more losses would result on other horses. For example, take the horse, Espedeco, which also qualified in a six-furlong race. This horse raced three times, following its qualifying race, at the same distance and lost each time. In its fourth race the horse was entered at 1 1/16 miles, and won at the nice mutuel of $15.50.

This method is very easy to follow and eliminates the necessity for examining past performances.

WORKOUT: *Winners From the Charts*

(November 27, 1953—January 15, 1953)

QUALIFYING HORSES

Date Qualifying	Horse	Chart Comment
11/27/52	Great Admiral	closed strongest
11/27	Eatontown	was getting to the winner
11/29	Sef's Bet	made up ground
11/29	Beech Hill	was getting to the winner
12/1	Suleiman	made up ground

Date Qualifying	Horse	Chart Comment
12/2	Some Lord	made up ground
12/5	Espedeco	made up ground
12/5	Semolina	closed with a rush
12/5	Perfect Power	making up ground
12/6	Prince Dandy	made up ground
12/6	Pampas Beauty	making up ground
12/8	Blue Grouse	getting to the top one
12/8	Blazing	closed considerable ground
12/9	Roman Jean	made up ground
12/10	Thwarted	wearing down the top one
12/10	For Rent	getting to the winner
12/11	Linda's Lady	getting to the top one
12/12	Deetzi	getting to the winner
12/13	Prize Ring	getting to the winner
12/15	Captain Gabe	getting to the top one
12/15	Colonel Phil	getting to the winner
12/17	Jantember	made up ground
12/17	Blaze	getting to the winner
12/20	Jet Fleet	made up ground
12/25	Gulf Stream	wearing down the winner
12/25	Marked Game	made up ground
12/26	Great Parham	wearing down the top one
12/27	Sirad	closed with a rush
12/27	Abbezac	getting to the winner
12/29	American Pilot	getting to the leader
12/29	Matchlock	getting to the winner
1/1/53	Tio Tito	wearing down the top one
1/1	Black Stream	closed ground
1/2	New Dream	closed considerable ground
1/2	Baggage Boy	closed with a rush
1/3	Blue Danube	gaining on the winner
1/3	War Antique	wearing down the winner
1/5	Mikeaby	closed ground
1/6	Little Falls	getting to the top one
1/7	Boston Gray	closed with a good burst of speed
1/8	High Trend	made up ground
1/9	Guy	closed ground
1/10	Empty Sea	made up ground
1/13	Hill Street	closed with a rush
1/14	Earmarked	closed ground
1/15	How	unleashed a cyclonic rush . . . made up ground

14.
PROFITS FROM WATCHING WORKOUTS

The workout is so important that every racing paper employs "clockers" to spot each animal's early morning efforts. The "works" are printed in the paper for the intelligent bettor's persual. It's an important adjunct in the racing information offered by these papers.

Not only do the racing newspapers pay strict attention to the horse's performance while working out, but individuals have been known to earn their livelihood at the practice of observing workouts.

Needless to say, since workouts are so important, it is imperative that this information should not be negelected by the astute bettor. The workouts are watched carefully. We can be sure of that. To benefit by this information through systematic play is another thing entirely. Here are a couple of systems that will show you how.

The Workout Angle

The workout is often the final test the trainer may make to discover whether or not his charge is ready for a good effort. Thus, a workout a few days before a race will sometimes signal that the horse is ready. Or it may reveal the equally important news that the animal was not prepared for a real attempt. In the latter event the trainer is hardly likely to endanger the future of his charge by asking for an all-out effort.

However, a horse that has shown good form in its last race—holding the lead in at least two of the four calls (as shown in the *Daily Racing Form*)—and has had a recent workout is likely to be an important factor next time out. Further, if the horse has demonstrated amply that he is suited to the distance, he becomes a reasonably sound selection.

By combining all the requirements into a set of rules we have a method of play that is sound and has shown excellent results. The rules follow:

RULES: *The Workout Angle*

1. Horse must have finished first or second last time out *or* within three lengths of the winner.
2. In its last race, the horse must have been in front for at least two of the four calls given in the *Daily Racing Form* past performance.
3. Horse must have raced within 15 days.
4. Must show a workout within seven days.
5. Of the races at *today's distance* shown in its past performances, horse must have won 25 per cent.
6. Past performances must show a minimum of two wins at today's distance—at least one of them within 100 days.
7. In case of tie, play horse with best win percentage in two years—shown at upper right of its past performances.
8. Selections are made after scratches are known.
9. Pass races for jumpers, two-year-olds and, of course, maidens.

The reader may not understand the logic behind the rules or they may not appear sufficiently clear. So to clarify things, let's go over the rules.

The first rule proves that the horse is in form, since the animal has either won its last race or finished close up to the leader. That the horse is in form is further emphasized in Rule 2, which requires that it must have been in the lead a good part of the way—first in at least two of the four calls.

Two weeks is about as long as a horse can be kept at his best form without a race. We have stretched this a bit and made our rule 15 days. If the horse is being given regular trials, this period of inactivity in competition should not be too long. It is to be remembered that recent workouts are a requirement of this method.

The workout specified in the fourth rule, is the trainer's angle. It gives us a hint as to whether the animal will be sharp.

Rules 5 and 6 go a little further and do not leave room for an accidental win. They test the horse by making the animal show

that the win at the specific distance was due to more than mere
luck. This also seems to show that the horse has a preference for
today's distance. A period of three months since a win at today's
distance was achieved would have sufficed, but to allow a little
leeway the prerequisite was stretched to an even 100 days. This
provision demonstrates clearly that the animal can win at today's
distance.

To separate ties, the seventh rule is provided. It also prevents
the acceptance of unproved horses.

WORKOUT: *The Workout Angle*

(July-August 1948)

Date	Race & Track	Horse	Win	Place	Show
7/1	7 A.P.	Carara Marble		Out	Out
2	4 Del.	Island Nymph			
3	3 Mth.	Sole Parate		$5.40	$3.20
5	2 Del.	Sir Toro			2.60
	6 Del.	Bam			2.40
	7 Del.	Going Airy	$5.60	3.50	2.40
	4 Nar.	Octorora			
	2 A.P.	Southern Pride	9.60	5.40	3.60
6	4 Mth.	Orange Sun			3.60
	4 Nar.	J. J. Lynch			
	6 Nar.	Plucky Boy			
	5 A.P.	Style Queen		9.00	7.00
7	8 Hdg.	Our Birthday			
	4 Mth.	Ariel Sweep		9.20	4.80
	5 Mth.	Flood Town		4.80	3.20
	6 Nar.	Tarpan	7.20	4.40	3.20
8	2 Mth.	Vim			
9	6 Aqu.	Energetic	6.30	3.50	2.70
	6 A.P.	Daily Dip			
10	8 Aqu.	Russian Action			
	3 A.P.	Tomos		11.80	6.60
	6 A.P.	Istan	16.60	6.40	4.40
13	8 Hdg.	Adonis			
14	4 Hdg.	Mad Pass			3.20
	4 Mth.	Eternal Flirt	5.40	3.60	3.00
	5 Suf.	Ogham	11.20	5.40	3.80
15	6 Hdg.	Oriole		3.60	Out
	2 Suf.	Gay Franka			
	5 A.P.	Rippey			Out
17	7 Aqu.	Nathaniel		3.00	2.40
	5 Suf.	Ogham	4.00	2.60	2.40

Date	Race & Track	Horse	Win	Place	Show
	3 A.P.	Preoccupy			
	5 A.P.	Countess In	19.60	7.00	4.60
19	7 Sar.	Motie Brand			
	1 Mth.	Carmus			2.60
	2 Suf.	Diego Red	4.00	3.20	2.80
20	6 Sar.	Jimmie			
	6 Mth.	Sole Parate			
	6 A.P.	Isa			
21	4 Sar.	Gay Song			
	5 Mth.	Erigeron		5.00	4.00*
22	5 Mth.	Eternal Flirt			
	7 A.P.	Southern Pride			8.00
24	1 Suf.	Gay Kiska			
	4 Suf.	Going Airy			
	7 A.P.	Hypostyle			
26	6 Sar.	Applause		9.60	4.30
	6 Mth.	Alexis			
27	3 Sar.	Coronet Star	3.70	2.80	2.30
	6 Sar.	Be Ready			
	2 Suf.	Diego Red			
	7 Suf.	Tillerette	8.60	4.20	2.80
28	5 Sar.	Gay Song			
	2 Mth.	Mist O'Dawn		4.60	3.60
	4 Mth.	Klamath		5.00	4.20
29	2 Sar.	Judy R.		2.80	2.40
30	2 Mth.	Carmus			8.00
31	5 Suf.	Tarpan			3.00
	1 A.P.	Sweep Gold			
8/2	5 Sar.	Grey Flight	16.30	9.00	5.90
	5 Suf.	Lt. Bill	9.20	5.40	4.20
	6 Suf.	Lolling			
4	2 Mth.	Kensington Gal.	5.60	3.00	2.60
	6 Mth.	Erigeron	14.20	7.00	4.00
	2 Suf.	Ariel Brigade			
	5 Was.	Loriot			
5	5 Mth.	Klamath			
	3 Suf.	Chalk	6.80	3.80	2.80
6	2 Sar.	Sunsation	3.50	2.70	2.50
	7 Sar.	Mary Ann		5.60	4.10
7	5 Suf.	Andy's Glory	10.00	5.00	4.00
	5 Was.	King Rhymer			
9	5 Atl.	Big Story	32.80	14.20	8.20
	6 Atl.	Even Break		6.80	4.20
	4 Suf.	Diego Red		7.00	5.20
10	2 Sar.	Parhelion	8.30	4.40	2.70
	4 Was.	Clevelander			
	5 Was.	Beneva			
11	6 Was.	Gala Revue			4.20

Date	Race & Track	Horse	Win	Place	Show
12	3 Atl.	Subdue			
14	2 Was.	Arab's Fancy			
	5 Atl.	Going Airy			2.60
16	2 Atl.	Carmus			
	7 Nar.	Adonis			
17	5 Atl.	Blue Fedora	28.20	11.60	6.60
	8 Atl.	I Did			
18	2 Sar.	Shifty Mae			2.40
	7 Sar.	Pipette	4.20	2.90	2.60
	5 Nar.	Grandpa Max			
	2 Was.	Replay			3.60
	6 Was.	First Whirl			
19	5 Sar.	Sunsation			
	8 Sar.	Combine			
	4 Rkm.	Reportable			
	4 Was.	Trust Fund		4.40	3.40
20	1 Was.	Topnotch			
21	7 Atl.	Big Story	9.80	4.00	3.40
	3 Nar.	Klamath		2.60	2.40
	1 Rkm.	Diego Red		3.80	2.60
23	8 Nar.	Generator	3.80	2.80	2.80
25	5 Atl.	Free Press			
	8 Atl.	Even Break		4.00	2.80
	7 Was.	Coaltown		4.20	3.20
26	6 Sar.	Pipette	7.70	4.20	2.90
	5 Atl.	All In Fun	6.80	4.20	2.80
27	3 Atl.	Min't O'Morn			3.00
	4 Rkm.	Diego Red			2.40
	7 Was.	Pelure			2.40
28	1 Nar.	Black Eagle	4.60	3.00	2.20
	3 Nar.	Klamath			
	4 Nar.	Gain A Foot			3.60
	7 Nar.	Transatlantic	10.80	5.80	4.20
	1 Rkm.	Suntos			
	2 Rkm.	Painted Arrow	4.40	2.60	2.20
	4 Rkm.	Shaffie	10.00	4.40	3.00
	7 Was.	Citation	2.20	Out	Out
30	4 Atl.	Layaway	5.40	3.60	3.00
	5 Nar.	Croupier	21.20	8.20	5.00
31	5 Atl.	Blue Fedora			
	6 Nar.	Cedar Bird	4.20	3.20	2.60

* Won—disqualified.
120 Win Selections—35 won—29%
118 Place Selections—54 placed—46%
116 Show Selections—69 showed—59%

	Win	Place	Show
Amount Returned	$331.80	$279.20	$249.40
Amount Invested	240.00	236.00	232.00
Profit	$ 91.80	$ 43.20	$ 17.40

WORKOUT: *The Workout Angle*

(February 1949)

Date	Race & Track	Horse	Win	Place	Show
2/1	4 Hia.	Yesnow			
	6 Hia.	Silly Gyp		$ 2.60	$2.60
	5 F.G.	Valdina Perion		11.60	7.00
	6 S.A.	Forever Amble			
4	5 F.G.	One Atom			
	6 F.G.	Bill Cogswell	$11.80	5.40	3.80
5	7 F.G.	Gestapo		2.80	Out
	5 S.P.	Suntos	14.50	5.40	3.00
7	6 S.P.	Auro Boro			
8	2 S.A.	Newsworthy		3.20	2.60
	5 S.A.	Jeannie	10.20	4.60	3.30
9	6 Hia.	Blue Border		3.00	2.20
	6 F.G.	Lovely Trace	9.00	4.60	3.40
	6 S.A.	Terry's Man			
10	4 Hia.	Ringador			
	7 Hia.	Liberty Babe	19.10	9.40	5.00
	4 F.G.	Donna M. G.			
	5 S.A.	Forever Amble			
11	6 Hia.	Cer Vantes	24.50	10.70	5.70
	2 F.G.	Sildonna			
	4 S.A.	Just Why			2.40
	5 S.A.	Top Sis			
12	2 F.G.	Tree Town			
	6 F.G.	Monterey		3.60	2.80
	7 F.G.	Bill Cogswell			
15	3 S.A.	Papagos	5.90	3.90	2.20
	6 S.A.	Tickingatit	14.10	5.70	3.60
16	7 S.A.	Burning Night			
	8 S.A.	Mantelite			
17	6 Hia.	Bab's Damion	12.90	6.00	4.50
18	5 S.A.	Grand La Grand			
19	2 F.G.	Nice Enough			3.20
	7 F.G.	Carmargo Bill			
	8 F.G.	Crisis ·			
21	5 Hia.	Tight Squeeze			
	6 Hia.	Cer Vantes			3.50
22	5 S.A.	Miss Cross S.			
23	4 Hia.	Cinder King			
	3 F.G.	Linden Belle			
	6 F.G.	Make It Easy			4.40
	6 S.A.	Forever Amble			
24	6 F.G.	Rodman Keenon		3.40	2.80
	4 S.A.	Bullreighzac	6.70	3.80	2.80

25	6 Hia.	Ichabod	3.80	2.70	2.30
	6 F.G.	Nimble Tiger	5.60	3.40	2.60
26	3 Hia.	Prefect	2.70	2.30	2.10*
	5 F.G.	Monterey		6.60	3.40
	5 S.P.	Suntos			2.50
	6 S.P.	Outrider	12.10	3.60	4.70

* Entry won—horse finished second

WORKOUT FEB. 1949 SUMMARY

49 Win Selections—14 won—29%
49 Place Selections—22 placed—45%
48 Show Selections—26 showed—54%

	Win	Place	Show
Amount Returned	$152.90	$108.30	$88.40
Amount Invested	98.00	98.00	96.00
Profit or Loss	$ 54.90	$ 10.30	$—7.60

The Workout Way

Most horses have to be raced into condition. In addition, the majority are also given workouts to hasten this desirable state. Certain trainers depend mainly on the workout way to get their animals into shape.

Horses that are given at least three workouts within a two-week period prior to their race, regardless of whether or not they have been in competition on the track during this period, are likely prospects to win today's event.

No trainer will use up his horse with so many works unless he feels, in so doing, that the animal will be better prepared to make a good showing.

Watching for horses with three workouts within the two-week period is a method which cannot help but click with winners. Operating at a profit with this logical idea is another matter entirely.

There are several ways for a system to prove its worthiness. One is a high winning percentage; another is a fair percentage of winners with sufficient longshots at intervals not too far apart.

The system to be presented here seems to be somewhere between the two. The percentage of winners is not high, yet not low, and the longshots are not too scattered.

Doubling the amount of money you invest at one track over a period of a month is not too bad a deal. This is exactly what the workout reveals for the play at Jamaica during April, 1950.

Obviously a good system must start with a sound premise. Very few of them, however, will work just the idea alone. The method must be garnished with other rational elements to round it out. This proceedure is true in practically all successful enterprises. Our system is no exception. Although not too garishly embroidered, sufficient necessary additions have been made to enhance its practicability.

For one thing the rules insist that the horse show a win or at least a place at today's distance in its past performances. This stipulation was made to prevent wagering on animals that evidently cannot perform well at today's distance.

RULES: *The Workout Way*

1. The horse must show three workouts within two weeks of today's race. (The workouts are to found at the bottom of the animal's past performances.)

2. The horse must show a win or place at today's distance somewhere in its list of past performances as shown in today's racing paper.

3. In case of a tie, take the horse with the highest class as listed anywhere in today's list of past performances. In looking through the past performances just check off the highest class for all those horses qualifying as selections and write it down somewhere next to the horse's name for reference.

   a. If still tied, choose the horse that raced most recently.

   b. If a tie still occurs, choose the horse with the best win consistency for the last year and this year combined.

4. Designate class as follows. The top one is to be considered highest, the bottom one lowest:

   a. Stakes

   b. Handicaps

   c. Graded Handicaps

    d. Allowances
    e. Graded Allowances
    f. Claimers, according to price
    g. Maidens

Do not consider any odd types of races such as weight-for-age, etc. However, if this is the only type of race the horse shows, qualify it as if it has the highest class.

Exception: If a horse has both allowances and claiming races in its past performances choose the highest claiming price as its class.

    IMPORTANT: If any horse has all allowance races or allowances and other races *not* claimers, but not of higher class than allowances (for example, maidens) and another horse has one or more allowance races and claimers listed in the past performances, consider these horses as still tied. This is so that one horse should not be disqualified because it has raced at a claiming price at one time although now racing in allowances. This horse might be a better animal than the one that never raced in claimers.

    5. Play no horse that has not won a race during the last two years. Play no maidens, no two-year-olds or jumpers. Play no Stakes or Name Handicaps. (Ordinary Handicaps are okay.)

    6. If a horse won its last race, do not select it if this winning race was two months ago or less.

    7. Play after scratches are known.

This system gets a considerable amount of play, which makes it ideal for track use. Of course it does not prevent wagering away from the track.

    There were many ties and the tie-breaking class rule became a very important adjunct. Combining other factors like consistency, recent form, the jockey, etc., should produce a greater percentage of winners but would also probably result in a decreased profit. This would also necessarily limit the action.

    For those players who prefer a higher percentage of winners and the increased feeling of security that goes with it, adding these factors should produce the desirable effects.

    The reader will notice that certain conventional rules such as a short time lapse from the horse's last race to the present, pace, a good finish in one of the recent races, etc., have been omitted. The method does not concern itself with such legitimate abstractions. For this reason alone it cannot help but reap a harvest of long-shots.

Untried horses, haphazard races, and animals that have long since ceased to be winners have been eliminated from consideration. Name Handicaps and Stakes races are hard to fathom, for the competition is usually too keen, and many times when an obviously superior animal appears in the lineup, the odds are too low to be acceptable.

Horses which won their last race often complete a cycle and are unable to repeat. There are some excellent systems based on horses repeating their winning effort, and I do not mean to imply that horses should never be played to repeat. Under the prevailing conditions of this method, in which workouts are used to prove fitness, a win in the horse's last race is often detrimental rather than beneficial. The system tries to avoid play on a recent winner.

Playing after scratches are known is important, because often there is more than one horse qualifying as a selection. The horse you have selected after figuring the tie-breaking rule might be scratched. If you ignore the other horse, which definitely figured according to the rules and should then be the selection, you might be bitterly disappointed to find that this animal won. The best way is to find out what horses have been scratched and cross them out on the racing paper.

It might be a good idea to demonstrate step by step how a play is determined. For this purpose it is not important to select winning races. However, I have selected two for analysis because they are excellent examples.

On April 3, 1950, we open our *Racing Forms* to the first race at Jamaica and start checking off those horses which qualify initially as selections.

We look for horses that show three workouts at the bottom of their past performances. These workouts must have been made not more than two weeks previous to today's race. We count back to determine what the latest workout date can be, which in this case is March 20.

Now we know that if a horse shows a workout earlier than

March 20 we can pass it by. We scan the workouts of each horse, not finding one that meets our workout specification until we come to Warden Jr. This horse shows workouts on March 31, March 28, and March 25. All workouts are within the required two-week time lapse. A little check is placed after Warden Jr.'s name.

Running down the list of past performances for each horse we next come to Birdie Lulley who also has three workouts within the required time. The workouts shown have been made on March 30, 25, and 23. Birdie Lulley gets a check. No other horses have the workout requirement.

Looking back at the two horses checked off, we find that Warden Jr. has not won a race for the last two years. This animal is therefore eliminated, leaving Birdie Lulley as the only possible selection.

Today's distance is at six furlongs and Birdie Lulley shows two wins and three places at today's distance. Since there are no other horses the tie-breaking rule is not necessary. Birdie Lulley is our horse. Birdie Lulley did not win its last race, so there was no concern about that. Remember that a horse showing a win in its last race cannot be chosen if that race was run within two months of today's event.

We find the first two horses in the third race are checked off because they meet the workout requirements. The fourth horse, Equipoisette, meets the workout prerequisite, but cannot be considered because she is a maiden.

Next we find Risking, Mr. Willie, Attrusa and Tunic, all showing three workouts within two weeks of today's race. Lucky Micky is also O. K., but he is a maiden and is discarded.

Risking and Attrausa won their last races. Risking won hers on February 28, less than two months ago, therefore she is eliminated. Attrusa's last race occurred on November 15, 1949, much more than two months ago. This animal must still be considered. Populace is eliminated, because it does not show a win or place at today's distance. Tunic was scratched.

This leaves Dark Miss, Mr. Willie, and Attrusa. Dark Miss and Attrusa show a win at today's distance. Mr. Willie's past performances record a place at the distance. Since the three are tied, the tie rule is used to separate them. The highest class race in Dark Miss' past performances is a $5500 claimer. Mr. Willie shows a $7500 claimer as his highest. The top race for Attrusa is $7000. Our choice is Mr. Willie.

Although only the Jamaica workout is shown here, the method was examined for every single track in the *Daily Racing Form* for the month of April, 1950. There were 306 selections, out of which 64 won for a $2 flat bet profit of $362.90.

Lack of space makes it impossible to show the entire workout, but the results should be sufficient. Although the percentages for all tracks showed a drop and the dollar for dollar return diminished, the system still maintained a healthy profit. An analysis of so many races would seem to show that the method has possibilities and should merit the system fan's serious attention.

WORKOUT: *The Workout Way*

Date	Horse	Race	Mutuel	Date	Horse	Race	Mutuel
4/1	Third Ace	2	....	4/15	Social Hour	2	....
	Ceara	4	....		Upbeat	5	....
	Pellicle	5	23.70		Starecase	7	4.00
	Questus	7	55.00	4/17	Enticement	4	....
4/3	Birdie Lulley	1	5.00		Persist	5	....
	Mr. Willie	3	13.70		Sky Miracle	6	....
	Luring	5	74.50		Marabout	7	....
4/4	Magic Words	2	4.60		Erosion	8	....
	Fabricate	5	....	4/18	Indian Barney	3	....
	Newsweekly	6	4.30		Third Ace	4	3.00
4/5	Hard Facts	1	....		War King	5	....
	Fourteen Grand	3	10.80		One Hitter	6	....
	Antagonism	5	....		Miss Comedy	7	....
	Lady Alice	7	6.30	4/19	Oilomacy	4	....
	Lucullus	8	....		Isocrates	7	....
4/6	Landlord	1	3.90	4/20	Vanetta	1	....
	By Heart	3	14.70		Pictoric	3	....
	Third Ace	5	....		Maijo	5	7.60
	Eatontown	6	20.80		Fighting Fan	6	3.80
4/7	Tunic	4	....	4/21	Wicki Wicki	2	....
	First Glance	6	9.90		Lickety Cut	3	....
	I Am	7	....		Piet	6	47.00
4/8	Ventolino	1	....		Royal Castle	7	....
	Major Kay	2	....	4/22	What	2	....
	Ceara	4	....		Busanda	4	....
	Next Move	5	3.10		Our Tommy	7	....
	Sagittarius	7	....		Shadow Shot	8	....
	Roseborough	8	....	4/24	Blue Row	2	....

Date	Horse	Race	Mutuel	Date	Horse	Race	Mutuel
4/10	Hopefully	1	9.60		Lady Marilyn	3	....
	Persist	4	....		Dee See Six	5	....
	Muzzle	7	....	4/25	Drifting Maid	5	....
4/11	Maid of Oz	1	....		Flying Missel	6	3.90
	Velvet Rhymer	3	....		Muzzle	7	....
	Ferd	6	9.50	4/26	Wicki Wicki	2	31.30
	Shoes	7	....		Tops All	3	....
4/12	Dark Miss	3	....		Didapper	4	....
	Antagonism	5	....		Thasian Hero	5	....
	Yankee Hill	6	....		Rope Trick	7	6.50
	Escador	8	....		Shadow Shot	8	....
4/13	Blue Row	1	....	4/27	Narviko	5	....
	Cornish Knight	3	....		Roseborough	7	....
	Gretna Green	4	....		Copito	8	4.30
	Watch Union	5	8.00	4/28	Lickety Cut	2	....
	Carmagnole	6	....		Fleet Vixen	4	....
	Lawful	7	....		Cochise	6	7.40
	Spider Rock	8	....		Royal Castle	7	6.50
4/14	Pittacus	1	....	4/29	Eternal Flirt	2	....
	Wicki Wicki	2	....		Sagittarius	5	5.70
	Kay Gibson	4	....		Blue Zac	7	....
	Sub	6	....		Shadow Shot	8	....
	Cencerro	7	....				
	Easy Chop	8	....				

102 Selections—29 won—28%

Amount Returned $408.40
Amount Invested $204.00

Profit on $2 Wagers to Win Only $204.40

15.
USING THE SPEED RATE
AS A TIME GAUGE

Numerous systems have been built around consistency, the ability of a horse to win a high percentage of its races or finish in the money frequently.

Nearly all racing experts will concede the fact that backing such animals will return more winners than wagering on those that have little or no consistency. Many experts maintain, however, that consistent horses are not profitable racing tools, because they do not command a high enough price when they win.

Although a large percentage of these consistent animals do run at short prices, you will find many that come in and pay excellent mutuels. Very often the reason for this is that there are more than one of these consistent horses in the race.

Such opportunties should not be lost by the vigilant bettor, for in such a race the animal's odds may be operating at a distinct overlay, and these overlays are always worth a bet.

Time Figures Rate Consistency

There is another way of judging consistency in an animal which has been woefully neglected. Horses are obviously consistent if they continually maintain a high rate of speed in their races. This can be judged either by the horse's final time or, to make it simpler, by the animal's earned speed rate.

It is frequently true that such animals are as consistent in their winning efforts as in their speed rates. We can often get a good price on a horse that looked bad or indifferent in its last race merely because of this factor. A horse may have competed against animals of high category in its last race and, although finishing out of the money, may have run a race of usual good caliber.

This can be seen by the speed rate the animal obtained for this particular race. If the speed rate earned was 80 or higher, or perhaps even in the nineties, we of course could not say that the animal ran a poor race even though it lost. Today's competition may be highly inferior and this would be a likely spot to look for a win.

Speed rates earned over different distances are not alike, so that it is necessary to select only those speed rates earned at the distance the horse is racing today. Should the last five races the horse has competed in show the same distance as today, with speed rates of 80 or higher, we can assume that the route is liked by the animal. Wagering on the animal at such a compatible distance should permit us to operate at an advantage. The tried and proven in all walks of life are always the more reliable.

Let's set down the rules now and then analyze them afterwards for purposes of clarification:

1. In order to be considered, the horse's last race must not have been more than ten day ago.

2. The horse's last five races must be at exactly the same distance as today's race, and show speed of 80 or over. (All five races must show speed rates and the horse must show at least five races in its past performances.)

3. Play no track where speed rates are not given.

4. Play no horse that finished farther back than fifth in its last race.

5. Play no horse that is carrying more than six pounds greater weight than it carried in its last race.

6. Play no maidens, two-year-olds or jumpers. Play no stake or name handicap races.

7. In case of tie, choose the horses that raced most recently. If still tied, choose the horse with the best last speed rate. If still tied, choose the horse carrying the least weight.

8. Play after scratches are known.

Many years of producing and checking systems seems to have brought conspicuous evidence for favoring the backing of horses that have raced within a period of ten days prior to today's event. So many winners come from horses that have raced within such a time lapse that it would be foolhardy to ignore this factor. For this reason you will find this ten-day last out rule so prominent in many systems.

Of course this may also tend to decrease the play, but it will inevitably enhance the prospect of a high percentage of winners. Because years of research has proven the ten-day time lapse rule sound, it was introduced into this method as an arbitrary rule.

There are times, of course, when a good winner may be procured by choosing a horse that shows a last race 11 or 12 days ago. This is something, however, beyond our control since systems by very virture of definition must be rigid and not flexible. In the long run this rigidity will prove beneficial, since it will also cast off many losers.

The speed rate element has been discussed previously and there is no need to go into it deeper. This element is the basic root of our system and comcentration on it without deviation is of utmost importance to successful play.

Although horses racing at minor ovals might show five speed rates of 80 or higher in their last five races (of course earned at other tracks, since minor ovals are not rated by the racing papers) this usually is a rarity. Since no speed rates are given for these tracks, a horse racing there for the second time would show at least one race without a speed rate. Only horses showing speed rates in all their last five efforts can be considered; therefore, such a horse could not qualify after one race at the same minor oval.

The only horses we could back would be those racing at this track for the first time. Such animals, at times, may be returned winners, but the rules for such play should be entirely different from our present method's. For the sake of convenience, to promote easier selections and to prevent erratic selections, minor ovals have been ruled out. They should not even be consulted for play. The waste of time in trying to find a suitable choice, as well as the possible hazards involved, stamp the minor ovals as impractical for our method.

Horses that have finished later than fifth in their last races are not attractive propositions. This does not mean that such a bad last performance cannot produce a win in the next effort, but the number of winners cannot effectively offset the losers. It is more profitable to avoid animals with last finishes worse than fifth in the method presented here. Methods that continually back horses with such poor final efforts do not, as a rule, obtain a high winning percentage. As far as price is concerned, we can still get good prices on horses that wound up no further than fifth.

Weight has always been a topic of controversy. Some horse-racing experts insist that since a horse is such a big, strong animal a few pounds more or less should not make much difference. Others, however, maintain that an animal can take just so much weight and that any further poundage is like the straw that broke the camel's back.

The records point to the soundness of the latter's logic. Time and again you will find horses beating each other and a close inspection will show that it was just a few pounds added or deducted that made the difference.

Track handicappers use weight assignments as a guide in their attemps to bring all the horses to the wire in a dead heat. All the reader has to do is to examine past performances carefully to prove this point.

There's a lot to this weight business and we should not disregard the known facts. This system has been fairly lenient with the weight rule, for it permits a horse to be considered even if it is carrying up to six pounds more than in its last race. Beyond this extra weight of six pounds we refuse to go. According to the rules of this system no horse can qualify if it is carrying seven or more pounds greater weight than it lugged in its last race.

There are some horses that are unreliable. Two-year-olds and maidens fall in this category. The former are too young and still in the formative stages where they can suddenly go either way, down or up in racing class. Maidens, obviously, have as yet proven nothing. They have failed to win a single race, and how are we to know that they ever will? Why risk your money on a question mark when there are many animals that have already proved their ability?

Another classification of animals that are difficult to figure are those racing in name handicaps or stakes events. These animals are of high caliber and too many of them will show 80 or higher speed rates in nearly all their races, if not all. Then, again, most of them will show varied distances in their past performances.

Name handicaps and stakes races are often run over greater than average distances, and since these animals show combinations of stakes, handicaps and merely preparatory races, the distances will be a mixture of all sorts.

Those horses that race only in sprint affairs, usually at six furlongs, will most likely have performed at 80 or higher speed rates in pratically all races, so that even if their races were always at the same distance it would be a difficult task to make a choice.

The tie rule is a necessary evil, since you will find two or more horses qualified. On occasion you will back the wrong horse, but in the main the tie rule is fairly sound and should work well. If, however, you don't mind playing more than one horse in a race and the odds are right there is no reason why you can't bet the way. This is left to the discretion of the player.

WORKOUT: *Time Figures Rate Consistency*

Date	Horse	Race & Track		Mutuel
July 2	U. S. Bound	5	Nar.	9.40
4	Bolo Mack	7	Mth.	...
5	Bated Breath	6	Nar.	6.80
7	Music	5	Mth.	...
	Scholarship	3	Nar.	...
	U. S. Bound	5	Nar.	...
	Little Step	6	Nar.	42.40
9	Bolo Mack	6	Mth.	...
11	Fern Gold	6	Nar.	...
12	Related	6	Nar.	14.20
13	Directoire	6	Mth.	4.60
14	Play Toy	5	Mth.	8.20
	Yes You	6	Nar.	...
18	Lawful	2	Nar.	...
	College Queen	4	Nar.	7.20
	Nor'west	6	Nar.	...
19	Lady's Delight	4	Emp.	6.00
20	Tripoli	4	Emp.	7.00
	Coveted	7	Emp.	15.40
23	Bated Breath	6	Nar.	...
24	Feudin Fightin	5	A.P.	...
25	Abbotstown	5	Nar.	...
26	Sir Sweep	4	Mth.	...
28	Suleiman	5	Mth.	...
	Bated Breath	5	Nar.	...
	Roy	6	Nar.	...

26 selections — 10 won — 38%

Returned $121.20
Invested $52.00
———
Profit on a $2 Win Wager $69.20

The last rule might not seem important, but to lose sight of it could make you want to tear your hair out after the race. Should you find two horses qualifying and one scratched, your choice is obviously the horse still in the race, even though the animal scratched was the selection according to the tie rule. Scratched horses should not be figured. They are not running and should be crossed out as if they had never been entered in the race.

It is good policy to refer to an actual race before permitting the reader to try to work the method on his own. Let's open the pages of our racing paper of July 2, 1951 (see workout), to the past performances of the fifth race at Narragansett where our first play is found.

This is a claiming race for four-year-olds and upward, so it can be examined for selection purposes. The easiest way to work the system is to look first for horses with five last consecutive races each of which shows a speed rate of 80 or higher.

Passing up the first seven horses listed, because they don't have the qualification, we finally come to U. S. Bound. This horse shows five consecutive races, starting from the top and working down, as follows: 81, 82, 84, 83, 85. All of these speed rates were earned at distances of ¾ of a mile. The horse's last race was on June 25th, just seven days from today's race. The weight it carried last time was 116 compared to today's weight of 112. The animal finished second in its last race. Since the event is not for jumpers and the horse is not a maiden, the animal qualifies in all respects.

The horse is checked off as a prospect. No other horse can be found in this race with five consecutive last speed rates of 80 or higher. U. S. Bound is the only possible selection.

If you will look at the workout you will notice that the horse won.

Rate 'Em

Slow and steady may win the race as far as turtles and rabbits go, but when you're betting dough on the ponies, brother, speed is what you've got to watch. That's one sound, logical reason for the speed rates appearing in the daily racing papers.

Although using straight time may be a more reliable index of measurement, it is difficult to determine accurately for all horses, because only the times of the winners are shown. Speed rates, however, are based on the record set at the individual tracks and take into consideration the element of ground condition. A good estimate of the horse's ability, the speed rate is a factor definitely worth inserting into handicapping procedure.

For purposes of obtaining winners, only current speed rates can be used profitably. A speed rate earned more than a month ago is stale and frequently unreliable. In order to ensure speed rates that can be used, only those races run within the period of a month from today's race should be considered.

It is not safe to assume that the horse with the highest speed rate for a period of a month will be the winner. Other considerations enter into the picture. The present condition of the animal is important to keep in mind. If the horse has raced recently we can assume that at least it has had the opportunity of going through a tightening race. Most horses have to be raced into condition, and will not usually win their first time out or if they have had a long layoff.

Workouts are important too. It does not always matter how fast the horse worked. Often when a trainer has a horse ready he will test it through a workout to determine whether or not the animal can live up to expectations. So, regardless of the time, a recent workout frequently tells us that the trainer is testing the animal to evaluate its potentialities.

One of the most vital tests for successful racing is the horse's consistency, the ability to win with a certain degree of frequency. An animal that can show a 20% or more winning percentage for the last two years combined is one that bears watching. This is the kind of horse that was really meant for racing.

Unfortunately, most horses are not stamped from such a mold. Thousands or more, probably millions of dollars, have been literally thrown to the wind on animals that can do no better than finish behind the winner. It is the opinion of many experts on horse racing that only the consistent animals are worth wagering on.

Let us look for a horse whose top speed rate, earned within one month of today's race, is at least one of the three best; a win consistency of 20% or better for the current and last year combined; a recent race, and a recent workout and we have a system that should stand up favorably. The results of our one month workout at Belmont Park seem to bear out our expectations.

RULES: *Rate 'Em*

1. *Before scratches* first select the horses who raced within a month from today's race and check off highest speed rate earned in any of the races within this period. Select the horses with

the three highest speed rates. All horses tied for third best speed rate are to be considered.

2. In order to qualify further the horse must have raced last out not more than ten days ago.

3. Horse must show a 20% or better win consistency for the current and last year combined.

4. Horse must show workout within eight days of today's race.

5. In case of tie, if race has ten or fewer horses, pick the horse with the lowest weight. If still tied, choose the horse with the best win consistency for current and last year combined.

6. If race has more than ten horses, pick the horse with the best win consistency.

7. Play no jumping races or two-year-olds. Play no name handicaps or stake races.

Selecting the horses may prove more difficult if you do not know how to go about it. It is not necessary to start with the first horse listed and to try to determine its highest speed rate earned during the period within a month from today's race.

Remember that only horses with a win consistency of 20% or better for the last two years combined, a recent race not more than ten days ago, and a workout within eight days of today's race, can qualify. If no animal meets all these requirements, we cannot have a play.

So, the person following the system should scan the charts for horses that show a 20% or better win consistency for the last two years combined. This step alone will often eliminate a race so that selecting the highest speed rates from the start is not always necessary.

Of course if the animal shows such a consistency, it would still be required to show a last race not more than ten days ago, and a workout within eight days of today's race. If you should discover at least one horse that meets the three necessary requirements other than the speed rate, then it is imperative to start checking all horses for everything.

It is important to keep in mind that the horse we finally select must show that its best speed rate earned within a month of today's race ranks among the top three of all the animals in the race.

Also do not forget that all horses tied for third best speed rate are to be considered.

Still further, remember that all calculations are made before scratches. If the reader wishes to try his hand at rating 'em after scratches I do not think that it will harm the method. Perhaps playing after scratches may prove beneficial, but the results of the workout shown here were obtained on the basis of figures determined before scratches. This makes for more simplicity in selection and raises no doubts when and if a qualified horse scratches. If our selection should scratch, the race is eliminated from further consideration.

On examination of system rules, the reader will notice that name handicaps and stake races have been eliminated from play. There are so many good horses running in these types of races that it is frequently difficult too make a selection based on any particular set of rules.

Horses that race in such events often do not need the same kind of treatment as their lesser brethren to prepare them for winning action. Yet in the 6th at Belmont on May 18, Resilient was one of the qualifying selections, and although this horse won, paying the nice price of $20.20, it would have been eliminated by the tie rules.

On May 25, the horse All At Once, 6th at Belmont, would have qualified as a selection. The animal went on to win at the neat mutuels of $28.60, $14.10, $8.70, across the board.

Playing stake racces and name handicaps would have increased the profit, because of the $28.60 winner, but would have lowered the winning percentage. All logic seems to point to the necessity of eliminating such races from consideration, but fact sometimes challenges logic.

Please pay special attention to the tie-breaking rules. Notice that when there are ten or fewer horses running, ties are broken on the basis of weight carried, whereas with events listing more than ten horses the separation rule calls for the animal with the best win consistency.

With a field of 10 or less horses the factor of weight is more important. This is a comparatively small field and there will not be as much jostling and elbowing for room. With the track more or less open, the element of weight may often tell the tale. With a crowded track a horse that knows how and wants to win will more likely come home first. To play the more win-consistent animal here is therefore a sounder policy.

For purposes of clarification it is essential in this type of system to actually demonstrate the process of selection by choosing a race at random and showing how the horse listed in the workout was chosen.

Let's take the 5th race at Belmont Park on May 6, 1954. It is an allowance event which is definitely a type of race that can be played. The first horse listed, Scent, shows three wins out of 14 for 1953, but no wins or races run for the current year. This horse obviously cannot qualify, even though its win consistency is better than 20%. We are looking first, as previously explained, for a horse with 20% or better win consistency, a workout within eight days of today's event, and a recent race not more than ten days ago.

The second horse, Trick Pilot, shows one win out of one for the current year and no wins out of three for last year. This gives the animal a 25% win consistency and it is eligible so far. Displaying a recent race on April 29, seven days ago, the horse still qualifies. However, it does not show a workout within eight days of today's race. April 26 is the date of Trick Pilot's most recent workout, and because this shows a ten-day interim, the animal is eliminated from consideration.

The next horse, Very Special also qualifies on consistency and current race, but fails to meet the workout requirement. Miss Weesie, a four-year-old filly, is also eliminated since she has not raced currently, although her consistency record is adequate.

Smart Apple, the horse that follows Miss Weesie in the past performance lists, has the necessary consistency and workout, meeting the requirements of our rules, but the colt raced last 14 days ago, so we throw this one out too.

Next comes Plus Fours with five wins out of 18 for 1953 and 1954 combined, four wins out of ten for the current year and one victory out of eight for the previous year. The animal raced last on April 30 and it shows a latest workout the day before the race on May 5. Plus Fours meets all the requirements and can be a

WORKOUT: *Rate 'Em*

(Belmont Park)

Date	Horse	Race	Win	Place	Show
5-1	Kaster	5	13.30	6.90	4.70
	Kinda Rough	8	...	...	...
5-3	Bold Man	5	3.00	2.60	2.30
	Palm Tree	6	6.60	2.90	2.40
	Scotstoun	7	...	...	...
5-5	Ham Bone	7	...	...	7.30
5-6	Red Relic	2	...	4.20	3.10
	Plus Fours	5	20.00	8.60	5.60
5-7	King Jolie	5	6.60	4.00	3.40
	Catspaw	7	10.40	4.90	2.80
5-8	Light Step	2	...	...	...
5-10	Iron Guy	2	...	...	...
	Indiana	5	5.20	3.00	2.50
	Kaster	7	...	4.00	2.70
5-12	Heed Me	4	6.30	4.10	2.90
5-13	Tortilla	7	...	...	...
5-14	Light Step	2	...	4.40	2.90
	Iron Guy	8	23.90	9.50	5.50
5-15	Diving Board	7	5.90	3.60	2.60
5-18	On Flight	7	...	...	...
5-19	Flying Rebel	2	17.60	8.10	6.30
	Hickory Hill	7	...	...	...
5-20	Speedy Wave	4	5.30	3.30	2.50
	Stone Saucer	7	...	3.20	2.40
5-24	Flying Rebel	4	5.70	5.20	3.70
	Diving Board	6	7.00	3.50	3.00
	South Point	7	10.90	6.60	3.70
5-26	Miss Weesie	4	13.40	5.60	4.40
5-28	Hoplite	7	...	3.20	2.50
5-29	All At Once	4	6.80	3.30	2.50
5-31	Royal Haste	3	...	...	...
	South Point	7	11.30	6.00	4.30

56% won	Amount Returned $179.20	110.70	86.00
72% placed	Amount Invested ......$ 64.00	64.00	64.00
75% showed	Profit on $2 Wagers $115.00	$46.00	$22.00

selection if its best speed rate earned within one month of today's race is one of the top three or tied for third best.

The top horse, Scent, has no races within one month of today's event. The second horse, Trick Pilot, shows only one race within a month. On April 29 it earned a speed rate of 89. This figure is its highest speed rate and we place this number next to its name. Very Special raced on April 30, 16 and 10. All these races are within the one month interim. The race on April 30 earned an 80 speed rate, while the 16th showed 92 and the 10th 91. Since 92 was the highest speed rate, this is the number placed next to Very Special's name.

Fly Wheel and Miss Weesie get no speed rate earnings, since they had not raced during the current year. Smart Apple gets 102 for its only qualifying race on April 22. Plus Fours receives a 94, Game Chance 92, Bradley 85 and Expletive nothing, since its last race was on December 5, 1953.

Smart Apple shows the highest rating, with 102. Plus Fours is next with 94, and Game Chance is tied with Very Special for third with 92. Very Special meets the consistency and current race rules, but is eliminated because its last workout was on March 20, much too far back. Game Chance does not have the necessary consistency.

Smart Apple has the consistency and workout tabbed correctly, but is eliminated because it raced last 14 days ago. Our only other possible selection, Plus Fours, meets all requirements, consistency, recent race and workout within eight days. This is our selection. Plus Fours won and paid $20.00, $8.60 and $5.60, across the board.

If you play this system, take your time and make sure you don't miss on any of the requirements. It is a sound, logical method that should bring you a great deal of satisfaction as well as profit.

16.
PLAYING HORSES
THAT SHOW PREFERRED DISTANCES

Horses like humans often have certain set preferences from which they find it difficult to deviate. Some horses are strictly routers, while others are adept only in sprints. Front runners are habitual in their desire to set the pace and, similarly, the stretch runner likes to come from behind. We can therefore often classify a horse because of its consistent type of performance, as for example, "stretch runner"—"front runner"—"router"—"sprinter"—etc.

The method to be presented here confines itself to animals that prefer specific distances, which are naturally reflected in their past performances. If you will examine any racing paper with past performances, you will notice that some horses always seem to run at the same distance.

The Preferred Distance Method

Six furlongs is by far the most common of preferred distances. This is so because more of these races are carded. Occasionally you will find that a horse has raced in nothing but $1\frac{1}{16}$ or $1\frac{1}{8}$ mile events.

Other distances are not common enough, so this system deals only with those just mentioned. The preponderance of selections will, nevertheless, come from the ¾-mile events.

Merely to select those horses which show the same distance throughout their past performances is not sufficiently sound to produce a successful method of play. There are still the elements of condition, form, consistency, etc., which must be considered before we can come to a logical conclusion.

To produce longshots, all these basic elements cannot be packed into the method, but we will stress at least one of them for each horse that is to be wagered on. One of these will be a requirement for the horse to be chosen as our selection: (1) Either our horse is a highly consistent animal, *or* (2) is in form, *or* (3) has raced recently enough to be in condition.

If our horse has raced within seven days from today's event, we will conclude that this is ample evidence of condition. A workout within three days of today's race will supply some manifestation of form. The conclusion here is that since the workout is of such recent vintage the trainer must think that the horse is ready.

To rely on the workout for form instead of a recent good effort permits room for longshots to develop. Horses that have shown poor last races either through connivance or for valid reasons may develop hidden form that can only be reflected by the animal's recent workout. The time of the workout is not important because the trainer may take various precautions to prevent a good showing, thus enhancing the possibilities of an excellent price.

A horse that has won at least 20% of its races for the current and last year combined is to be considered highly consistent. Such an animal can be thought of as a good bet on its consistency alone.

To prove that our horse is fitted to today's distance, we will use its list of past performances as shown in today's paper. The distance must be *exactly the same* and no "about" distances can be considered, At some tracks, especially minor ovals, races are run at about ¾ of a mile or about $1\frac{1}{16}$ of a mile. We cannot consider these distances, since they are obviously not the same.

If an animal does not show at least six races at today's distance it cannot qualify as a habitual performer and is not to be contemplated for selection.

A horse that shows only three or four or even five races in its past performances, regardless of whether they are all at the same distance, does not show sufficient proof of its likes or dislikes. In order to qualify the animal must show at least six races at the designated distance in its past performances.

RULES: *Preferred Distance Method*

1. Play races at the following distances only: ¾, $1\frac{1}{16}$, 1⅛ miles.

2. The horse's last race must have been not more than a month ago.

3. Check off all those horses that raced at the same distance as today's race in every race as listed in today's list of past performances. At least six such races must be shown in the past performances for the horse to be considered.

4. Do not accept "about" distances. Any race at about the distance run today is to be considered as a different distance.

5. Our horse must show at least one of the following: *a.* at least 20% win consistency for the current and last year com-

bined; or, *b.* a race within seven days of today's race; or *c.* a workout within three days of today's race.

6. Do not play Stakes races or "Name" Handicaps.

7. Play no two-year-olds or jumpers.

8. Play after scratches are known.

9. In case of tie, play the horse with the best in-the-money consistency for the current and last year combined. If still tied, play the horse that raced most recently.

Finally, if our selection is carrying more than three pounds greater weight than it carried in its last race, *pass* the race. If our selection is over eight years old, *pass* the race. *Disregard disqualifications.* If the horse won the race, it is counted as a winning one, regardless of whether the judges decided to disqualify it. (This is optional, and if the reader chooses to disregard it he may.)

The method clicked with many four-figure winners, quite a few at exceptionally long prices. The reason for this is obvious. We are sometimes playing horses that showed miserable performances in their last race.

Vital, in the 7th at Delaware, June 6 (see workout), paid $43.50 after losing its last race by 16 lengths. It's the longshots that are bound to come along in this method that make it worthwhile playing.

There were 142 plays for the month of June, 1951, and this may be a little too much for the average player. For those who like spot plays, the following diversion of this method might prove adequate.

Play *claiming* races *only,* choosing those horses selected by our method which show a win anywhere in today's list of past performances at a claiming price at least $500 higher than today's entered price. The qualifying winning race must be a claiming race. No other type of race can be considered. Disregard disqualifications. We are only interested here in the horse's ability to win, regardless of whether or not there is an infraction of rules, intentional or otherwise.

Use the same rules to get your selection. After it is obtained, however, check to see whether it has won at a claiming price at least $500 higher. If not, the race is passed.

Using this added rule, 23 horses met the requirements, eight of them winning. Among them were a couple of longshots, which produced a tremendous profit and percentage won on investment. This condition might not always prevail, but the added rule seems logical enough to procure a greater percentage of winners and it will definitely reduce the number of plays to a bare minimum.

The reason for using claiming races only will seem more obvious on closer inspection. Only by comparing the raw figures can we be sure that the animal can do better or is in company that it ought to beat. A horse that has won in a $3000 claimer should be able to wrest a victory when entered among $2500 platers. If the qualifying race was won in an allowance or other race, not a claimer, it would be difficult to ascertain this.

Of course there may be other horses in the race that have won at a higher claiming price, and this is an angle that system fans may be able to utilize in conjunction with this system. The investigation here has not gone so far. Sometimes the further one digs the worse the method gets. The situation might not be so here, but the rewards shown seem to bear out a basic soundness in the method.

The reader will notice that stakes races and "name" handicaps have been excluded from play. Systems based on such races must employ different rules in order to extract winners. The competition is too keen and there is less room for an angle to be used, since the larger purses arouse enough incentive to make every trainer try to win.

WORKOUT: *Preferred Distance Method*

Date	Horse	Race & Track	Mutuel	Date	Horse	Race & Track	Mutuel
6/1	Shine On	2 Del.	19.70		King Mowlee	5 Del.	....
	Windflower	6 Del.	22.30		Definitely	6 Del.	....
	Be Proud	2 Suf.	....		Gaby H	2 Suf.	....
	Daughter C	6 Suf.	....		Chall Wind	4 Suf.	....
	Pnut Vendor	6 L.F.	3.80		Tiny Admiral	5 Suf.	....
6/2	Betsy Marie	1 Bel.	53.30		Bidandmade	6 L.F.	....
	Mobile Belle	3 Bel.	....	6/13	Algie	1 Bel.	....
	Big Story	5 Bel	....		Birchie	3 Del.	....
	Galla Babe	2 Suf.	....		Annie's Choice	1 Suf.	....
	Equihaze	7 Suf.	15.60		College Queen	4 Suf.	....
6/4	Yes You	7 Del.	....		Wise Choice	1 L.F.	....
	Be Proud	1 Suf.	....	6/14	Little Falls	6 Bel.	....
	Jean Meter	2 Suf.	14.60		Galla Babe	2 Suf.	....

Date	Horse	Race & Track	Mutuel	Date	Horse	Race & Track	Mutuel
	Fiorentina	3 Suf.	....		Alsiral	5 Suf.	19.20
	Woodstone	5 L.F.	....		Lefty Jim	6 Suf.	....
6/5	On Guard	2 Del.	....	6/15	King Twig	1 Suf.	....
	Up Beat	5 Del.	....		Punks	5 L.F.	....
	Troy Road	2 Suf.	17.80	6/16	Easy Whirl	2 Bel.	....
	Shirley's Pride	4 Suf.	....		Music	5 Mth.	....
	Little Flossy	5 Suf.	....		Tea-Maker	7 Mth.	....
	Delta Eagle	5 L.F.	12.20		Surpass	2 Del.	....
6/6	Vital	7 Del.	43.50		Shine On	3 Del.	....
	Custody	3 Suf.	....		Gold Apple	3 Suf.	....
	Idio	4 Suf.	....		Best Degree	5 Suf.	....
	Pnut Vendor	7 L.F.	....		Thunderjet	5 L.F.	....
6/7	Wolf Whistle	2 Suf.	3.40	6/18	Betsy Marie	4 Bel.	....
	Summer Cruise	5 Suf.	....		Gay Ten	2 Mth.	....
	Bonrilla	5 L.F.	....		Darby D'Amour	2 Del.	3.70
6/8	Windflower	5 Del.	9.70		Lotoftown	3 Del.	....
	Silver Reward	2 Suf.	....		Gaby H	1 Suf.	....
	Asphalt	7 L.F.	7.00		Tintina	2 Suf.	....
6/9	War Phar	3 Del.	....		Lawful	4 Suf.	....
	Eagle Eye	6 Del.	....	6/19	Balla-Duke	6 Del.	....
	Play Toy	7 Del.	6.10		Grey Beard	1 Suf.	....
	Galla Babe	1 Suf.	....		Fiorentina	2 Suf.	....
	Idio	3 Suf.	5.00		College Queen	5 Suf.	15.60
	Punks	4 L.F.	....	6/20	On Guard	2 Mth.	....
	Spring Chimes	6 L.F.	....		Senoril	4 Mth.	4.00
6/11	Heddy B	1 Del.	....		Head Stream	5 Mth.	....
	Surpass	2 Del.	26.80		Play Toy	6 Mth.	....
	Jolirab	4 Del.	....		Spring Chimes	3 A.P.	....
	Fiesta	2 Suf.	....		Jean Meter	2 Suf.	....
	Hoo Is It	4 Suf.	....	6/21	Mary Like	1 Mth.	....
	Ringneck	5 Suf.	....		Will I	2 Mth.	....
	Lawful	6 Suf.	4.80		Little Harp	5 Del.	....
6/12	Hard To Get	3 Del.	86.50		Scheming World	6 Del.	....
	Ackley	2 Suf.	....		Sailcloth	1 Del.	....
	Golden Mean	3 Suf.	....		Librab	2 Del.	11.90
6/22	Suptela	2 Mth.	....		Annie's Choice	4 Suf.	....
	Mobile Belle	5 Mth.	....		Sky Ranger	4 A.P.	....
	Bold Jo	6 Mth.	....		Holly Sweet	5 A.P.	....
	Here's a Dream	5 Suf.	....	6/28	Diamond Head	1 Mth.	....
	Signal Code	4 A.P.	....		Shirlson	2 Mth.	....
6/23	Betsy Marie	2 Aqu.	....		Balinakill	2 Del.	....
	Gallalad	8 Mth.	9.20		Little Harp	5 Del.	....
	Windflower	4 Del.	5.90		Gams	1 Suf.	16.60
	Doby	2 Suf.	....		Mocha	4 Suf.	....
	Alsiral	3 Suf.	....		Ydear	1 A.P.	....
	Mr. Joe Puck	5 Suf.	....		Signal Code	6 A.P.	9.20
	Wise Choice	1 A.P.	....	6/29	Tea Maker	6 Aqu.	....
6/25	Wingy	4 Mth.	....		Blue Fedora	2 Mth.	....

Date	Horse	Race & Track	Mutuel	Date	Horse	Race & Track	Mutuel
	Lotoftown	1 Del.	....		Flower Hat	5 Mth.	....
	My Ruthie	4 Suf.	....		Recline	7 A.P.	....
	Idio	6 Suf.	....	6/30	Tea Deb	5 Mth.	....
	Spring Chimes	3 A.P.	13.40		Carolina Star	1 Suf.	....
	Asphalt	6 A.P.	....		Gift Package	2 Suf.	....
6/26	Sugar Alley	2 Mth.	....		Alsiral	4 Suf.	....
	Warmoud	3 Del.	....		Bated Breath	5 Suf.	....
	Mahoon	4 Del.	....				
	Annar	4 Suf.	....	142 Selections—28 won, 20%			
	Brownskin	5 Suf.	....	Amount Returned $468.60			
	College Queen	6 Suf.	....	Amount Invested $284.00			
6/27	Flying Weather	4 Mth.	7.80				
	Laran	5 Mth.	....	Profit on $2 wager $184.60			

17.
HOW TO FIND FORMFUL HORSES
AND MAKE THEM PAY

Revealed form is a luxury every racing fan relishes. The trouble with revealed form alone, however, is that it is often misleading. Although a horse may be ready to win, there are other factors which enter into the picture and tend to confuse us.

The simplest of these factors is not only the current, but the actual, condition of the animal at the time of the race. Is the horse feeling his oats? Is he up to par, eager to run a winning race?

Unfortunately, this is something that no one can predict or determine. No one has as yet discovered a way to communicate with a horse. As a rule, though a horse that is in good condition and form, and has a reputation as an animal that likes to win, will do as expected, provided of course that the horse is not hindered in any way.

"Hindered" can mean several things. First it may depend on the element of racing luck. The animal may be caught in a pocket, may trip, be pushed, or find itself behind horses with no opening through which it can go. Then again, the stable may not want the horse to win today, hoping for a better price in the future, and the animal may not be extended by the jockey, or the horse may even be pulled to halt its efforts to finish ahead. Perhaps even the jockey assigned to do the riding may be of inferior ability and unable to give the horse the ride it deserves. These are some of the hidden factors, prevalent in many races, which make revealed form alone inadequate in determining a horse's chances of winning.

Regardless of all these drawbacks, it is helpful to be cognizant of an animal's condition and form. The idea is to discard as many animals as possible, but to select the choicest, those which will give you a decent chance of cashing a bet.

The Form Finder

When a horse shows high win consistency, especially for the current year, we have a type of animal that can be backed with comparative confidence. When it not only demonstrates a high degree of win consistency, 20% or better winning efforts for the current year, but shows more than one win, the horse is even more reliable.

Consistency and form alone may prove unprofitable, if the element of speed is not considered. The horse may be good when it's raced only against extremely inferior animals, but if it should be raised in class, the horse may prove to be an unsound investment.

The *Daily Racing Form* Speed Ratings are excellent criterions of a horse's speed index. If the horse displays a speed rating of 80 or more, the animal is definitely one to be reckoned with. It must be considered as a contender in most races. The exceptions, of course, are in the high-purse Handicaps and Stakes races, where speed rates over 90 are commonplace. Usually most horses entered in such races will show speed ratings of 90 or higher, and in the majority of cases the animal chosen as our selection in the system presented here will have a speed rating of 90 or more.

The only speed rating we are concerned with in this system is the very last one. The speed rating must have been earned within ten days of today's race. To allow any extended period to elapse between the interval of the last race and today's event would decrease the value of the speed rating, because if the horse staled off, or is in bad form or condition today, the speed rating certainly would not be a true estimate of the horse's ability.

An in-the-money effort usually implies that the horse is in form, and may be all set to go for a win, perhaps in the next race. This next race must be very soon or the animal may cool off and lose its good condition. Every good trainer is aware of this fact, and when he knows that the horse has been ground to razor sharpness he will act quickly.

The trainer will look for a race where he can spot his horse at an advantage. Frequently he searches for a spot where the horse can get in under a weight advantage. Above all he does not want his horse to spot the other animals any weight. Often the trainer will be content if he can get away with exactly the same weight the horse carried in its last race, in which the animal finished in the money.

You'd be surprised at what a few pounds more or less can do in a race. Take a little time to examine the weights carried by many winners. You'll find horses losing and winning against each other, with just a few pounds more or less being the determining factor.

Since all racing abides by the scale of weights, there must be plenty to this business of weight advantage. If a horse is dropping weight, the speed rating earned in its recent last race surely becomes more significant.

With this system a player does not have to be concerned about a rise or drop in class. In fact the element of class should absolutely be ignored. For example: May Reward, on August 9, in the 5th race at Del Mar, was going up in claiming price from $4000 in its last race to $5000 today. Yet this did not prevent May Reward from winning at the handsome mutuel payoff of $30.70. (See workout.)

Because of this indifference to class, the system will frequently click with real, bankroll building prices. The betting public at the track is usually wary about a horse going up in class. Especially is this true when there is another highly consistent horse in the race. There may be other horses in the same race that are of good calibre, and perhaps they are being dropped in class today. Most of the play will go on these animals, so that our selection, when it does romp home, pays off at a juicy figure.

The element of distance is to be disregarded too. Remember that we are placing considerable faith in the trainer's intentions, and this faith will very often be paid back with a good priced winning mutuel.

We are not playing mediocre animals here. The player must also be aware of the fact that the animal selected for play has just finished in the money in its last race, not more than ten days ago. So let the other players choose the favorites, or any other kind which they have tagged to win, while we wager on a solid, sound, not heavily burdened animal.

Now let's consolidate and see how our system stacks up. First we will try to find a horse that is in form. We will consider a horse to be in form if its last race was an in-the-money effort. The horse must be in good current condition. For this reason we have provided a maximum time lapse of ten days from its last race. An animal that has raced so recently is more likely to be in condition. The average horse does not win until it has been raced into form and condition.

To make sure that our horse is not an ordinary animal, and that it has recently shown ability to run at a fast clip, we will require a speed rating of 80 or more for its last race. Our animal will not be excessively burdened. Since the horse has already demonstrated that it can finish in the money carrying a designated weight, we will refuse to accept the animal for play unless the weight carried today is the same as, or less than, that carried in its last race. With this stipulation we are working in line with the trainer's intentions, for under such conditions the horse is more likely to be sent for the purse.

Our horse will have a high winning consistency for the current year. A one-time winner this year will not be acceptable. With a horse that has already demonstrated its ability to win more than once, the chances of repeating such an effort is more likely. This type of animal shows that it likes to win, and given the proper opportunity, it will probably live up to its reputation. Win consistency established in the distant past is not a true test of the animal's present value. A horse is even more subject to physical frailties and mishaps than a human being.

Our selections, as you see, are shaping up as substantial, reliable betting tools. The results of the workout seem to imply as much. Many excellent prices were obtained, and a similar pattern does not seem to be unlikely for other months. However, the fact that we are playing horses in form seems to point out that play may be more profitable during the summer months when form is much better.

Nevertheless a great deal of the system's success depends on the trainer's intentions, so that the question of the method's all-year-round practicability is not completely settled. Further investigation for this purpose is essential. If the reader wishes to play this system in months other than the summer, he should test it before risking any money. Remember, the workout here was made during the month of August.

RULES: *The Form Finder*

1. The horse's last race must have been run not more than ten days ago.

2. The horse must show an in-the-money effort in its last race (1st, 2nd or 3rd).

3. The horse must show at least 20% win consistency for the current year, with at least two wins.

4. The horse's weight carried today must not be higher than the weight it carried in its last race. If the horse is carrying exactly the same weight as it carried in its last race, the animal does qualify.

5. The horse's speed rating earned in its last race must be 80 or more. If the horse does not show a speed rating in its last race the animal cannot be considered.

6. Play no maidens, two-year-olds, or jumpers.

7. In case of tie, choose the horse with the highest speed rating in its last race. If still tied, play the horse with the best win consistency for the current year. If still tied, play the horse that raced most recently.

8. Play after scratches are known.

WORKOUT: *The Form Finder*

Date	Race	Horse	Win	Place	Show
1	2	Amigo X	$35.90	11.00	5.30
	5	Dina Bam	13.60	6.20	4.30
	7	Tar Flat	....	....	....
	8	Time's Scarce	....	....	....
2	2	Over Fast	5.40	2.90	2.50
	4	War Pep	....	....	....
	8	Gustaf	28.30	10.30	5.70
8	4	Toubo Chilla	....	....	3.20
	7	My Chief	....	....	....
	8	Long Pull	....	....	....
9	2	Honor System	....	....	2.70
	4	Matizar	5.10	3.40	2.70
	5	May Reward	30.70	8.10	4.90
11	6	Dina Bam	....	....	3.30
13	3	Sea Novice	....	....	4.60
14	6	Barbara Brown*	12.10	6.90	4.10
15	4	Willow Way	....	....	....
16	3	Cone	13.30	6.20	3.90
	6	May Reward	....	....	....
18	5	Abe's Birthday	28.60	10.50	4.80
	7	Matizar	....	....	....
19	5	Shedon't Smoke	....	....	....
20	6	Ascribe	....	....	....
	8	Van Ness	....	....	....
21	4	Kings Moll	....	....	....
22	5	Bangster	....	3.70	4.20
25	6	Flash Burn	....	3.70	3.10
26	6	Tingling	....	....	....
	7	Bombay Duck	....	3.30	3.00
27	6	Countess Speed	....	....	8.10
28	5	Lon's Choice	8.00	4.00	3.70
29	5	Matizar	9.50	3.90	3.40
30	4	Black Silk	....	....	3.30
	7	Ze Pippin	7.80	4.10	3.00

*Entry won

	Win	Place	Show
Amount Returned	$198.30	$88.20	$83.80
Amount Invested	68.00	68.00	68.00
Profit	$130.30	$20.20	$15.80

34 selections
12 won — 35%
15 placed — 44%
21 showed — 62%

18.
SHORT AND SWEET

Every horse player would like to make a profit every time he makes a wager. The longshot bettors cannot expect to do this. Most of these players would be content to win 10% of the time providing they can get a substantial return on those horses that do come in for them.

But playing longshots necessarily means that the bettor must inure himself to long strings of consecutive losers. This obviously is a situation which the average bettor cannot stand very long. The result is that often when the losers start rolling down the assembly line, the strain will cause the bettor to drop his method of play and switch to shorter prices. This only leads to further confusion and greater loss.

It is the rare player who can stick to his plan under the conditions that prevail when playing longshots. The strings of consecutive losers that are bound to go along with this type of play are too disconcerting for the average person.

Short and Sweet

If you would like to win as frequently as possible, it is imperative that you stay away from longshots. It is sometimes possible to get all kinds of prices and a high percentage of winners, but at best such play is limited.

With a high percentage of winners as a goal, together with decent prices, the spots where play will occur should be few. To obtain such a high percentage under these circumstances is also difficult, because there are no known quantities from which to start the basis of the figures.

For example, if we were playing favorites we would know that our chances of winning would be about 33%. Playing Consensus Best Bets would bring about 40% winners. If we could start on some such basis, knowing with a fair degree of accuracy what minimal returns to expect, it should buoy up our confidence and enable us to reach a logical, profitable conclusion.

Sweep is the fellow who grades the horses for the *Daily Racing Form*. He lists the probable odds that each horse will go off in each race.

It is sound policy, if you are going into business, to choose a partner with plenty of experience. Sweep has been grading the horses for the *Daily Racing Form* for a long time and he has proven that he definitely knows what he is doing.

We can go along with Sweep on certain things. If Sweep lists a horse at 8-5 or less, we can figure that the chances of the horse winning would be approximately at the odds suggested, or let us say, to be safe, that the odds against the horse winning will be somewhat less.

However, if we could pick Sweep's first choice at 8-5 or less and then carefully examine each of these horses, running at these probable odds, making sure that our animal has a good chance, we should stack up a better percentage of winners than Sweep.

Sweep's 8-5 or less selections alone should bring in about 40% winners. This would not be sufficient for profitable play, but with our additional digging into the horse's possibilities we ought to increase the average and make it a lucrative venture.

If you expect to reap vast sums of money from the method of selection to be presented here, you are bound to be disappointed. For those who would be content with a 30% or better return on their investment the method holds promise. In what business or investment is it possible to make 30% dividends on each dollar put up? If you treat race wagering as the business venture one can assume it to be, you are more inclined to be successful.

RULES: *Short and Sweet*

1. Horse must be Sweep's first choice at 8-5 or less.
2. Horse must have been first, or second by less than two lengths, or third by less than one length in its last race.
3. Horse must have been leading at any of two calls in its last race.

4. Horse must show at least 20% win consistency for the current and last year combined or for the current year only, providing the animal raced at least six times this year. *Exception:* If the horse is a two-year-old, do not set any limitations on the number of races for the current year.

If the animal did not race this year, consider the two previous years combined, and consider the last year it ran as if it were current. If less than six races were run that year (for example, 1957) then consider the combined previous years (for example, 1956 and 1957).

5. Play no horse that won its last two races.

6. Do not play jumpers, name handicaps, or stakes races.

By starting off with Sweep's first choice at 8-5 or less, we are reasonably assured of a good percentage of winners, when we further add the ingredients of a good finish in its last race, ability to set the pace, and consistency, it seems logical to assume that our chances will be enhanced.

Although there is no stipulation that the horse must have been racing recently (very often a sound rule), with the type of horse played here there should not be too much concern about condition. Often when a horse has raced considerably and has shown that it is a worthy animal, the trainer may decide to rest the animal but still condition it away from the track. The fact that the horse is fit is already shown by the low estimated odds Sweep has figured the animal to go off at.

A consistent animal, tried and proved, is always a better risk than one that seems to be in excellent condition and form, yet shows little ability to win. Constant check has provided proof that a horse which can lead somewhere in the race at more than one call, even though it does not win the race, but finishes within striking distance of the leader, is likely a threat in the future. All it needs is to extend this pace-setting ability a little further—which it frequently does.

With the higher type of horses, those entered in name handicaps or stakes races, it is a different thing entirely. There the competition is so keen that it is difficult to fathom who the winner may be. This system, therefore, eliminates such races from consideration. The risky jumping races are also discarded for obvious reasons.

By tightening up the rules so that our horse will be even more of a standout, a greater percentage of winners can be obtained. For those people who are still not satisfied with the percentage of winning return a further group of restrictions have been added. Here they are:

1. The horse must show at least 50% win plus place in today's list of past performances, or 33⅓% win. Disqualification races are to be considered as lost. If horse won race and was placed second, consider the finish as second.

2. The horse must not be going up in class off its last race unless it won its last race by four lengths or more. Consider class as follows:

   a. Stakes (any kind)
   b. Handicaps (any kind)
   c. Allowances (any kind)
   d. Claimers (according to price)
   e. Maidens

Remember that these rules are only added and that the previous set of rules still apply. The horse must qualify off the first set of rules before being considered further.

The first tightening rule needs a little clarification. Let's take a selection or two (see workout) and see how they were chosen for play. On April 3, 1950, in the 6th race at Gulfstream Park, we find Growing Up listed as the first choice of Sweep at 8-5 in an allowance race. Under the first set of rules the horse is a perfect selection.

Now let's see how the animal will make out with our initial restricting rule. We look at Growing Up's list of past performances. We notice that there are eight races listed. In one race (the seventh listed) the horse finished third but was placed second on a disqualification. This race should be considered as if the horse actually appeared second at the finish. Out of the eight races the horse won three, which would already be sufficient to qualify it, since three wins out of eight is 37½%, somewhat more than the necessary 33⅓% needed to qualify.

The horse placed twice, which gives it a win plus place average of 62½% (five out of eight), more than sufficient to qualify on that score. If you will consult the workout, you will see that the horse won the race. In fact, under these added rules, only six horses failed to win. Of course these added rules reduced the action, but they brought a greater dollar for dollar profit.

Little Harp was our selection under the first set of rules on April 10, in the 6th race at Havre DeGrace. The horse's list of past performances consisted of nine races. The gelding had only won two of them, not nearly enough to qualify on a win percentage. However, out of the remaining seven races, the animal had come in second six times. Six places plus two wins gave the animal a win plus place average of 89⅝%, obviously qualifying the horse. It went on to win the race at a mutuel of $3.40, $2.60, $2.40, across the board.

The system can still be made to produce a better win percentage by further tightening the rules. Add the further stipulation that the horse must have won its last race by three lengths or more and see what happens. The action is cut down greatly but the win percentage is increased tremendously. There were only eight selections, but only one horse lost, finishing second.

By forcing the selection to show a win by four lengths or more, only five plays showed up during both months. All of them won.

WORKOUTS: *Short and Sweet*

(April-May 1950)

A

Date		Horse	Race & Track	Win	Place	Show
April	1	Guillotine	4 Jam.	3.30	2.90	2.40
	3	Sweet Dream	6 Jam	4.50	3.00	2.40
		Growing Up	6 G.P.	5.10	3.70	3.10
	5	Big and Better	4 G.P.	10.20	5.10	4.40
	6	Our John Wm.	6 Jam	....	2.10	Out
	10	Little Harp	6 Hdg.	3.40	2.60	2.40
	11	Eagle Eye	6 G.P.	5.30	3.70	2.80
	13	Next Move	6 Jam.	2.50	2.30	2.10
	14	Landlord	1 Jam.	4.40	3.00	2.20
		Eddie Leonard	6 G.P.	....	....	2.70
	15	Starecase	7 Jam.	4.00	3.00	2.60
	20	Empty Sea	5 G.P.	5.20	3.10	2.50
	22	Brazen Brat	3 Hdg.	3.20	2.60	2.40
	24	Rudy's Star	5 L.D.	....	....	....
	25	Flying Missel	6 Jam.	3.90	2.40	2.10
	26	Fabricate	4 Jam.	....	2.70	2.30
May	1	Starecase	6 Jam	....	....	2.50
	5	Black Ed	3 Suf.	....	....	....

Date		Horse	Race & Track	Win	Place	Show
	8	Gorget	9 Suf.	5.60	3.80	3.00
	10	Tea Deb	4 G.S.	....	2.40	2.40
	11	Bakersfield	6 Bel	5.90	2.50	2.20
		East Indies	5 G.S.	6.00	3.80	3.00
	13	Wisconsin Boy	4 C.D.	....	2.60	2.20
	16	Excelente	8 Suf.	....	4.00	3.00
	17	Jack The Great	5 Pim.	....	3.00	2.20
	19	King Wilson	6 Suf.	3.60	2.40	2.20
	22	Little Bones	7 Pim.	....	2.60	2.40
	29	Loyal Legion	4 Del.	....	2.70	2.20
	31	Phantom Heels	1 L.F.	....	4.60	3.20
Amount Returned				$76.10	$76.60	$66.90
Amount Invested				$58.00	$58.00	$56.00
Profit				$18.10	$18.60	$10.90

55% won—86% placed—93% showed

B

Date		Horse	Race & Track	Win	Place	Show
April	1	Guillotine	4 Jam.	3.30	2.90	2.40
	3	Growing Up	6 G.P.	5.10	3.70	3.10
	10	Little Harp	6 Hdg.	3.40	2.60	2.40
	13	Next Move	6 Jam.	2.50	2.30	2.10
	14	Landlord	1 Jam.	4.40	3.00	2.20
	15	Starecase	7 Jam.	4.00	3.00	2.60
	20	Empty Sea	5 G.P.	5.20	3.10	2.50
	22	Brazen Brat	3 Hdg.	3.20	2.60	2.40
	24	Rudy's Star	5 L.D.	....	....	....
	25	Flying Missel	6 Jam.	3.90	2.40	2.10
	26	Fabricate	4 Jam.	....	2.70	2.30
May	1	Starecase	6 Jam.	....	....	2.50
	8	Gorget	9 Suf.	5.60	3.80	3.00
	10	Tea Deb	4 G.S.	....	2.40	2.40
	11	Bakersfield	6 Bel.	5.90	2.50	2.20
	11	East Indies	5 G.S.	6.00	3.80	3.00
	16	Excelente	8 Suf.	....	4.00	3.00
	19	King Wilson	6 Suf.	3.60	2.40	2.20
	22	Little Bones	7 Pim.	....	2.60	2.40
Amount Returned				$56.10	$49.80	$44.80
Amount Invested				$38.00	$38.00	$38.00
Profit				$18.10	$11.80	$ 6.80

68% won—89% placed—95% showed

C

Date		Horse	Race & Track	Win	Place	Show
April	3	Growing Up	6 G.P.	5.10	3.70	3.10
	10	Little Harp	6 Hdg.	3.40	2.60	2.40

Date		Horse	Race & Track	Win	Place	Show
	13	Next Move	6 Jam.	2.50	2.30	2.10
	14	Landlord	1 Jam.	4.40	3.00	2.20
	20	Empty Sea	5 G.P.	5.20	3.10	2.50
	22	Brazen Brat	3 Hdg.	3.20	2.60	2.40
May	8	Gorget	9 Suf.	5.60	3.80	3.00
	10	Tea Deb	4 G.S.	....	2.40	2.40
Amount Returned				$29.40	$23.50	$20.10
Amount Invested				$16.00	$16.00	$16.00
Profit				$13.40	$ 7.50	$ 4.10

87½% won—100% placed—100% showed

D

Date	Horse	Race & Track	Win	Place	Show
April 13	Next Move	6 Jam.	2.50	2.30	2.10
14	Landlord	1 Jam.	4.40	3.00	2.20
20	Empty Sea	5 G.P.	5.20	3.10	2.50
22	Brazen Brat	3 Hdg.	3.20	2.60	2.40
May 8	Gorget	9 Suf.	5.60	3.80	3.00
Amount Returned			$20.90	$14.80	$12.20
Amount Invested			$10.00	$10.00	$10.00
Profit			$10.90	$ 4.80	$ 2.20

100% won—100% placed—100% showed

19.
LATCHING ONTO OVERLAYS

Many horseplayers find beating the ponies as difficult as knocking over an elephant with a pea shooter. The reason for this is erratic, poorly orientated play.

The average player does not start from a firm foundation; nor does he base his play on logical contentions. If he confines his bets to favorites, he finds that he has to obtain a lot more than a third winners to make a profit. Betting on favorites without any concrete plan must lead to inevitable loss.

However, the bettor can get around this playing of favorites by applying rational rules to enable him to raise his winning percentage. If his approach is from such an angle his play is no longer erratic.

Wagering on Best Bets has its distinct advantages if worked properly. If the Best Bets are based on the *Daily Racing Form* Consensus, the bettor can console himself with the fact that over the long haul these Best Bets will average about 40% winners. Should he be able to increase the percentage, say to 60%, his chances of operating at a profit are enhanced.

Of course the question of price still remains an important factor. The prices must be equivalent to those ordinarily obtained by betting any consensus Best Bet. If the prices are on a lower level, naturally the added winning percentage becomes worthless.

The intelligent bettor always has in mind the formidable elements of taxes, track take and breakage. These elements dip deeply into your potential profit. It has always been good sense to confine play, as much as possible, to those tracks where taxes and other deductions are smaller. Many fans will say that they don't care about these factors. They are only interested in winners. But statistics show that these factors are often the difference between profit and loss.

At many tracks, if there were no deductions, wagering on the favorites alone would produce a profit. But take my word for it— these subtractions *do* play an important role in successful wagering.

The Overlay Way

The overlay way has always been a rational approach to successful play. If you bet on a horse that should go off at 2-1, and find the actual odds are 6-1, you've got yourself a nice overlay. Overlays occur frequently because sound factors do not always determine the odds. Rather, they are produced by the often erratic judgment of the betting public.

Many emotional factors may rule the play of a bettor at the track, where the actual odds are produced. We all know bettors who will place their money on a horse because it is carrying the name of his best gal or his wife. We know bettors who use a number system or who indulge in stick-pin methods to let Lady Luck come up with the winner.

The reason for mentioning these haphazard, irrational methods is to show the reader what sort of people are helping to make the odds. All this money, bet foolishly on animals that most likely don't figure to win, raises the odds on logical contenders.

Sometimes, of course, these senseless methods do pick winners. But according to the law of averages one is bound to come up with a winner sometime, no matter how he picks them. All of us know that people have won on the "Sweepstakes" when their chance of winning were one in thousands.

The system presented here backs horses rated by Sweep in the *Daily Racing Form*. Why was Sweep chosen? Because Sweep has shown that he has better judgment of probable odds than most selectors. Of course it is not necessary to use Sweep's graded selections. It is possible to get better results after scratches are known. If the reader wants to use this type of morning line (made after scratches) he will have to resort to other sources. Many players can do excellent jobs themselves in reaching such pre-race conclusions. A good scratch sheet's morning line can also be helpful.

Sweep's ratings are not the only factors used to obtain an overlay in this system. Resorting to Sweep's pre-race odds alone does not seem likely to culminate profitably. We still must go back to the other selectors who determine the consensus.

If at least one of the selectors has chosen the animal for second or third then a play possibly can be made—all this, of course, provided that the horse is actually going off at a minimum overlay price.

It is important to remember that Sweep in the consensus is to be considered as one of the selectors. In other words, if Sweep has selected the horse as his second or third choice, the horse is eligible, even though none of the other selectors have mentioned the animal in these positions.

Consider the consensus as something entirely removed from the grading of probable odds. Should the horse be listed as any one of the selectors' first choice, the bettor must be wary. You will discover that if such a horse becomes an overlay it will most likely lose.

Why this is so is sometimes hard to deduce. Perhaps it is due to the fact that a horse chosen as first by a selector should normally be low priced. The public usually follows the selectors and many of them would back it. The rush of the horse's price upward means that most of the money is being bet on the other horses in the race. If the horse's probable odds were high to begin with, this would be another matter.

This overlay horse (selected as first by one of the handicappers making up the consensus) may frequently be an animal who has suddenly become unsound, and the increase in odds may reflect a certain uncanny knowledge that seems to sweep like mental telepathy through the racing spectators.

Scanning the workout, you will find only 14 winners out of 95 selections, yet look at the profit on a $2 flat bet basis. Could you get such a substantial return on any other method with probably much more difficult rules?

The system can definitely be tightened to procure a higher percentage of winners. *This was deliberately not done.*

Go back to the workout and check it. You will notice that the prices are comparatively low—none higher than $42.60, paid by only one horse, Four Jacks, August 6th, in the seventh race at Saratoga. Most of the winners are payoffs in the twenties.

This definitely proves that one or two or even three horses are not responsible for the total profit. The profit was built up gradually with each successive longshot winner.

There are no tie-breaking rules in this system. If more than one horse qualifies as a selection, all should be played. It is exceedingly improbable that more than two will ever become selections, but if this does occur, remember every horse is on its own. We repeat— there are no tie-breaking rules. If the reader, after sufficient investigation, can figure out a workable separation rule, however, there is no reason why it cannot be used.

RULES: *The Overlay Way*

1. Check Sweep's graded selections. Mark off all those horses listed at odds of 9-2 or less.

2. Look back at the selectors' choices that make up the consensus. The horses selected in Rule 1 must be the second or third choice of *at least one* of the selectors. If any of these selectors choose the qualifying horse for first, the animal is to be discarded.

To simplify matters, automatically eliminate the horse listed first in Sweep's Graded Handicap listing, since that animal will be Sweep's number one choice. Remember that Sweep is also one of the selectors who make up the consensus.

3. If we have a qualifying horse, the animal must show actual odds of 10-1 or better. Play all horses that meet all prerequisites. No tie-breaking rules are observed.

4. If not playing at the track, play after scratches are known. At the track you will know, naturally, whether or not a horse is running.

The reader will notice that only horses running at actual odds of 10-1 or greater are ever backed. Since on this scale, we can never receive less than $22 as our mutuel return, even a winning percentage of 10% would be adequate to ensure profitable proceeds. However, we can safely assume that the average mutuel return will be in excess of this minimum, therefore a 10% winning average should provide a much greater profit.

Now certain questions may pop up into the reader's mind. "Why can't I play horses at shorter odds?" he may ask.

There is no doubt in my mind that a method of play can be worked out which will obtain shorter as well as real box-car mutuels. We must never lose sight, however, of the fact that successful wagering is always based on logical deduction and a sound framework from which to build. It is extremely dangerous to make distracting allowances that are not strictly implied in the system.

With a system we do not allow ourselves room for personal judgment. Because of this aspect alone, the system often proves itself superior to personal handicapping. It does not permit room for extreme error due to human frailty. This does not mean that a system, in itself, does not have inherent weaknesses.

However, with a system you can spend considerable time in ironing out flaws and perfecting it so that the method operates as soundly as time, concentration, logical deduction, and the human mind can make it.

But let's get back to the problem of obtaining horses that are running at less than 10-1. If we were looking for such horses, the original odds as rated by Sweep or any other proper source would have to be lower.

The question we ask ourselves now is, "What is a safe margin for determining a valid overlay?"

If we figure the horse's chance to win at 2-1, are 4-1 odds sufficient to rate it an overlay? There must be some margin of safety. Our calculations may be slightly off, so that the horse rated at 2-1 may more safely be figured at odds between 8-5 and 3-1, or perhaps even from 1-1 to 4-1. Therefore, we cannot arbitrarily assume that the odds of 4-1 are really an overlay price.

When the price we accept is at least more than twice the price of the horse's estimated chances, there is more reason to assume that we are getting an overlay, especially when we base our minimum on odds of 10-1 or better. We need only comparatively few winners to obtain more than an ample return on our investment. For this reason, odds of 10-1 or more should prove more than adequate.

WORKOUT: *The Overlay Way*

Aug.	Horse	Race & Track	Mutuel	Aug.	Horse	Race & Track	Mutuel
1	Sky Rings	6 Dmr.	....	15	Stone Saucer	4 Sar.	32.60
2	Merryman	1 Dmr.	....	16	Golden Sickle	7 Dmr.	....
	Competing Beau	7 Dmr.	24.50		Venerable ⎫	9 Dmr.	....
	Queen of Cairo	1 Was.	....		Tripper ⎰	9 Dmr.	....
	Foxpoise	9 Was.	....		Eolus	5 Sar.	....
4	Mi Amante	4 Dmr.	25.00		New Stream	3 Was.	....
	Battle Count	5 Dmr.	....		Vi Dog	5 Was.	....
	Purse Seiner	8 Dmr.	....		Peter Vinegar	8 Was.	....
	Mahatma	3 Sar.	....	18	Galgo	1 Dmr.	....
	Cotton Top	5 Was.	....		Mr. Pilate	5 Dmr.	....
	Dead Duck	6 Was.	....		Oh Dear	1 Was.	....
	Mincemeat	8 Was.	....	19	Barbara L	3 Was.	....
5	Fleet Orphan	3 Dmr.	....	20	Helio Sky	1 Dmr.	....
	Lord North	2 Sar.	....		H. Bone	8 Dmr.	....
	Night-Phara	6 Was.	....		Recatado	4 Sar.	....
6	Marclif	6 Dmr.	....		Konza	6 Was.	....
	Chanty Man	3 Sar.	....	21	Jade B's Babe	1 Dmr.	....
	Kaster	6 Sar.	....		Daphne	6 Dmr.	....
	Four Jacks	7 Sar.	42.60		Ramasari	7 Dmr.	....
	Judge J. B.	6 Was.	....		Level Lea	4 Sar.	....
7	Canute	4 Dmr.	31.50		Dottie McC	8 Sar.	....
	Sea Novice	8 Dmr.	22.40	22	Magic Note	7 Dmr.	34.80
	Our Jan	2 Was.	....		Puddler	2 Sar.	....
	Barbara L ⎫	3 Was.	....		Slippy	5 Was.	....
	Duchess-Ev ⎰	3 Was.	....	23	Round Stitch	7 Dmr.	30.60
8	Recur ⎫	3 Dmr.	....		Honor Deck	4 Was.	....
	Prince Sirte ⎰	3 Dmr.	22.50		Foxpoise	9 Was.	....

Aug.	Horse	Race & Track	Mutuel	Aug.	Horse	Race & Track	Mutuel
	Oleada	4 Dmr.	....	25	Mary's Jeffrey	8 Dmr.	....
	Pnut Vendor	2 Sar.	....		Stray Gift ⎱	1 Sar.	....
	Copper Plate	3 Sar.	....		Hoop Roller ⎰	1 Sar.	....
	Blue Bar. ⎱	8 Was.	....	26	Practise	4 Sar.	....
	Lady Ridgewell ⎰	8 Was.	25.40		Show Ring	1 Was.	....
9	Snooks T	7 Dmr.	....		Holly Sweet	8 Was.	....
	Fleet Rose	5 Sar.	....	27	Toronto	3 Was.	....
11	Sea Flora	1 Dmr.	26.60		Necklace ⎱	5 Was.	....
	Bullet Proof	6 Dmr.	....		Miss Wabash ⎰	5 Was.	....
	Felsparoo	3 Sar.	....		Boo Boo Shoo	9 Was.	....
	Blue Square	6 Was.	....	28	Lothario	6 Dmr.	22.90
12	Hoop Roller	4 Sar.	....		Duke Fanelli	7 Sar.	....
	Red River	3 Was.	....		Burnt Look	3 Was.	....
	On Wings	8 Was.	....		Mon-Pharo ⎱	6 Was.	....
13	Pronto's Image	2 Dmr.	....		Fleeter Than ⎰	6 Was.	....
	Octavia	5 Dmr.	....	29	Kentom	6 Dmr.	....
	Laughing Fox	4 Was.	25.80		French Admiral	7 Was.	27.40
14	Oleada	3 Dmr.	....		Gallant D	8 Was.	....
	Ritz	6 Dmr.	....	30	Tricopa	1 Was.	....
	Ed-Ell's Gal	1 Sar.	....		Fancy Dancer	3 Was.	....
					Isomur	4 Was.	....

95 Selections—14 Won—15%

Amount Returned	$394.60
Amount Invested	$190.00
Profit	$204.60

20.
HOW DUTCHING CAN BUILD A BANKROLL UP FAST

It's naturally easier to pick a winner if you bet on three horses than if you stick your money on one. However, in such a situation your investment is six dollars. This fact prevents the vast majority of horse players from using an attack that has proved successful ever since betting on racing was an accepted sport.

Most bettors forget that the winning percentage is greatly increased. Many times a race is a toss-up between two or three animals and if the bettor could put his money on all three he would be certain to collect on one of his wagers. However, if you don't know how to dutch your bet, you can lose your shirt.

The following method is one actually used by the author. I like it because of the many times you can collect. I also like it because I feel safe in the thought that I'm usually getting the animals that show promise of winning the race.

Modified Dutching Method

For the person who can earmark $500 as a bankroll for speculation over the period of one month at any one track, the following method of play may produce a substantial return.

The method lends itself to the type of progression play to be suggested, because very often more than one horse is played in a race. This may appear to be sacrilegious to some horse players, since many of them believe it to be poor policy to risk added money when actually only one horse can win.

The logic of betting on only one horse in a race is not as sound as you might think. In the majority of cases it depends on the type of horses running. If there is an odds-on choice in the race or where two horses or even three are held at short odds, it is self-evident that betting on more than one can produce little or no profit. It is in open races where anything can win that dutching (betting on more than one horse in a race) can be employed more effectively.

For example, if twelve horses (let us assume that they are all of equal ability) were entered in a race and we bet on one of them, our chances of winning, obviously, would be one out of 12. But if we wagered on three of the horses, it is quite evident that our chances would be increased three-fold and we would now have one chance in four of winning.

Of course, we will be investing $6 instead of $2 to achieve our objective. Should one of the horses win and pay $30, the $24 won instead of $28 seems worthwhile. The main object in playing the races is to get winners at a profit and if you can do it by playing two or three horses, the aim has been accomplished.

By modifying the dutching method and proceeding on the basis that if one or two horses stand out we will not resort to a play on another horse, a very effective system of play can be developed. For those who are squeamish about progressive play, flat bets should also prove productive.

The winners according to the 230 selection workout at Narragansett during September, 1950, came in so frequently that it is bound to satisfy. The method was tested at other tracks and proved highly satisfactory. It seems that the best results were obtained at those tracks where the take is not too high. It is only common sense to assume that where the take is higher the average mutuels will be smaller.

This is not a strict dutching system, since we do not always play more than one horse in a race. In the vast majority of cases the plural wagering occurs and the winners increase in proportion. We can, therefore, basically consider it as a dutching method.

The speed ratings, as used in the *Daily Racing Form,* are a fairly reliable index of a horse's ability. They take into consideration the track record at the distance as well as the prevailing track conditions. Using speed ratings is a simplified method of deducing speed, which is an important aspect of the horse's winning possibilities.

The speed ratings can be more effectively used in sprint races, where speed is a more important factor. In route races endurance seems to play a greater role.

The six-furlong affair is the common type of sprint race, and therefore, using this type of distance exclusively it is possible to obtain a more valid approach to the speed angle. Sticking to ¾-mile races assures us ample testing grounds to secure possible winners.

A horse which has approached, in its last race, within three points of its highest speed rating earned within the last three months, appears to be rounding to form. Such an animal has good possibilities of taking its next heat. Also a horse that has reached, in its last race, the top speed rating it has ever obtained during the last three months, would also seem eligible for the winning lists in its next venture.

As a rule, races run more than three months ago cannot be considered. Three months is a fairly long period for a horse and many things may have happened during this time to change the animal's racing ability. It might have been injured or developed an illness. The horse may even have changed its attitude about racing with the advent of a new "guinea" or stable boy or the boy that gives it workouts or any other new person with which it is now in contact. These things may develop for the better or for worse.

This may not always be true, and there are horses that showed a good race a year ago and since then demonstrated nothing, only to come back to form suddenly in today's race.

Systems, however, must have arbitrary rules and since constant check has shown that horses producing good efforts during this confined three-month period are more often returned winners, it is best to adhere strictly to this rule. Its importance in the system would eventually define itself.

We will discard all horses, therefore, that have not reached a rating within three points of the highest received not more than three months from today's race.

RULES: *Modified Dutching Method*

1. Cross off all horses that have scratched.
2. Eliminate all horses that have not raced at ¾ of a mile in their last race or do not show speed ratings in their last efforts.
3. Discard all maidens from consideration.
4. Discard all horses that have not raced within one month of today's race.
5. For each remaining horse check off the highest speed rating earned at ¾ of a mile at any time within three months of today's race.
6. Look at the horse's last speed rating. This speed rating must be within three points of the horse's highest speed rating obtained within three months of today's race. If the last speed rating was the highest ever made, the animal is definitely under consideration.
7. For those horses qualifying write down the highest speed rating earned within three months next to the horse's name, right above its past performances. Eliminate all horses that do not have highest speed ratings within three points of the animal with the top speed rating. Play horses that still qualify. Do not play

more than three horses in a race. If more than three qualify, use the following tie-breaking rule.

8. If tied for third choice, select the horse with the best consistency for the current and last year combined. If horses are two-year-olds, naturally only the current year's consistency is figured. If still tied, choose the animal with the best finish in its last race as far as distance ahead or lengths behind is concerned. (A horse finishing fourth beaten by two lengths would be preferred over a horse finishing third beaten by three lengths.)

Note: If two or more horses in an entry of field qualify consider entry of field as if they were one horse, since only one bet wins on either.

Selections are made in this manner:

First we cross out those horses that have scratched. Then we proceed to eliminate those horses which show other than ¾-mile races in their last outs, or where no speed ratings are shown in their last effort.

Next, horses that have not run for over a month are discarded. Maidens are never considered. Should one horse have a speed rating more than three points higher than the others, this horse alone would be our selection and the others would be eliminated from consideration. (Remember, the speed rating we are talking about here is the highest speed rating the horse has ever earned within three months. This and only this speed rating is the one that is listed next to the horse's name, above its past performances.) For example, if horse A had a speed rating of 86, horse B had 82 and horse C had 81, we could only choose horse A as a selection, but if the horses are marked as follows: A-86; B-85; C-83, all three would be picked.

If more than two horses are tied for third consideration, the tie-breaking rule would have to be employed. This rule was obviously made to avoid play on more than one horse when there is a conspicuous standout in the race.

With this system a modified progression can be used effectively, increasing the profits tremendously. Of course, there is always the danger of a losing streak coming along which will burn up a bankroll fast. However, checking this system under progression seems to indicate that a bankroll of $500 would be sufficient. During September, 1950, at Narragansett the greatest sum ever needed would have been $347.60.

Using a progression of merely adding $2 to the amount bet on each horse until a profit is accrued, previous losses can be recouped quickly. To clarify the use of the progression suggested let's look back at the workout to see how the wagering is done. A lot depends on the prices paid.

The progression is continued until a profit is earned on the play, regardless of whether or not a winner occurs. Our losses are not always recovered by the first winner appearing on the scene.

Let's start off with the first day's races at Narragansett, September 2, 1950. In the first race two qualifying horses appear—Sunshade and Flaming Acres. We bet two dollars on each one. They both lose and so far we are out the sum of four dollars.

In the second race we also have two horses, Here'sa Dream and Mestiza. Adding two dollars more on each horse (we must understand that two dollars will always be our initial bet) we are now betting four dollars on each horse. Here'sa Dream wins at $13.20 and we collect $26.40 on our four-dollar bet. Since we had invested $12, the profit is $14.40.

Our profit objective has been met and now we are ready to start all over again with a two dollar bet on any of the horses qualifying in the next race.

The wager on each horse is always two dollars more than the amount wagered on each horse in the previous race, provided no profit has as yet been made on the play.

Readers will find the Modified Dutching Method sound in every respect. Even if one is not inclined to regard it with favor in system form, the selection method will prove a valuable handicapping aid in arriving at the contenders in six-furlong sprints.

WORKOUT: *Modified Dutching Method*

Date	Horse	Race	Mutuel	Date	Horse	Race	Mutuel
9/2	Sunshade	1	. . . .		Blue Sage	5	. . . .
	Flaming Acres		. . . .		Rip Snort		11.00
	Here'sa Dream	2	13.20		Atom Ride		. . . .
	Mestiza		. . . .		Vital Sun	6	. . . .
	Glorious Maxim	4	. . . .		Ted M		. . . .
	Flicka Foot	5	4.20	9/18	Tarawa	1	10.40

Date	Horse	Race	Mutuel	Date	Horse	Race	Mutuel
	Gold Eagle		....		Theodore		....
	Vital Sun	6	....		Rite Easy	2	....
	Supper Date	7	4.20		Phoebe S		....
9/4	Gay	1	....		Daleen	4	....
	Sir Stephen	3	....		Daughter C		....
	Rampageous		....		Quick Buck		....
	Idio		....		Sir David	5	....
	Stargram	4	....		Vagrant Cloud	6	....
	Dinghy	5	....		Fort Miflin		7.60
9/5	Sandy Atlas	1	....		Power Drunk		
	Stratojet		35.40	9/19	Bold Knot	1	8.80
	Mesmerized	3	....		Mike M	3	....
	Miss Rhoda		....		Zeeland	4	....
	Gingham		....		Fighting Buddy		....
	Irish Channel	4	....		Orbit	5	....
	Miss Marlo		....	9/20	Big and Better	2	....
	Dash For Cash		14.80		Sorisky		....
	Charlotta K	5	....		My Ruthie		....
	Air Attack	6	....		Beam O' Light	3	....
9/6	Sun Baby	1	....		Supper Date	5	5.40
	Mighty Son	2	....		Pittacus		....
	Nitro Dugan	4	....		Pensava	6	6.20
	My Ruthie	5	....		Crown Me		....
	Big and Better		....		Sassy's King	7	7.60
	Eternal Way	6	....		Time Roll		....
	Ima Scholar	7	....	9/21	Blue Falcon	1	6.00
9/7	Maid of Kent	1	9.20		French Lure		....
	Sorisky	2	....		Quiz Me	3	....
	Hustling Oaks		....		Althor		....
	Reynard		....		Locks	5	5.40
	Benjomike	4	....		First Honey		....
	Zeeland		....		Duke's Gal	6	....
	Dauntedid	6	....		Evening Rose		....
	Chancescript		....		Dauntedid		....
	Anamia		....	9/22	Rembird	1	8.20
9/8	Beau's Nurse	1	....		Maruca		....
	Dinghy	4	....		Hurinow		....
	Step's Girl		21.40		Miss Marlo	2	....
	Bold Pat	5	....		Rhubarb	5	....
	Wixted		....		Bold Bolo	6	....
9/9	Azure	1	....	9/23	Court Ace	1	....
	Casein		....		The Prophet		....
	Gerham	2	....		Joe's Gal	3	36.00
	Wendigo	3	....		Rab's Son		....
	Musical Lady		....		Suffinth		....
	Eternal Great		....		Daughter C	4	4.60
	Faneuil Miss	4	....		Quick Buck		....
	Evening Rose		14.20		Worldly Wise		....
	Wisenheimer	5	....		Sickle's Image	6	4.80

Date	Horse	Race	Mutuel	Date	Horse	Race	Mutuel
	Red Ring		....		Blue Roxy		....
	Jacodema	6	3.40		Swift Swiv		....
9/11	Joie De Vivre	1	....		Supper Date	7	4.20
	Pencell		23.40		Beaming Light		....
	Blue Falcon		....	9/25	Four Speeds	2	....
	Juana	2	....		Concert Piece		7.40
	Why		....		Ann's Step		....
	Roffie		11.20		Librab	4	....
	Four Speeds	3	....		Rodeo		....
	Ann's Step		6.80		Eternal Great	5	....
	Nitro Dugan		....		Musical Lady		....
	Bounding Ace	4	....		Model King	7	5.40
	My Freedom		17.40		Nor'west		....
	Blue Roxy	5	3.20	9/26	Rudy's Star	1	....
9/12	Confection	2	....		Gay		....
	Azure	3	....		Butterweed	3	4.40
	Gay		....		Tea Token	4	....
	Galla Babe	5	....		Royal Duke		....
	Mr. Beiltro		....		Northern Deb	5	....
	Jobie		....	9/27	Mesmerized	1	....
	Wisenheimer	6	....		My Ruthie		8.00
	Nor'west		....		Woodstone	4	....
9/13	Foster's Pride	1	....		Jeep Gypsy		12.40
	Marse Robert		....		Rhubarb		....
	Southern Eve	2	....		Yogurt	5	....
	Marymigirl		14.80		Queen Zac		....
	Here'sa Dream		....		Lou de Latour		....
	Floco	4	....		Vagrant Cloud	6	....
	Musical Lady		10.60		Merry Risk		....
	Red Ring	5	....		Auntie		6.60
	Fly Around		14.20		Chancescript	7	....
	Chancescript	6	....		Best Punch		....
9/14	Ruling Time	1	....		Little Captain		5.40
	Still Champ		....	9/28	Gavilan	1	....
	Swinging Star		....		Miss Emileo	2	....
	Cresson Knight	2	....		Bold Knot	5	....
	Copacabana	5	....		Winged		....
	Paper Mill		....		Suprograph		....
	Idio		10.00	9/29	Beau's Nurse	1	....
9/15	Judy R	1	....		Censured		....
	Rudy's Star		9.20		Melody Miss	2	....
	Esta Vez		....		Whirling Bat	4	14.60
	Wild Cat	2	17.20		In Taste		....
	Glorious Maxim		....		Royal Duke		....
	Miss Emileo	3	....		Ima Scholar	5	4.80
	Merry Risk	6	....	9/30	Ackley	1	....
	Auntie		....		Gray Brook		11.60
	Evening Rose		....		Maruca		....
9/16	Big and Better	1	....		Bad Hombre	2	....

Date	Horse	Race	Mutuel	Date	Horse	Race	Mutuel
	Casein		....		Nitro Dugan		9.20
	Portentous		9.60		Sweep Tiger		....
	Dinghy	2	....		Shining Deed	3	....
	Step's Girl		....		War Toro		....
	Quiz Me		14.00		Sickle Sue	4	....
	Bounding Ace	3	16.00		Gams		....
	Wardril		....		Musical Lady		7.60
	Annar		....		Roy	5	9.20
	Doll Foot	4	....		Dauntedid		....
	Fair Game		....		Pensava		....
	Sickle's Image		9.40				

Amount Returned $2 Flat Bets $539.80
Amount Invested $2 Flat Bets $460.00

Profit .... $ 79.80

230 selections—51 winners—22%

Amount of money won if progression was used $869.00
Largest capital needed on progression $347.60
(period from Sept.5—5th Nar. to Sept. 9—4th Nar.)

21.
HOW TO DETECT HOT HORSES

A horse that is ready, a horse that is in form, a horse that is set to go—this is the kind of animal that every bettor is constantly on the lookout for. Obviously, this is not easy to find. The trainer is not usually eager to let every one know that his horse is hot. Sometimes he doesn't care, especially if the stable is a big one, and it is not interested in price. Even this type of trainer may not wish to disclose the horse's condition for fear that extra efforts may be made to hamper his animal. Purse money is the real bread and butter item that makes horse racing so attractive.

Naturally there are ways and means of finding out which horses are hot. The system detailed here sets out to give the fan an opportunity to get in on some of the killings. It is the ability to detect the hot horse that often makes the difference between a winner and a loser.

Get 'Em While They're Hot!

Don't be fooled by the above caption. We are not selling hot dogs—it's hot horses we're after, the kind you so frequently find at the top of the result charts.

Statistics have proved that a large percentage of winners come from the ranks of horses that have shown a fairly recent good effort. Good form is a distinct asset for a horse, and it is often primarily because of this factor that an animal of inferior class is able to defeat superior horses.

If trainer manipulations never entered into the picture it would be much easier to beat the races on the element of exposed form alone. Since there are such things as betting stables, racing luck, temperamental horses, poor jockeys, the business of picking winning horses becomes so much more difficult. No matter what booby traps have been set up to snare the unwary bettor, good form is still an important consideration in determining the probable winner.

To make sure that our horse—selected in the method to be presented here—is in good form we will insist that the animal show at least two in-the-money efforts in its last three races. Also an in-the-money effort in the horse's last race is a requirement that will enhance the possibility of our selection's current form quality. We are now pretty sure of backing a formful animal.

Condition, as everyone knows, is also an important factor. Horses that are ready to win often have already run one or two warm-up races. These races may or may not have been good tries; however if the animal showed a good effort, even so far as to come in-the-money in these events, the prospect of the horse's winning today is really bright. If a horse looks sharp, he is often hustled back into competition as soon as possible. The reason for this is that the average horse does not maintain its form for a long time; the trainer knows that if he wants to win with this animal he had better send him to the races while the horse is hot.

That's why so many winners come from horses that have raced last not more than eight days ago. You'll find that the eight-day last out time limit occurs frequently in good systems. This is because there is a strong feeling that when a horse is sent back to the races so quickly a win is on the trainer's mind. Obviously one of the most important elements for profitable play is to know the trainer's intentions.

To prevent the backing of horses that may have sneaked into the money in two of their last three races, and have also managed by luck to meet the requirement of coming in-the-money in the last race, two additional barriers have been set up. The first barrier halts usually poor performers that cannot really run a good race and that have managed to meet the requirements by sheer co-incidence and chance.

By insisting that the animal show speed rates (as given in *Daily Racing Form*) over 75 in its last three races, or the last three races where speed rates are shown in the horse's past performances, we know that we are backing a good animal. If the horse does not show at least three speed rates in its past performances, the animal cannot be considered as a possible selection.

Since the element of speed rating is to be used, it is necessary to apply it only to distances that can be most suitably rated. Route races are more likely to be a matter of endurance rather than speed. Such races, therefore, cannot be considered in our system. The six-furlong (¾-mile) event lends itself to speed ratings more easily. The tracks usually card most of their races, especially sprints, at this distance. The six-furlong race is ideal for speed rate interpretation. It provides for sufficient action as well as reliability for determining speed ability. Only the six-furlong races were, therefore, considered in this system.

The other barrier to freakish selection is consistency. Horses that can win at least 20% of their races are not ordinary animals. They are genuine competitors, and their reliability deserves a bettor's backing under numerous conditions. A highly consistent animal should always be considered as a threat, no matter what the prevailing form or condition the animal displays. Should such an animal also show good form and condition, then it becomes even harder for the schooled handicapper to overlook.

Many horses have their own distinct likes and dislikes for particular distances. If you will examine the past performances of certain animals, you will discover that some seem to run at the same distance all the time. There are horses that are never raced in sprints, while others seem to dodge routes. Sometimes a confirmed router is placed into a sprint race for other reasons than winning. The animal may be sent out in a conditioner, a race that acts like a workout. Then again the horse may be entered with the firm intention of showing a poor performance so that the stable may obtain a good price in a future race.

There are animals that can slide up and down the distance scale, but certain other factors tell the observant player when the situation is safe. On the whole, however, it is better to stick with horses that have shown a distinct taste for a certain distance. To enhance the prospect of a win, another requirement was inserted into the already formidable list of rules. Our horse must show not one but two winning efforts at exactly today's distance (six furlongs) in its list of past performances. Only the past performances recorded in today's racing paper can be used for this purpose.

You can now see how our rules are building up for a solid selection method. The horse's last effort must not have been made more than eight days ago, and the animal must have finished no worse than third. The animal must show at least two in-the-money efforts out of its last three races. All the speed rates of these last three races (or any last three speed rates shown) must be over 75. The animal must display its ability to win at today's distance by showing at least two wins at this particular route; and finally the horse must be highly consistent, displaying at least 20% win consistency for the current and last year combined.

Maiden races are never considered. Obviously a maiden can never be selected, since one of our requirements is for at least two wins at today's distance. Two-year-olds are still unproved and are, as a rule, considered precarious betting propositions. Jumping races are too unreliable, since barriers have been deliberately erected so that a horse, even though leading, may stumble and fall, losing the race. Handicap and Stake races require different rules for selection. They are distinctly races that belong in another category entirely and are run under dissimilar conditions from ordinary races, by animals that are of considerably higher class. Unless an obvious standout looms up, it is more difficult to determine the winners of such events. Handicaps and Stakes races cannot be played with this system.

Not to stretch our luck too far, horses that have won their last three races are not to be considered for selection. If our horse shows two consecutive wins, we will risk another chance, but no more. To repeat twice is a rather difficult task, but the type of horse we are backing does it so frequently that we have not discarded the possibility. To repeat three times is another matter, and we are not willing to take such an added risk.

RULES: Get 'Em While They're Hot

1. Play six-furlong (¾-mile) races only.
2. The horse must have shown at least two in-the-money efforts out of its last three races.
3. The horse must have finished in-the-money in its last race.
4. The horse must show at least 20% win consistency for the current and last year combined.
5. The horse's last race must not have been run more than eight calendar days ago.
6. The horse must show at least two wins at exactly today's distance anywhere in today's list of past performances.
7. The horse's last three speed rates (not necessarily the speed rates of the last three races) must be *over* 75. If the animal does not show three speed rates in today's list of past performances it cannot be considered for possible selection.
8. Eliminate all horses that have won their last three races.
9. Play no Handicap or Stake Races.
10. Play no two-year-olds or jumpers.
11. In case of a tie choose the horse with the highest last out speed rate. If still tied, pass the race.
12. Play after scratches are known.

WORKOUT: Get 'Em While They're Hot

Date	Horse	Race & Track	Win	Place	Show
3	Andy's Glory	1 Bel.	4.00	3.10	2.60
	Ten Forty	3 Del.	9.00	4.60	2.80
	Senator Joe	6 Del.	3.60	2.80	2.10
	Idio	7 Suf.	4.40	2.80	2.40
4	Charley Foy	2 Del.	13.20	6.70	4.40
	Mr. A. B.	5 Suf.	19.20	9.20	7.40
6	Bee A. H.	5 Del.	....	....	7.70
	Jones Brook	6 Suf.	....	4.00	3.60
7	Congo King	3 Bel.	4.70	3.30	2.40
	Hay Edy	5 Suf.	5.80	4.00	3.20
	Dauntedid	6 Suf.	....	....	....
10	Penocc	5 Del.	....	4.40	2.50
	Idio	7 Suf.	....	....	....
11	Congo King	5 Bel.	....	....	....
14	Bee A. H.	7 Del.	11.70	5.80	3.70
	Our Bully	2 Suf.	8.80	4.40	2.80
16	Penocc	6 Del.	....	2.50	2.20
	For Rent	3 A.P.	9.20	4.80	3.60
17	Third Ace	4 Del.	....	....	....
	Prepared	7 Del.	3.90	2.80	2.50
18	Scholarship	1 Suf.	....	....	2.60
19	Hay Edy	6 Suf.	3.40	2.60	2.20
20	Goodwillow	4 Del.	....	2.90	2.50
21	Rehearser	4 Mth.	....	....	....
	Scholarship	1 Suf.	14.00	6.80	4.00
23	Mae West	5 Aqu.	....	....	....
	Pisgah Road	5 Mth.	6.40	4.20	3.20
	Penocc	7 Mth.	4.60	3.20	2.60
24	Mighty Quest	5 Aqu.	....	....	2.30
	Bakersfield	4 Mth.	....	2.60	2.40
25	Devilkin	5 Mth.	6.20	3.80	2.80
	Phoenicia	7 Mth.	....	....	....
	Scholarship	2 Suf.	....	....	....
26	Frenabilbepa	4 Mth.	3.20	2.20	2.20
	Roman Fair	6 A.P.	....	....	....

	Win	Place	Show
Amount Returned	$135.30	$93.50	$82.70
Amount Invested	70.00	70.00	70.00
Profit	65.30	23.50	12.70

35 selections—18 won—51%
23 placed—66%
26 showed—74%

$10 flat win bets shows $326.50 profit

22.
WATCH THE BIG STABLES
FOR WINNERS

When looking for winners, there is no better place to start than with the leading money-winning stables. Big horse outfits are similar to business corporations. Big business invests heavily to insure success. Likewise, the big money winners in horseracing make every effort to get the best horses. In baseball, the Yankees spend prodigally to get the best players, that's why they have won so many pennants and World Series. The same is true with regard to stables. The stables that earn the most money and win the most purses are those with the "winningest" horses. Fundamentally horse racing is no different from any other enterprise. A stable that has good horses earns money. It is natural, then, that the bettor should choose horses from such stables. By picking such animals he is assured of many winners.

Spotting the Stables

Of course basic handicapping factors must be considered. Even in successful stables, though, there are horses that rarely find the winner's circle. Such runners are not media for profitable play. It is necessary, therefore, to examine the past performances of each animal to determine whether or not it is capable of winning the particular race.

It is usually more advisable to give greater consideration to current winning performance, rather than to what was accomplished in the past. However, in the method to be described here, a rating of the horse's potential is what we seek. Thus our horses were selected on the basis of recent performance, because many of the races in which they figured were stakes. Many good animals, competing in such events, do not race frequently, and may be conditioned mainly through workouts, so we require a recent workout. A morning trial shows that certain preparations have been made for the present race.

Stress was placed on the animal's consistency record for the current and last year combined, and its ability to race at a sufficiently high speed, as well as to its earnings for either of the two years.

RULES: *Spotting the Stables*

1. Make a list of the Leading Money-Winning Owners. Such a list is found in the *Daily Racing Form* usually between the 25th of the month and the first of the next month. Any other source for obtaining this list may be used, but confine yourself to not more than the top 15 owners.

2. Play only races with purse value of $4000 or more.

3. The horse must show 20% or better win consistency and 50% or better in-the-money consistency for the current and last year combined.

4. As listed in the horse's past performances, 50% or more of its *Racing Form* speed ratings must be 85 or more.

5. Horse must show a workout within seven days of today's race.

6. Play no jumping or quarter-horse races.

7. Horse must have won $25,000 or more last year or $10,000 or more this year. A $100 leeway is allowed, so that, for example, if our horse only earned $9,900 this year, the horse can be considered.

8. In case of tie, choose the horse with the best win percentage for the current and last year combined. If still tied, play the horse that earned the most money for both years combined.

9. Selections are made after scratches are known.

The list of leading money-winning owners changes from month to month, so that it is imperative to take a new list as it is published.

You will notice that we confine operations to those events offering purses of $4000 or more. Here we will find the more consistent animals, and we can be more sure that the horse we back is properly placed. Consistency is a virtue not possessed by too many horses racing on our tracks today. Many experts are of the opinion that

only consistent animals should ever be played. However, no amount
of consistency will help an animal if it is mismatched. If the horse
can show speed ratings of 85 or better in at least half of its races,
it can be considered a better-than-fair individual. Our system,
therefore, stresses this condition as one of the requirements for
selection.

To make sure his animal is ready, the trainer often employs the
workout some short time before the race. The time of the work
is not always important, for every trainer has his particular method,
so too much emphasis on the time of the workout may lead to
trouble.

The ability to win money is what makes the horse valuable to
his owner. If it cannot show within $100 of $10,000 won for the
current year, or at least $25,000, with the $100 leeway, earned
last year, it does not appear to be a substantially worthwhile horse.
You will notice that the earnings expected last year are greater than
the current amount of money. Obviously it took the animal all year
to earn this $25,000, whereas with our $10,000 requirement the
animal may have only raced a couple of months.

To clarify the method it is necessary to demonstrate the actual
process of selection.

First the list of leading money-winning owners is typed in
alphabetical order. The one used for this workout came from the
Los Angeles issue of the *Daily Racing Form* of April 1. Using
the same paper, we find that the first track is Golden Gate Fields.
The initial step is to search for purses of at least $4000. For this
day Golden Gate has no races with such a minimum purse.

As there is no Thoroughbred racing in Southern California at
this time we turn to Jamaica, where the second race carries a purse
value of $4000. This is a maiden race and no horse qualifies.

The fourth race is endowed with a purse of $4000, so we look to
see if one of our stables is represented and find that J. W. Brown
has a horse in. As it shows only one win out of ten for the current
and last year combined, it cannot be considered.

The fifth race is an allowance event with a purse of $4500. In
this there is a qualifying horse—Sometime Thing, owned by A. G.
Vanderbilt. Her consistency record shows three wins and five in-
the-money efforts in five starts, which meets our consistency re-

WORKOUT: *Spotting the Stables*

(April 1955)

Date	Horse	Track	Win	Place	Show
Apr. 1	Sometime Thing	5 Jam.	$8.20	$4.10	$3.40
	Bobby Brocato	6 Jam.	40.90	13.10	5.10
2	Joe Jones	7 Bow.	2.60	2.20	2.20
6	Sometime Thing	6 Jam.	4.40	3.00	2.30
	Peter Lane	7 Jam.	7.00	2.90	2.90
8	Capeador	6 Jam.			
9	Social Outcast	7 Bow.	19.40	7.40	out
13	Poona II	7 G.G.		4.80	3.10
14	Miss Arlette	5 Kee.			
15	Gandharva	5 Jam.	2.80	2.60	2.20
	Peter Lane	6 Jam.		2.60	2.80
16	Joe Jones	6 Jam.		3.00	2.80
	Sea O' Erin	6 Kee.	5.80	3.20	2.40
18	Miz Clementine	6 Jam.			
19	Peter Lane	7 Jam.			
	Lap Full	5 Kee.	3.40	2.60	out
21	Sometime Thing	5 Jam.		2.60	out
23	Determine	8 G.G.	4.00	2.30	2.30
	Nashua	6 Jam.	4.20	2.10	out
	Sea O' Erin	6 Kee.	3.00	2.20	out
25	Sailor	6 Bel.	13.90	5.60	3.00
	Paper Tiger	7 Bel.	5.40	4.20	3.00
26	Gandharva	5 Bel.	4.90	3.40	2.80
27	County Clare	7 Bel.	13.20	6.60	4.10
28	Sometime Thing	6 Bel.		3.80	2.70
30	Swaps	6 C.D.	2.60	2.20	out
Amount Returned			$145.70	$86.50	$47.10
Amount Invested			52.00	52.00	40.00
Profit			$ 93.70	$34.50	$ 7.10

26 selections—17 won—65%
26 selections—23 placed—88%
20 selections—17 showed—85%

quirement. The filly has won $9,925, just $75 short of $10,000, so that we can qualify it on the money earned currently basis, since it passes because of our $100 leeway. Speed ratings for its five races listed are 89, 92, 88, 72, 84. She still is eligible, since 60% of her speed ratings are 85 or over. Sometime Thing shows a workout on March 30, two days before today's race, so we can chalk this animal up as a candidate for selection.

The demonstration given is sufficient to show just how play is made. However, the player should be cautioned about certain specifics. Remember that if the horse does not meet the earning requirements for the current year, it still may be eligible on the basis of the money won last year. Don't forget that both for this year and last year a $100 leeway is allowed.

Because of the high calibre of many horses running in the races chosen we will often enough obtain good prices. This can be seen in the workout.

23.
WATCHING THE EARLY RETURNERS

When a horse is sent right back to the races only a few days after its last effort, it is generally a signal that the stable thinks the animal is ready. Of course, the horse may be sent back so quickly because the trainer thinks it needs conditioning, and there is often no better way to do this than by actual racing competition. But there are certain factors that will aid the player in determining when to bet or not to bet. At times mere analysis of the horse's last race will provide a clue. If the horse was able to stay close to the pace, or showed definite improvement over the race before its last, or is dropping in class today, it can be assumed that it has possibilities. It is the overlaid mutuels many times realized on such runners that makes following this type of play so profitable.

Bringing 'Em Right Back

A horse that won its last race often has completed a form cycle. This is especially true of platers. Although there are many good systems based on repeaters, even where claimers are used, it has been found in this study that it is best to avoid last-time winners, unless the winning effort showed extraordinary results.

Two methods, closely related, will be outlined in the paragraphs that follow. Both hinge largely on current form as exemplified in performance in a very recent race.

In that race the horse, to become a selection, must have been able to stay with the pace, or have showed improvement over the previous race, or must be dropping down in class.

Usually those who devise systems begin by barring all maidens. In Plan A, which gives enough action to satisfy almost everyone, maidens are considered, if they are entered in races other than those exclusively for non-winners.

Under Plan B, maidens are eliminated from consideration.

RULES: *Bringing 'Em Right Back*

PLAN A

1. Play only claiming races.
2. Horse must have raced within four days.
3. Horse must qualify under any one of clauses *a, b* or *c* (below).

a. Horse was first, second or third at any of the first three calls of its last race, as shown in the *Daily Racing Form* past performances; or finished second or third in its last race. If the horse *won* its last race, it is eliminated.

b. Horse is today being dropped in class from its last race or is being entered at a lower claiming price. All races other than maiden are to be considered higher than claimers. Maiden races are considered lower than claiming. If dropping in class or claiming price is the horse's only qualification, it must have finished not more than eight lengths behind the winner in its last race. If the horse qualified under clause *a,* this length rule is nullified.

c. Horse improved in its last race over its previous race in its finish, according to lengths. The previous to last race must not be more than two months ago. For example: If one horse finished fourth, beaten by 1½ lengths, and another finished third beaten by two lengths, the former would get the nod. Consider the lengths behind only, not position. If improving from last race to present is the only qualification, the animal must have finished not more than two lengths behind the winner in its last race. If the animal should qualify under an earlier clause, this length rule would be void.

In all cases (clauses *a, b,* or *c*) do not play the horse if its weight assigned today exceeds the weight carried in its last race by *more* than five pounds. Play no horse that lost its last race by 12 lengths or more.

3. Do not play any horse whose last race was at a minor track and is today racing at a major track.

4. Do not play two-year-olds or jumping races.

5. In case of tie choose the animal that shows a workout within seven days of today's race. If still tied, choose the horse with the best win consistency for the last two years combined. If still tied, choose the horse with the best in-the-money consistency for both years.

6. Play after scratches are known.

The reader will notice that the drop-in-class rule has been qualified. The drop alone is not sufficient to make us believe that the horse is properly placed. If the horse finished far back in its last race the drop in class may just be a move to find the correct company for the animal. Similarly, if the horse does not show adequate improvement from its last race, it certainly does not deserve our attention.

The simplest way to operate this method is to first check horses that raced last not more than four days ago, remembering, of course, that play is only made in claiming races.

Now check the last race of each horse that has qualified so far. If the horse won its last race, it is eliminated. If the horse was first, second, or third at *any* of the first three calls, or finished second or third, it still remains under consideration.

Now look for horses that are dropping in class or claiming price from their last race. Remember, all races that are not claimers, except maidens, are to be considered higher than claiming races of any value. If the horse is dropping in class or claiming price and has not already qualified by another clause, it remains under consideration only if it did not lose by more than eight lengths.

Now look among the horses that raced not longer than four days ago and that have not qualified under previous clauses, for those which improved in last race over race before. These must have been no farther back of the winner than two lengths. In case of such improvement, this previous to last race must not have been more than two months removed from its last race. If this qualifying race was six months old, for example, the improvement certainly would have no value.

If more than one horse remains under consideration, the separation rule is employed.

For those players who crave less action, Plan B may be more appropriate. These rules are based primarily on the horse's ability to show that it can stay out front at some period of the race. The last race has been designated for analysis. The time lapse has been extended slightly, otherwise the action would be altogether insufficient. One day more under the circumstances will not make too much difference, especially when the maximum time from the last race is only five days.

PLAN B

1. Play only claiming races.

2. Horse must have raced within five days.

3. The horse must have been first at any of the first three calls *(Daily Racing Form)* of its last race and lost the race, but by less than 12 lengths. Also play horses that finished first by two lengths or more and were first at any other call.

4. Play no maidens, jumpers or two-year-olds.

5. In case of tie, choose the horse with the best win consistency for the last two years combined.

6. Play after scratches are known.

24.
USING METHODICAL PROCEDURES
FOR PROFIT

There are so many factors which the player may probe before making his decision to back a horse that it is impossible to put them all together into one system. Methods of play are as varied in character as the humans they appeal to. "One man's meat is another man's poison," is an old saying which is as true in horse racing as anywhere else. That is why one fan scoffs at another's playing tactics. The bettor who stays with horse racing long enough will soon develop his own style of selecting. Once he falls into it he finds it very difficult to change. Although there are numerous, logical ways of procuring winners, many fans will come up with "systems" so ludicrous that it is impossible to classify them. Selections may be based on superstition or faulty deduction.

The dictionary defines the word "method" as: 1. A *general* or *established* order of doing. 2. suitable and convenient arrangement. 3. orderly procedure.

If a method fits the definition of the word and has logical concepts, it should prove effective. How effective depends on the amount of research employed.

Tri-Factor Theory

When analyzing a horse's chances in a race, it is important to know what is on the trainer's mind. It is obviously best to go along with the trainer, rather than against him. A trainer, when he feels the horse is nearly ready, will often give the animal several workouts and then drop it into a race in which the horse will be at an advantage. If he can find a race in which the horse will be dropping weight from its last effort, the trainer will be more than glad to accept the concession. If the horse has been worked at least three times in the last weeks prior to the race, it is often a signal that a spot has been found for the horse to go all out in a winning effort.

A *Daily Racing Form* speed rating of 80 or better obtained by a horse stamps the animal as rather a good sort. Since the horse is capable of hitting such a good speed rate over any standard distance, we can feel that the animal has the necessary ability to win. Lower speed rates are not sufficiently assertive, unless, of course, the animals in the race are of a very inferior type. Should such a good effort be made in the horse's last race, earning a speed rate of 80 or higher, we can acknowledge the animal as worthwhile. In some cases, as in turf races, or when the going is very heavy, a horse will earn no speed rating at all. When this occurs, if the *last* speed rate *shown* for the horse in today's list of past performances is 80 or greater, we will accept the animal for consideration.

A horse, however, can not be played if its past performances show *no* speed rates.

Three factors, therefore, must be considered before the horse can be selected for play.

1. Three or more workouts within three weeks of today's race.
2. A drop in weight.
3. A last speed rate of 80 or more.

Few horses win after a long layoff, so the rule holding the animal to a time lapse of two months (see rules) was applied to prevent needless losers. Maidens, two-year-olds, and jumpers also were avoided.

RULES: *Tri-Factor Theory*

1. Horse's last race must have been within two months.
2. Horse must have finished no father back than sixth in last race.
3. The weight the horse carries today must be *less* than the weight carried in last race.
4. Weight carried today must not be more than 120 pounds.
5. *Daily Racing Form* speed rating of last race (or last race where speed rating is given) must be 80 or higher. If no speed ratings are given in any of the horse's past performances, the animal is not considered.
6. Horse must show three workouts, all within three weeks of today's race. For example, if today's date is July 23, and the third workout back was on July 2, it is acceptable—21 days. A workout on July 1 would not be acceptable. Workouts are listed under past performances.
7. Play no maidens, jumpers, or two-year-olds. Play after scratches are known.
8. In case of tie, choose the horse whose third workout back is most recent. This is the workout farthest removed in time from today's date. If still tied, pass the race.

Horses carrying over 120 pounds in today's race are not considered. More than 120 pounds is usually a weight disadvantage, even though the animal carried more poundage in its last effort. Also horses that finished worse than sixth in their last race are not acceptable. A horse that has shown such a poor last performance is usually not worth considering.

As a whole, the method is very simple and selections can be made quite rapidly. The most important things to watch for are the three basic factors.

To make the system clearer, we will examine a race and show how selections are made.

On July 24 at Arlington Park, the first race was for two-year-old fillies, so it was passed.

A claiming race for three-year-olds, the second event was suitable for selection purposes. To speed up the operation, it is advisable to look first for a last speed rating. Since the last speed rate shown must be 80 or higher the horses will cancel out rapidly in cheaper races. In this way, the first seven horses listed are eliminated, since they all have last speed ratings lower than the qualifying figure. Two of the seven disqualified are maidens, therefore, there was no need to even look at their speed ratings.

Romanda, listed eighth in the past performances, shows a last speed rating of 80. She is, therefore, a possibility. Her last race was on July 17, 1951, seven days ago, definitely within two months. In her last race, she carried 117 pounds; today her burden is only 109. There is no further concern about today's weight, since it is under 120 pounds.

Romanda finished fifth in her last race and qualifies on this score (the last finish must be no worse than sixth).

Three workouts are shown under the animal's past performances. From left to right, the dates are as follows: July 23, July 16, July 9. The earliest date, July 9, is only 15 days from today's date, July 24. Our horse is a perfect selection.

Moving down the list in the same race, we find the colt, Open Way, with a last speed rating of 83. He is carrying 122 pounds today, and would be disqualified because of this alone. No workouts were shown under its past performances, so that the horse could not be considered even if the weight was suitable. The next horse, Left Bank, shows a last speed rate of 83, but is carrying 122 pounds, and it too is eliminated. Prince of Evil showed a speed rate of 80, but, being a maiden, was passed by. Romannda was the only qualified horse and became our selection. (See workout.)

WORKOUT: *Tri-Factor Theory*
(July 1951)

Date	Track	Race	Horse	Win	Place	Show
7/2	Aqu.	5	Self Assurance	$32.90	$ 9.80	$ 4.60
	Aqu.	6	Banjoist	9.40	3.50	2.90
	Del.	1	White Bones	11.20	6.80	5.30
	Del.	4	Psychic Dream	6.20	4.10	2.80
	Del.	6	Midyear	5.40	3.80	2.90
	A.P.	5	Enforcer			
	Nar.	6	Sagittarius	4.00	3.60	2.60
3	Aqu.	6	Shy Bim	6.30	3.70	2.90
	Aqu.	7	Fairy's Gem			
	Mth.	5	Occupancy	21.00	9.00	5.00
	Del.	1	Solid Trick			
	Del.	5	Zeeland			
	A.P.	1	George Gains	44.60	16.80	12.60
	A.P.	4	Timus	16.60	5.60	4.20
	A.P.	7	Peter Vinegar		8.20	5.40
	Nar.	4	Galedo	18.40	7.40	4.60
	Nar.	6	Count Off		8.00	5.00
4	Aqu.	2	Algie		4.30	3.10
	Aqu.	5	Sister Louise			
	Aqu.	6	Northern Star			
	Mth.	2	Eternal Great			7.40
	Mth.	3	Speedy Van			
	Mth.	7	War King			
	A.P.	6	*Royal Mustang	8.60	4.40	3.40
	A.P.	7	Blue Hills			
	Del.	7	Tus One		8.30	3.20
	Nar.	5	Dockstader			
	Nar.	7	Swadelle	26.20	8.80	5.40
5	Aqu.	1	Argyle	5.00	3.10	2.70
	Aqu.	6	*Cardsandspades	4.30	2.60	2.10
	Aqu.	7	Easy Whirl			
	Mth.	4	Suptela			
	Mth.	7	Directoire	7.60	3.40	2.40
	Nar.	6	Atom Ride			
	A.P.	3	Cathy Jo			
	A.P.	7	On Velvet			
6	Aqu.	5	Liveletlive			
	Aqu.	6	Midanite			
	Mth.	6	Sky Prince			
	Nar.	6	Tilenny		3.80	2.80
	A.P.	7	Chariot Wheels			
7	Aqu.	3	Away Away		2.30	2.10
	Aqu.	5	Versify			
	Aqu.	6	Hull Down			11.50

Date	Track	Race	Horse	Win	Place	Show
	Aqu.	7	Brandy Punch			
	Mth.	4	Mobile Belle	6.40	3.40	2.80
	Mth.	6	The Pincher			3.60
	Nar.	2	Blue Sage		5.00	3.40
	Nar.	4	Princess Hope		4.80	3.60
	Nar.	6	Royal Duke			
	Nar.	7	Mr. Joe Puck			3.00
	Nar.	8	False Front			
	Nar.	9	Liteco	8.00	3.20	2.60
	A.P.	5	Marse George		6.00	4.00
	A.P.	6	Coffee Money	18.20	6.80	4.00
9	Aqu.	4	Battle Royal			
	Aqu.	7	Toto			
	Mth.	6	Suleiman			
	A.P.	5	Lady Indian			4.60
10	Aqu.	5	On The Mark			
	Aqu.	6	Lights Up			
	Mth.	3	Bolog			
	Mth.	4	Flower Hat			2.80
	Nar.	6	Shadow Start	3.40	2.60	2.20
	Nar.	7	Mirthmaker			
	A.P.	6	Little Captain			
11	Aqu.	6	Ruddy			
	Aqu.	7	The Battler			
	Mth.	3	Sky World			
	Mth.	5	Puppet			
	Mth.	6	Banjoist			3.60
	Nar.	4	Adelantado			
	Nar.	5	Lefty Jim			
	Nar.	7	Charleston			
	Nar.	9	Gay Courier		3.40	2.60
	A.P.	5	Officious	6.60	3.60	3.20
12	Nar.	1	Nassau		3.20	2.80
	Nar.	6	Montmartree II			
	A.P.	6	Bernwood	9.40	4.40	4.00
	C.T.	5	Bachelor Belle	5.40	3.60	2.40
13	Aqu.	6	Barrage			
	Mth.	4	Lucky Ned			
	Mth.	6	Tom Q			3.20
	A.P.	5	Last Venture			
	A.P.	6	Ballydam		8.00	5.20
	A.P.	7	Beauty's Tiger			3.60
	C.T.	2	Bourbon			
14	Aqu.	2	For Jon			
	Aqu.	5	Mangohick			
	Aqu.	6	Busanda			
	Mth.	5	Binky B			
	Mth.	6	Marta	5.00	3.40	2.40
	Mth.	7	Vamanos			

Date	Track	Race	Horse	Win	Place	Show
	Nar.	7	Bold Bolo			
	Nar.	8	Mel Hash			
	A.P.	2	Roman Road			
	A.P.	4	Lasting War	23.80	11.60	8.20
	A.P.	5	To Market	10.00	5.20	3.80
	A.P.	6	Recline			
	A.P.	7	War Talk			6.80
	A.P.	8	Bill Ross			
16	Emp.	3	Rampallion			
	Emp.	4	Vulcania			
	Emp.	5	Nosun			
	Mth.	6	Bullow			4.60
	Nar.	6	Knight's Knave		9.00	4.40
	A.P.	3	Lily Lark			2.20
	A.P.	5	†Snuzzle		5.00	3.00
	A.P.	6	Rose Beam		4.20	3.20
17	Emp.	1	Maximal			
	Nar.	6	Homing Pigeon		13.20	6.60
	Nar.	7	Two Feathers			
	A.P.	3	Extortionist			
	A.P.	6	Cuore			2.40
18	Emp.	4	Carry Me Back			4.40
	Mth.	5	Vamanos	25.80	10.60	5.80
	Mth.	6	†Why Not Now		3.40	4.60
	Nar.	1	Tintina			
	Nar.	4	Marymigirl			
	Nar.	5	Flaming Bush		9.80	6.20
	Nar.	6	Vagrant Cloud		7.20	4.80
	Nar.	7	Loridale	8.40	5.60	5.40
	A.P.	5	French Admiral		4.40	3.60
	A.P.	7	Brillance	35.60	16.20	10.40
19	Emp.	6	Graphic			
	Mth.	2	Brown Fox			2.60
	Nar.	4	Princess Hope		3.20	2.60
	Nar.	6	Option	13.80	6.60	4.60
	Nar.	7	Sigh Man	8.60	5.20	3.60
	A.P.	2	Under Pressure			
	A.P.	5	Jacoboy			
	A.P.	6	Recline			
20	Emp.	4	Tripoli	7.00	4.30	3.30
	Emp.	6	Who Dini			
	Emp.	7	Saxony			3.80
	Mth.	6	Tuscany		2.80	2.80
	Mth.	7	Cutting Edge			
	Nar.	7	Jaialai			3.20
	A.P.	6	Tidy Sum			
21	Emp.	2	Ballachulish			2.70
	Emp.	6	Bryan G	4.30	5.50	3.50
	Mth.	1	Kalluki	10.00	5.40	4.00

Date	Track	Race	Horse	Win	Place	Show
	Mth.	5	Father Link	6.60	4.00	3.20
	Mth.	6	Yildiz			
	Mth.	7	Reigh's Double			
	Nar.	5	Shoe Shine			
	Nar.	7	Roy			
	A.P.	3	Some Friend			
	A.P.	7	Longleat			
23	Sar.	4	Fanborough		3.40	2.90
	Sar.	6	Away Away			Out
	Sar.	7	Jam Session	7.70	4.70	3.50
	Mth.	5	Stepchild	4.60	3.00	2.60
	Mth.	6	Guillotine	3.20	2.80	2.20
	Mth.	7	Relic Gold	30.00	12.40	6.60
	Nar.	2	Flying Mile	11.40	5.80	3.20
	Nar.	5	Direct Mister			
	Nar.	7	Knight's Knave			
	A.P.	2	Royal Challa			
	A.P.	5	Party Request			
	A.P.	6	Volcanic			
	A.P.	7	Bob's Betty		11.40	5.40
24	Sar.	6	September			
	Mth.	7	Benbow			
	A.P.	2	Romanda		5.40	4.00
	A.P.	5	Hand Finished			
	A.P.	6	Will You Dance	53.20	16.20	7.60
25	Sar.	3	Satartia	6.90	4.20	3.20
	Sar.	4	Frigid			
	Sar.	5	Mangohick			
	Nar.	2	Capt. Gallagher	10.80	4.40	3.80
	Nar.	3	Top Foot			
	Nar.	5	Finder Keeper			
	Nar.	6	Quiz Song	5.80	3.40	3.00
	A.P.	4	Town Sheik			3.20
	A.P.	5	Convidado		3.20	2.60
	A.P.	6	Circus Clown			2.80
26	Sar.	3	Quick Deal	5.40	3.30	2.50
	Sar.	6	Hull Down		2.80	2.30
	Mth.	6	Miss President			
	Mth.	7	On		5.40	3.80
	Nar.	2	Dagger Point			
	Nar.	6	Good Egg	10.40	5.60	3.20
	Nar.	7	U. S. Navy		4.80	3.80
	A.P.	4	Spring Chimes			
	A.P.	8	Slip Around			
27	Sar.	6	Sagittarius			2.10
	Sar.	7	Aleatory		8.80	6.30
	Mth.	7	Rataplan		2.60	2.40
	Nar.	6	Apennine			
	Nar.	9	Hi Bunty			

Date	Track	Race	Horse	Win	Place	Show
28	Sar.	5	Self Assurance		5.10	2.90
	Sar.	6	Mandingo		Out	Out
	Sar.	7	Frost Bitten			2.40
	Sar.	8	Burt's Reward			3.30
	Mth.	5	Suleiman			
	Nar.	4	Queen Zac		8.00	5.60
	Nar.	5	Charing Rock			
	Nar.	6	Sedgeview		3.60	2.80
	Nar.	7	Abstract			2.80
	Nar.	8	Alairne	12.60	6.20	4.20
	A.P.	5	Look Here			
	A.P.	6	Jet Fleet		5.00	3.40
	A.P.	7	One Hitter			
	A.P.	8	Clevelander			
30	Mth.	5	Laran	9.40	3.20	2.40
	Mth.	6	West Milton			
	Rkm.	2	Tyrol			5.60
	Rkm.	3	Annar			6.40
	Rkm.	8	I Forgot			
	Was.	5	Nightmarish			3.40
	Was.	6	Prop			
	Was.	8	Miss Nap			
31	Sar.	3	Besita			
	Sar.	4	Mayes Riley			
	Sar.	6	Sagittarius			
	Rkm.	1	Heath Fire			
	Rkm.	2	Ruling Time			3.80
	Rkm.	4	Cencerro			
	Rkm.	6	Talltown	14.60	6.80	4.40
	Rkm.	7	Five Passes			
	Was.	6	Graham			

*Entry won.
†Entry placed.

	Win	Place	Show
Amount Returned	$624.00	$486.60	$443.20
Amount Invested (222 plays to win)	444.00	442.00	440.00
Profit	$180.00	$ 44.60	$ 3.20

49 won—22%
84 placed—38%
112 showed—51%

(April 1952)

Date	Track & Race	Horse	Win	Place	Show
	Jam.				
4/1	7	Schroon	$ 7.20	$ 4.00	$ 3.00
4/3	4	Deflation	6.90	4.20	3.20
	7	Seaflash			4.60
4/4	7	Jacodema		2.80	2.20
	8	Blue W.			
4/7	6	Armageddon			
4/9	7	Armagh			3.20
4/10	5	Sun Rene			
	6	Combat Boots	24.50	9.50	4.40
	7	Eye For Two			
4/11	6	Thelma Berger			
	7	Bob's Alibi	6.40	4.20	2.80
	8	Sweet Naomi			
4/12	4	Maijo			4.00
	5	Suggested	9.80	4.70	2.50
	6	Sky Ship			4.40
4/14	7	Vain Puritan			
4/15	7	Daiquiri	6.30	4.10	3.10
4/16	4	Bakersfield	7.30	3.60	2.20
	6	Tea-Maker	22.40	12.00	7.30
4/17	5	Bedazzle		5.50	3.60
4/18	6	Risque Rouge			
4/19	3	Bay Hash			
	5	Safety			
	7	Our John Wm.	9.20	4.80	3.40
4/21	4	High Dive			2.10
4/22	6	High Bracket		10.50	5.20
	7	Utopia			
4/23	1	Kathy Mendel			
	3	Hoplite	7.90	4.60	3.60
4/24	6	Fresh Air		3.50	2.90
	8	Mission			4.60
4/26	5	Seaflash			
	Bel				
4/29	2	Magic Words	5.40	3.10	2.40
	5	Sufie	10.80	3.60	2.90
	6	Jet Master			
	7	Parading Lady	4.40	3.30	2.40
	8	Brave Spirit		3.30	2.20
Amount Returned			$128.50	$91.30	$85.10
Amount Invested			76.00	76.00	76.00
Profit			$52.50	$15.30	$ 9.10

12 Won—34%
18 placed—47%
25 showed—65%

25.
HOW TO BEAT
THE OPTIONALS

_____

"You bets your money and you takes your choice." This is an old Cockney aphorism which needs no dispute. In racing you put your money on your selection, and then hang on to your mutuel ticket hoping for a win.

Yet, many players have certain preferences when it comes to playing a race. Some horse bettors confine themselves strictly to claimers, while others prefer allowances. Still others won't bet on anything but handicaps. No matter which type of race a bettor selects for handicapping, he knows that certain rules are applicable.

Frequently you can't use the same rules for allowance races that are employed with claimers. Similarly, handicap races have to be analyzed in an individual manner. If a player sticks to a particular type of race, such as a claimer, allowance, etc., he does not have to be too much concerned about using a false premise.

Optionals Can Be Beaten

What can a guy do about optionals? You can't designate this type of race as a claimer or allowance. It's a two-headed animal, and you'd have to call upon ambidextrous rules if you want to make them fit both the claimer and allowance races. However, by using good horse sense you *can* get around this type of race.

If you treat optionals as a distinctly different type of race, with a label all its own, you've made your first step in the right direction. The rest is not too difficult.

Most intelligent bettors use some sort of guide to determine the horse they will bet on. For this purpose the past performances in a good daily racing paper like the *Morning Telegraph,* or the *Daily Racing Form* are perused by many.

Now when a punter tries to handicap a race by delving through the past performances he is always somewhat conscious of the label, "Class." Just what the term means is sometimes hard to define. However, the player knows that it implies an inherent quality that makes one horse superior to another.

The average horse bettor finds it easier to use the class angle when he is trying to analyze a claiming race. Why? Because he merely uses the indexed amount of money for which the animal has been entered, and for which it can be claimed out of a race.

This is frequently not a substantial criterion for determining the animal's class. Usually the claiming tag is only the owner's estimate of the animal's worth to him. Whether or not this is so, the bettor can determine by examining the price tags of the races in which it has appeared. But the very imperfection of this device is sometimes sufficient to make a bettor hesitate to use claiming prices as a basis for determining class.

Now some tracks have come up with a new mechanism of torture, the optional claimer. In the optional claimer a horse can either be entered at a claiming price, or run free of any chances of being gobbled up by a new stable. With such a situation the horse, when it is not entered at a claiming price, is racing as an unknown quantity.

We don't know the horse's value, unless we can accept previous claiming tags, if there are any in its list of past performances. This way the trainer does not risk the loss of his animal by entering it in a cheap race.

Under such circumstances you would figure that the horse not entered at a claiming price would have an edge. Yet this is not always true, for there may be other conditions in the race which tend to offset this.

Since the bettor finds it very difficult to rate a horse on the element of class, there is much confusion. He starts a whirlwind of fearful rationalizing. First he may say to himself, "Is this beetle really out to win this race, since he has no claiming tag on him?" Or he may think, "Gosh, horse A is entered at a claiming price, but horse B isn't. Does that make horse B equivalent to an allowance racer, and therefore of higher class?" He becomes too wary and loses his sense of judgment.

With the optionals there is no clearcut defined choice. The horse bettors don't know whether they are trying to figure a claiming or allowance race.

But again, let's reiterate, you can avoid this by figuring optionals as a different type of race altogether, and so avoid the confusion surrounding interpretation of whether the race is a claimer or an allowance.

You can disregard the element of class completely, by excluding all price tags from your mind and concentrate mainly on one factor, the ability to win, or to perform sufficiently well at today's distance.

When a horse shows that it can favorably negotiate a particular distance, we can assume that its chances of winning are adequate, especially when it has been victorious in such a race. The system presented here stresses this factor.

In order to qualify, the horse must show a win, place or show at the distance of today's race somewhere in its list of past performances. In every instance the win qualification, rather than place or show, was met by all the selections in our workout.

However, a winning race at today's distance is not completely necessary. If no horses in the race show a win they still can be qualified on the basis of a place race, or if none of the animal's reveal a place race at today's distance, then a show finish is sufficient.

Systems, as a rule, provide for more than one factor, although stress may be laid on a single point. To be content with past results and neglect recent races would make the system hazardous.

To protect ourselves against animals that have shown little in their most recent engagements, the system demands at least one winning effort, at *any* distance, in the horse's *last two* races. If the animal should show *more* than two consecutive victories in its last three races the horse is *not* to be considered.

To expect the type of horses that run in optionals to win more than three in a row is really to stretch our luck too far. Also horses that have lost races by ten lengths or more are to be disregarded. Such a bad performance usually points to lack of form.

As you can see, our selections never can be considered hopeless outsiders. At the worst, the animals chosen must be figured as contenders.

RULES: *Optionals Can Be Beaten*

1. Check off all horses that *won* at today's distance anywhere in today's list of past performances. (Remember that we are only playing Optional Claiming Races.)
2. If no horses show winning races at today's distance, then select them on the basis of place finishes at today's distance.
3. If no horses show either winning or placing races, select them on the basis of show finishes at today's distance.

WORKOUT: *Optionals Can Be Beaten*

Date	Horse	Race	Win	Place	Show
Dec. 1	Tumbling After	5	15.60	9.00	5.80
3	Top Brass	7	25.80	11.40	6.00
8	In Class	5	5.80	3.40	2.80
9	Tiger Toi	3	...	...	...
10	Bugles Dream	4	...	...	...
16	Hug Up	2	...	...	...
	Hardhack	4	7.40	5.00	3.60
	Seventh Tribe	7	...	...	...
17	Tiger Toi	5	11.80	6.40	4.80
18	Red Speed	7	7.40	4.00	3.00
22	In Class	6	...	...	...
	Cullerton	7	7.40	7.60	5.80
25	Tiger Toi	5	...	...	...
	Rags to Riches	6	...	4.60	3.60
	McBezzill	8	5.60	3.80	3.20
30	Red Speed*	8	...	2.60	2.40
31	Flying Gypsy	4	...	...	...

			Win	Place	Show
Amount Returned			$86.80	$57.80	$41.00
Amount Invested			34.00	34.00	34.00
Profit			$52.80	$23.80	$7.00

*Entry placed   17 selections
                         8 won—47%
                        10 placed—59%
                        10 showed—59%

4. If no horses show either win, place, or show races at to-day's distance then *pass* the race.

5. Play after scratches are known.

ELIMINATIONS

I. The selection must have won *at least* one of its last two races.

II. Eliminate from consideration any horse that won its last three starts.

III. Eliminate any horse that lost its last race by 10 lengths or more.

TIE-BREAKING RULES

1. In case of tie, choose the horse that shows the best win consistency for the current year.

2. If still tied, select the horse with the best in-the-money consistency for the current year.

3. If still tied, play the horse that raced most recently.

26.
PLAYING FAVORITES
AND BEATEN FAVORITES

They're off! A longshot at 30-1 is out front, legging it to beat all blazes and finishes on top—the winner! Where is the favorite? You guessed it, left at the post. But "there's many a slip 'twixt the cup and lip," as the saying goes, so don't sell the public choice short just because it landed down the river on this occasion.

Favorites run to about 33% winners year in and year out, taking all kinds of races into consideration. There isn't a public selector alive who can equal this feat. The reason the races cannot be beaten by playing all favorites, as everyone knows, is the mutuel system and the resulting short prices.

The bettor can do two things about this rough situation. He can try to be selective about the favorites he does pick and so raise his winning percentage, or next time out he can play the favorite that lost, with the chance of getting a much better payoff. The following system will show you how to play beaten favorites. Later we'll demonstrate a method of selecting favorites for play during the tough winter months.

Selected Beaten Favorites

It's a good idea to play losing favorites next time out. Since many of them tailed most of the others in their losing effort, the public will not be inclined to wager on them to any extent. If the beaten favorite wins next time out, and they do this quite often, the tote board may record a juicy payoff and leave many a player with his mouth wide open.

You can't, however, play all losing favorites in their next race and expect to beat the game that way. As in all successful methods you must pick your spots carefully, avoiding any deadwood.

Time is an important element and if the player hopes to play the type of horse discussed here, he cannot afford to wait too long for its next race. We want a horse that is in condition. The recent race has given our animal friend a feel for the track and if it is the kind of consistent animal that we intend to back it should have developed a desire to win.

The public, which has very aptly been called "ace handicapper," has already pointed our animal out as one with the necessary ability to win. If our beaten favorite is now entered in a race not more than six days from its last effort and if it shows that it has been in the money in at least one half (50%) of its tries for both this year and last year combined, the time has come to take the rubber band off the bankroll.

RULES: *Selected Beaten Favorites*

1. The horse's last race must not have been more than six days from today's race.
2. The horse must have been the favorite in its last race and must *not* have won that race.

3. The horse must show that it was in the money in at least 50% of its races for the current and last year combined.

4. In case of tie, choose the horse whose last race was most recent. If still tied, choose the horse that is carrying the least weight in today's race.

5. Play no maidens, two-year-olds or jumpers.

Why do horses run out when they are favorites and then win in the next race or a couple of tries later? There are almost as many reasons for this happening as there are excuses given for any horse that fails to win. Here are just a few of the more valid ones.

First, the stable may not have liked the short price and may have purposely not tried that day. Another possible reason is that the horse may have gotten into a pocket or maybe the jockey did not give it a good ride. The horse may have broken too late to get up and was not ridden out to save it for another race.

In order to make the method perfectly clear let's take a gander at a selection to see how it was chosen. We used the *Daily Racing Form* here.

We pick up the first paper in February (see Workout). The first track we encounter is Hialeah. The first race is for two-year-olds. It is a maiden claiming race. We pass this race for two reasons: we do not play maidens nor do we wager on two-year-olds. The next race is for three-year-old maidens, so we give this the go-by too.

We look at the third race carefully and notice that not even one horse was the favorite in its last race. This race is also out. The same situation holds true for the fourth at Hialeah.

However, in the fifth race, there are two horses that show a little triangle after the odds of their last race. We check off these two horses, Dimit and Imperator. Of course the race is not for two-year-olds, maidens or jumpers, nor are our horses maidens. Even maidens not in a maiden race cannot be considered.

Dimit's last race was on January 19. Since today is February 1, this would have been 13 days ago. Therefore, we eliminate Dimit, since its last race was more than six days from today's race. Even if the horse's last race was within our six-day time limit, it would not qualify, since the animal won the race when it was favorite, and is, therefore, not a losing favorite.

Imperator's last race was on January 27, exactly five days ago. This horse is considered, since its last effort was not more than six days ago, in fact one day less. The animal had lost its last race when it was favorite, thus making it a beaten favorite.

Imperator's record in the right hand corner of the past performance chart shows that it was third in one of its two tries this year. Last year the horse raced ten times, won three, placed once and finished third once. This gives the animal an in-the-money performance record for this year and last year combined of 50% (six in-the-money races out of 12). Here is his score board:

| 1949 | 2 | 0 | 0 | 1 |
| 1948 | 10 | 3 | 1 | 1 |

The horse became our selection and won, paying $13.90.

Anyone could compile a list of beaten favorites with just a few minutes work on the charts each night. But to follow each and every one is to court disaster. Evidence that our method keeps us on the live ones and off the dead ones can be seen from a glance at the results we achieved in a two-month check.

Our very worthy system rolled up a profit of $251.70 on only a $2 across-the-board play. It grabbed longshots as well as repeating favorites, a necessity if we are going to stay in business.

Since the rules are so important to our success, perhaps it is a good idea to review them in detail so as to avoid any uncertainty as to why they were formulated.

Rule 1 is designed to catch our horses while they are still sharp. It stands to reason that a trainer who has a fit horse which was beaten last time out through accident will lose no time in getting him to the races again.

Rule 2 steers us off a lot of short-priced horses. Certainly, we all know that a horse that won its last start always receives strong public support the next time it runs, unless it is up against stiffer competition.

Rule 3 helps us to avoid those paddock good things that go off favorite on the strength of a fast work, or even just plain rumor. If they haven't shown themselves capable of fighting for the

WORKOUT: *Selected Beaten Favorites*

(January-February 1949)

Date	Horse	Race & Track	Win	Place	Show
Jan. 1	Prince Favor	7 F.G.	...	...	4.20
	Top Sis	2 S.A.	...	4.40	2.80
4	Grandpere	7 S.A.	...	3.10	2.50
5	Big and Better	5 Trp.	...	...	...
	War Bam	2 S.A.	4.30	3.20	2.50
6	Snatched	6 F.G.	...	2.60	2.40
7	Rippey	7 S.A.	...	...	2.60
11	Kantar Run	1 Trp.	...	...	5.00
	Irish Sun	5 Trp.	7.50	3.90	3.10
12	Snatched	5 F.G.	8.60	5.80	3.40
	Little Delph	4 S.A.	...	...	...
	Tickingatit	7 S.A.	...	...	...
13	Rare Jewel	5 Trp.	4.60	3.20	2.80
	Junior Wolf	6 F.G.	...	...	...
	Dick Manners	7 F.G.	...	...	...
14	Vicksburg	8 S.A.	6.40	3.60	2.90
15	Castle Oak	5 S.A.	...	...	4.00
20	Dagon	5 F.G.	...	...	...
21	Great Beyond	4 F.G.	...	...	...
22	Joan's Robin	4 Hia.	...	...	...
	Howdy Rowdy	2 F.G.	68.20	23.20	10.20
24	Vaudeville	5 Hia.	...	...	...
	Green Bowler	8 Hia.	...	...	...
25	Bar News	6 S.A.	...	...	...
26	Reveille	5 Hia.	...	...	...
29	First Draft	8 Hia.	...	...	...
	Jade C	2 S.A.	11.50	6.70	4.10
31	Piping By	4 Hia.	...	...	...
	Buck Ash	6 S.P.	...	5.80	3.70
Feb. 1	Imperator	5 Hia.	13.90	6.50	4.70
	Top Boots	1 S.P.	11.00	4.60	2.90
	Gold Jig	6 S.A.	23.60	11.40	4.70
	Inroc	7 S.A.	7.80	4.70	2.90
	Pay N Takit	8 S.A.	...	9.10	4.90
2	Brooke Argo	1 S.P.	...	...	...
	New Hour	3 S.P.	...	...	4.10
3	Odd Goods	3 S.P.	...	4.40	3.40
5	Model King	3 Hia.	14.90	6.80	4.90
	One Only	7 S.P.	...	2.50	2.10
8	Rodman Keenon	5 F.G.	...	...	2.60
	Gyrette	7 F.G.	...	...	...
	Gabe	4 S.P.	...	...	...
9	De Luxe	3 Hia.	...	...	...
	One Only	6 S.P.	...	...	...
	Hopeful Play	8 S.P.	...	...	...

Date	Horse	Race & Track	Win	Place	Show
10	Day After	5 S.P.	...	3.20	2.80
12	First Draft	8 Hia.	...	...	...
14	Tight Squeeze	6 Hia.	4.90	3.10	2.40
	Alfios	2 S.P.	...	...	2.40
	True Blue	7 S.P.	...	2.90	2.20
15	Miss Tartan	4 Hia.	31.20	10.00	6.20
	Cordon	6 S.P.	3.80	2.40	2.10
16	Hopeful Play	8 S.P.	33.50	10.00	7.10
17	Top Sis	5 S.A.	13.80	7.00	5.60
18	Colonel Mike	6 Hia.	10.70	5.40	4.90
	Alfios	5 S.P.	6.20	3.20	2.40
	New Hour	7 S.P.	...	...	...
	Soon Again	8 S.A.	6.80	3.80	2.90
19	Free America *	6 Hia.	2.20	2.10	Out
	Some Pigeon	6 F.G.	...	...	...
	King Gail	8 F.G.	...	...	...
	Quarterinch	1 S.P.	...	2.60	2.20
	Harpstrings	6 S.P.	...	3.20	2.40
	Ebro	7 S.P.	8.50	4.90	2.80
21	Kitchen Police	5 Hia.	...	...	...
22	De Luxe	4 Hia.	3.30	2.80	2.70
	Flower Bed	7 S.A.	...	...	...
23	Brooke Argo	2 S.P.	4.40	2.90	2.40
26	Repentance	4 Hia.	...	...	2.80
	Donna M. G.	1 F.G.	...	7.40	4.00
	Normrich	4 O.P.	4.70	4.70	4.10
	Hoosier Boy	7 O.P.	...	6.90	5.60
28	Big Wig	6 F.G.	...	6.20	3.80
	Cowlan	1 O.P.	...	...	...

* Entry won

Number of Selections		74	74	73
Number won — placed — showed		25	39	46
Percentage: won — placed — showed		34%	53%	63%
Amount returned		$316.30	210.20	167.20
Amount invested		148.00	148.00	146.00
Profit		$168.30	62.20	21.20

money at least fifty per cent of the time, we want no part of them.

Rule 4 is a necessary separation rule in the event two or more beaten favorites are entered in the same race. Followers of this method may use sound handicapping principles such as best jockey, post position, mudding ability, etc., if they so desire. Experience and good judgment should be employed at the discretion of the player.

Rule 5 needs no elaboration. Maidens and two-year-olds are bad risks and should usually be avoided.

The writer has enjoyed considerable success following beaten favorites selected for quality and dependability. If the reader exercises care and patience in using the method outlined here, he will find himself equipped with a system which will give him ample action on well-meant horses.

Playing Winter Favorites

Favorites are usually poor bargains any time. That is, if you play favorites indiscriminately. Yet everyone knows that favorites do hang up better than ⅓ winners, taking into consideration all the tracks throughout the nation, year in year out. The player has something substantial to latch onto when he bets his money on the favorite.

Even though he will eventually lose his shirt if he consistently backs all the favorites, he knows that he is sure to get winners and approximately at a one-out-of-three batting average. This percentage of mutuel payoffs is hard to beat, yet the whole set-up is just so much "sucker bait."

However, the favorite is very frequently a solid bet, but the take and breakage manage to eat up any profits that these selections might ordinarily produce. The take and breakage also get in an extra bite to insure a loss. This makes playing favorites all the time sheer lunacy.

Yet something has to be the favorite, and if we could sort the good from the bad and produce a higher percentage of winners, our operations might become profitable. If the punter could get 50% or better winning favorites, he would soon find the folding money accumulating in his pockets.

Form frequently produces the favorite, and it is during the summer months that good form usually seems to be found. It is true that horses of all ages and categories, are usually more formful in the warmer seasons. The difficulty in finding the form horses during the wintertime lies with the players' lack of know-how. You simply can't play horses during the winter in the same fashion as you would in the summer. You must play a solid, seasoned, race-hardened animal in the wintertime.

The younger horses, the two- and three-year-olds, won't do. This is not meant to imply that these youngsters don't sometimes beat the older horses. They do, but the odds are in your favor if you stick to the four- and five-year-olds.

The older horses, like the younger ones, can be similarly discounted. The four-year-olds are now practically mature, and the five-year-olds are at the peak of their life cycles. Some readers may not agree. They may point out particular three-year-olds that have beaten older horses frequently.

This is true, but we are classifying the animals as a group. We are not concerned with individuals. Research has proved that this age group (four-year-olds—during the winter—and five-year-olds) is physically superior, and we'll go along with that.

Further, the workout presented with this system seems to confirm the statistics. Don't forget that these are winter favorites, and this is the time when form is not supposed to hold true. But— you'll find that form will tell in the winter as well as the summer if you back the proper animals.

Now how do we go about determining whether a horse is in form during the winter? Does the method differ from summer probing? Not exactly. Form is usually determined by recent good efforts, and sometimes form is merely determined by the animal's last three performances regardless of date.

What is a good effort? For our purposes an in-the-money effort will be sufficient. A horse that finished close up might be good enough too, but it is preferable to stick to those animals that came in among the first three.

It is not necessary for this in-the-money effort to be the horse's last race. However, we will not be content with just one in-the-money performance. If the horse shows at least two in-the-money efforts out of its last three races the animal meets our form requirement.

Though our system calls for a recent last race or workout, none of the horse's most recent efforts need be of current vintage. As long as the animal shows in-the-money efforts in at least two out of these three races the horse has paved the way for us to make it our system selection.

We are frequently backing a favorite with hidden form when our selection is finally made. For one thing, the horse's last effort may have been a dismal failure, with the animal finishing way back. Or then again, all three last races, or at least two of them, may be performances made quite some time ago.

Yet, more likely than not, the fact that the animal is the favorite and that it shows either a very recent race, not more than one week ago, or a workout within five days of today's event, is evidence to point out that the in-the-money races needed for qualification are potent signs of the animal's retained present good form. So there is really no need to be concerned about how far back these races were run.

Of course, when it comes to horses that have won their last two races we would really be stretching our luck to expect another win. Such performances, three or more consecutive wins, do occur, but they can be expected only from exceptional animals, and there are not too many of these to be found on the race tracks. Repeating a winning performance is not unusual, but three or more victories in a row is comparatively rare.

The bettor, naturally, is only interested in turning a profit on his wagering, and although he may obtain some winners by backing animals that have won two or more of their last races, he will get many more losers. In the long run backing such horses is a losing proposition. It is only logical to try to avoid any extra risks, so that if the horse has won its last two races, it cannot be accepted for play.

The distance factor is always an important one to consider. If the horse is a sprinter and is entered in a route race, how can we be certain that it can cope with the distance? And if the animal should prefer a route, what can we expect if it is entered in a sprint?

To avoid backing horses that are entered at a distance they cannot handle, specific requirements have been erected. The horse must show, not one but two in-the-money efforts at exactly today's distance. This ought to satisfy us that the animal can successfully negotiate the distance of today's race.

Now let's take a gander at the kind of horse we are backing here by summarizing the necessary requirements. We have an animal that is the favorite, which gives us at least a 1-3 chance to start with; the horse has a recent race or workout under its belt; it shows at least two in-the-money races out of its last three; and finally it has successfully negotiated today's distance at least twice, finishing not worse than third.

RULES: *Playing Winter Favorites*

1. Play the favorite only if it meets the following conditions:

a. The horse is four or five years old.

b. The horse is not a maiden, nor is it participating in a jumping event.

c. Either the horse's last race was not more than seven day's ago or it shows a workout within five days of today's race.

d. The horse shows at least two in-the-money efforts out of its last three races.

e. The horse shows anywhere in its past performances two in-the-money efforts at exactly the same distance as today's race.

f. The horse did not lose its last race by five lengths or more.

g. The horse did not win its last two races.

2. If the horse is tied as a favorite, it cannot be considered the favorite. The animal is not playable.

There is much to be said for systems that obtain a high percentage of winners. Usually such a method should reduce the number of possible consecutive losers.

This method gets more winners than you would obtain if you played odds-on horses exclusively. Of course if you played horses at less than even money you would surely eventually find yourself in the red. It is possible to get some fairly good prices playing favorites. For example, Miss Meggy, fourth at Tropical, on December 8, paid $10.00. There were a couple of winners that paid better than $8.00. (See Workout.)

Many fans have been raising the roof, howling against optional claimers. On the whole, I would say they have reason for complaint. Yet frequently a stand-out play can be discovered, based on the rules of this system, that will obviate any reason for discontent, even with optionals.

WORKOUT: *Playing Winter Favorites*

(1953)

Date	Horse	Track	Win	Place	Show
12-1	Siren Song	1 Bow.	7.00	3.40	2.60
	Landseair	5 Bow.	4.20	3.00	2.40
	Imalright	7 Trp.			
	Sun Tan Gal	6 F.G.	5.00	3.60	3.00
12-2	Hoop Roller	2 Trp.			2.40
	Hierarch	7 Trp.	5.30	3.10	2.40
12-3	Triograph	1 Trp.			
	Dover Coast	4 Trp.	3.60	2.80	2.40
12-4	Deep River	5 Bow.	6.40	3.80	3.20
	Brazen Brat	6 Bow.	4.40	3.20	2.20
	Merry Thought	2 Trp.			2.30
12-5	Jack The Great	5 Bow.			
	Battle Wave	7 C.T.		2.80	2.40
12-7	Sir Cross	8 Trp.	4.80	3.10	2.50
12-8	Miss Meggy	4 Trp.	10.00	5.10	4.00
	Next Stop	6 Trp.			
	Miss C Sue	8 C.T.			2.60
	In Class	5 F.G.	5.80	3.40	2.80
	Sun Tan Gal	6 F.G.	4.00	2.40	2.40
	Mock Battle	7 F.G.	5.00	3.40	3.00
12-10	Bayou Boy	8 Trp.	3.40	2.50	2.20
12-11	Shallow Brook	6 Trp.	6.60	3.60	3.40
	Whitleather	8 Trp.			
	Battle Wave	6 C.T.	3.60	2.60	2.20
12-12	Ignition	5 Trp.	4.80	3.40	2.60
	Andre	7 Trp.	7.90	5.20	3.50
	Hiram Jr.	6 F.G.			
12-14	Avion	7 Trp.	8.10	6.30	3.30
	Dorothy G.	7 C.T.	5.60	4.00	3.00
12-15	Triograph	1 Trp.	4.50	2.40	2.30
	Hasty Tiger	3 F.G.			2.80
12-16	Shallow Brook	4 Trp.			
	Dover Coast	6 Trp.	5.40	3.30	2.70
	Sir Cross	9 Trp.		3.40	2.70
	Seventh Tribe	7 F.G.			
	Little Bookie	8 F.G.	5.40	2.80	2.80
12-17	Marked Game	7 Trp.			
12-19	Diamond Jimmy	7 F.G.		2.80	2.30
12-21	Avion	7 Trp.			
12-22	Ignition	7 Trp.	6.50	3.30	2.50
	McBezzill	5 F.G.	5.80	3.40	2.80
	Cullerton	7 F.G.	7.40	7.60	5.80

Date	Horse	Track	Win	Place	Show
	Tony's Trouble	8 F.G.	8.20	4.40	3.80
12-23	Mollie Fagan	9 Trp.			
	Highway	2 F.G.	7.80	3.80	3.60
12-24	Vertrees	7 Trp.			2.40
12-25	Imalright	6 Trp.			3.10
12-26	Sand Fly	2 Trp.	4.60	3.20	2.70
12-28	Our Kite	8 Trp.	4.70	2.60	2.60
12-29	Monacoan	9 Trp.			4.70
12-30	Arizona K.	4 F.G.			
	Fuzzhead	4 S.A.			
12-31	The Eagle	7 Trp.		3.20	2.70
Amount Returned			$165.80	$116.90	$115.10
Amount Invested			$106.00	$106.00	$106.00
Profit			$ 59.80	$ 10.90	$ 9.10

53 selections
29 won 55%
33 placed 62%
40 showed 75%

27.
SOLID ALL THE WAY

Every horse player has cherished the dream of finding the perfect system—the key that would unlock a treasure chest brimming with gold. The perfect system would pick the winner in any and every race. All the owner of this miraculous method would have to do is gleefully cash stacks of mutuel tickets, cramming the long green stuff into all his pockets.

Dreams, beautiful dreams—yet still *dreams*.

Solid All the Way

For the fellow who can afford to plunk down a fifty-dollar bill to show on a certain type of horse that I will describe later, such a dream may become a little less distant. This method won't make the fifty-dollar bettor rich, but it can make him about $70 per week with the greatest of ease an with very little sweating over a racing paper.

The system is simple, easy to operate and purely mechanical. It must, however, be operated at the track or wire room, where odds can be obtained.

The favorite pays off in the show spot about two-thirds of the time. With this knowledge in hand a system can be devised for increasing the percentage to 90% or more. This I feel certain can be done. Playing odds-on choices would probably do this, but the action would be so limited and the prices so small that our wagering would show a loss anyway. It is necessary to get sufficient action, otherwise the method would not be worth playing.

The system to be outlined here is based on track wagering only, therefore the rules were set up to give sufficient action without confining ourselves to Best Bets. At the same time there was an attempt to obtain a fair show price. For this reason our play never went on a horse running at less than even money to win.

RULES: *Solid All the Way*

Play the favorite and only the favorite for *show* if it meets the following requirements:

A. Consistency: The horse must show any *one* of the following consistencies:

1. 50% *in the money* for the current year. In order for the horse to qualify fully it must have raced at least 4 times this year. If the horse has made less than four starts this year its current in the money consistency cannot be considered.

2. 20% *win consistency* for the current year. There is no minimum or maximum amount of races for the horse to run here. All that is required is that the horse show 20% win consistency for this year.

3. 50% *in the money* for the current and last year combined. There is no minimum or maximum amount of races to be run for both years.

B. Our home must have a speed rating at today's distance equal to one of the top three speed ratings at any time listed in the past performances. Merely look for the highest speed rating earned at today's distance in the past performances of each horse and record the number next to its name. Our horse must have a top speed rating among the three highest.

C. If our horse does not have 20% *win* consistency with at least 2 wins for the current and last year combined and there is at least one horse in the race that has this consistency and has raced recently (within 25 days) pass the race.

D. Our horse's last race must have run within 90 days.

E. Do not play the horse if it is a maiden.

F. Do not play the horse if it is a two-year-old.

G. Do not play the horse if the odds to win are less than even money.

H. Do not play the horse if it does not show a race at today's distance somewhere in its past performances.

I. Do not play the horse unless it shows an in the money effort in at least one of its last two races.

J. If the race is a claiming race our horse must not be going up in claiming price more than $500 over the highest of its last three claiming tags. If our horse did not race in claiming races in its last three races this rule does not apply.

K. Pass up all races with more than twelve starters.

L. Do not play the horse if it is a female racing against males. Females are to be considered only if racing solely against other females.

M. Horse must have won at least 1 race for both years.

N. Pass up any race where there are three or more horses with 20% win consistency or higher for the current and last year combined and who show at least two wins for this two year period.

To make the system as clear as possible, let me elaborate on the rules.

A favorite that can show 50% in-the-money consistency or 20% win consistency for the current year or current and last year combined is very likely to be a true favorite. The added stipulation that it must show a race at today's distance with a speed rating among the three best, points out the animal as at least having the ability to finish third.

If our horse did not show 20% win consistency for both years, we refuse to play it if another horse in the race has this consistency and has been racing recently.

We insured the win consistency percentage to be true by insisting that it be based on more than one win effort. It is very dangerous to wager against such consistent animals, so our system was built to refuse to take this risk.

As for maidens or two-year-olds, they are best left alone, since they are not reliable.

Those animals that have failed to win a single race for this year and last year are not much better than maidens. They were ignored as too hazardous to wager on.

The necessary in-the-money effort in at least one of the horse's last two races was inserted to obtain some semblance of form. This rule is not perfect, since it does not specify a time limit, but as intensive spot checks proved its value, the rule is to be accepted and no attempt should be made to discard it.

Females racing against males have proved, in the long run, to be at a disadvantage, therefore we ignored them when they were racing against the opposite sex.

The more contenders in a race the more difficult it is for any horse to win. Knowing this, we limited the field to 12 and no more.

28.
THE LAST LAP

It's important in summing up to stress the virtues of patience and effort. You can't just sit back and garner profits without doing a little work yourself.

The systems here are varied intentionally, because not all people are the same. What may be a perfectly good method for one person is not worthwhile to another. Let's face these facts. Choose those methods that suit your fancy. Don't try to play all of them at once. If you like longshots, pick out the systems that deal specifically with this idea in mind. Should you prefer favorites or you want to feel safe by backing methods that bring in a high percentage of winners, don't try the others. Your character should reflect the method of play you prefer.

Remember that you can't usually find a winning method that does not employ the use of past performances. Although there definitely are some good ones that eliminate the use of past performances, you should always be able to consult the sources of information that permit you to see more than the surface of selection.

Sometimes what is true today can prove the opposite tomorrow. So test the method currently. See what its possibilities are now. All the methods in this book can be employed with success. However, a good method may lose its value when too many bettors employ it, because the prices become shorter. Especially is this true of the simpler methods, which naturally find more followers.

Based on sound handicapping principles a system will prove profitable if used right. Don't forget to stick to the rules. Deviation may prove fatal. Every system has been checked and double checked; almost every one has a workout displaying specific profits.

Many bettors will chuck away a perfectly sound system just because, at that particular instance of wagering, the method unfortunately ran into an unexpected streak of losers. After dropping the method a player may feel like tearing his hair out by the roots when the winners start popping in.

So remember, patience, and perhaps a little work on the past performances will pay off. Things are apt to be a little difficult at the beginning, but when you get the hang of the method you are playing, selections will roll off smooth as butter, Racing is a tough game to beat, but it pays off for those in the know, those who can persevere and work for success.

Some bettors like to use methodical handicapping procedures, while others are interested purely in the time factor. Rate them or weight them, the fundamental principles are what count. Get into the swing of things by sticking to a strict set of rules. This way you are sure of betting right, leaving no room for guess work.

WILSHIRE SELF-IMPROVEMENT LIBRARY

ASTROLOGY

___ASTROLOGY—HOW TO CHART YOUR HOROSCOPE Max Heindel 7.00
___ASTROLOGY AND SEXUAL ANALYSIS Morris C. Goodman 10.00
___ASTROLOGY AND YOU Carroll Righter 5.00
___ASTROLOGY MADE EASY Astarte 7.00
___ASTROLOGY, ROMANCE, YOU AND THE STARS Anthony Norvell 10.00
___MY WORLD OF ASTROLOGY Sydney Omarr 10.00
___THOUGHT DIAL Sydney Omarr 7.00
___WHAT THE STARS REVEAL ABOUT THE MEN IN YOUR LIFE Thelma White 3.00

BRIDGE

___BRIDGE BIDDING MADE EASY Edwin B. Kantar 15.00
___BRIDGE CONVENTIONS Edwin B. Kantar 10.00
___COMPETITIVE BIDDING IN MODERN BRIDGE Edgar Kaplan 7.00
___DEFENSIVE BRIDGE PLAY COMPLETE Edwin B Kantar 20.00
___GAMESMAN BRIDGE—PLAY BETTER WITH KANTAR Edwin B. Kantar 7.00
___HOW TO IMPROVE YOUR BRIDGE Alfred Sheinwold 7.00
___IMPROVING YOUR BIDDING SKILLS Edwin B. Kantar 10.00
___INTRODUCTION TO DECLARER'S PLAY Edwin B. Kantar 10.00
___INTRODUCTION TO DEFENDER'S PLAY Edwin B. Kantar 10.00
___KANTAR FOR THE DEFENSE Edwin B. Kantar 10.00
___KANTAR FOR THE DEFENSE VOLUME 2 Edwin B. Kantar 10.00
___TEST YOUR BRIDGE PLAY Edwin B. Kantar 10.00
___VOLUME 2—TEST YOUR BRIDGE PLAY Edwin B. Kantar 10.00
___WINNING DECLARER PLAY Dorothy Hayden Truscott 10.00

BUSINESS, STUDY & REFERENCE

___BRAINSTORMING Charles Clark 10.00
___CONVERSATION MADE EASY Elliot Russell 5.00
___EXAM SECRET Dennis B. Jackson 7.00
___FIX-IT BOOK Arthur Symons 2.00
___HOW TO DEVELOP A BETTER SPEAKING VOICE M. Hellier 5.00
___HOW TO SAVE 50% ON GAS & CAR EXPENSES Ken Stansbie 5.00
___HOW TO SELF-PUBLISH YOUR BOOK & MAKE IT A BEST SELLER Melvin Powers . . 20.00
___INCREASE YOUR LEARNING POWER Geoffrey A. Dudley 5.00
___PRACTICAL GUIDE TO BETTER CONCENTRATION Melvin Powers 5.00
___PUBLIC SPEAKING MADE EASY Thomas Montalbo 10.00
___7 DAYS TO FASTER READING William S. Schaill 7.00
___SONGWRITER'S RHYMING DICTIONARY Jane Shaw Whitfield 10.00
___SPELLING MADE EASY Lester D. Basch & Dr. Milton Finkelstein 3.00
___STUDENT'S GUIDE TO BETTER GRADES J.A. Rickard 3.00
___YOUR WILL & WHAT TO DO ABOUT IT Attorney Samuel G. King 7.00

CALLIGRAPHY

___ADVANCED CALLIGRAPHY Katherine Jeffares 7.00
___CALLIGRAPHY—THE ART OF BEAUTIFUL WRITING Katherine Jeffares 7.00
___CALLIGRAPHY FOR FUN & PROFIT Anne Leptich & Jacque Evans 7.00
___CALLIGRAPHY MADE EASY Tina Serafini 7.00

CHESS & CHECKERS

___BEGINNER'S GUIDE TO WINNING CHESS Fred Reinfeld 10.00
___CHESS IN TEN EASY LESSONS Larry Evans 10.00
___CHESS MADE EASY Milton L. Hanauer 5.00
___CHESS PROBLEMS FOR BEGINNERS Edited by Fred Reinfeld 7.00

____CHESS TACTICS FOR BEGINNERS Edited by Fred Reinfeld 10.00
____HOW TO WIN AT CHECKERS Fred Reinfeld 7.00
____1001 BRILLIANT WAYS TO CHECKMATE Fred Reinfeld 10.00
____1001 WINNING CHESS SACRIFICES & COMBINATIONS Fred Reinfeld 10.00

COOKERY & HERBS

____CULPEPER'S HERBAL REMEDIES Dr. Nicholas Culpeper 5.00
____FAST GOURMET COOKBOOK Poppy Cannon 2.50
____HEALING POWER OF HERBS May Bethel 5.00
____HEALING POWER OF NATURAL FOODS May Bethel 7.00
____HERBS FOR HEALTH—HOW TO GROW & USE THEM Louise Evans Doole 7.00
____HOME GARDEN COOKBOOK—DELICIOUS NATURAL FOOD RECIPES Ken Kraft 3.00
____MEATLESS MEAL GUIDE Tomi Ryan & James H. Ryan, M.D. 4.00
____VEGETABLE GARDENING FOR BEGINNERS Hugh Wilberg 2.00
____VEGETABLES FOR TODAY'S GARDENS R. Milton Carleton 2.00
____VEGETARIAN COOKERY Janet Walker 10.00
____VEGETARIAN COOKING MADE EASY & DELECTABLE Veronica Vezza 3.00

GAMBLING & POKER

____HOW TO WIN AT POKER Terence Reese & Anthony T. Watkins 10.00
____SCARNE ON DICE John Scarne 15.00
____WINNING AT CRAPS Dr. Lloyd T. Commins 10.00
____WINNING AT GIN Chester Wander & Cy Rice 10.00
____WINNING AT POKER—AN EXPERT'S GUIDE John Archer 10.00
____WINNING AT 21—AN EXPERT'S GUIDE John Archer 10.00
____WINNING POKER SYSTEMS Norman Zadeh 10.00

HEALTH

____BEE POLLEN Lynda Lyngheim & Jack Scagnetti 5.00
____COPING WITH ALZHEIMER'S Rose Oliver, Ph.D. & Francis Bock, Ph.D. 10.00
____HELP YOURSELF TO BETTER SIGHT Margaret Darst Corbett 10.00
____HOW YOU CAN STOP SMOKING PERMANENTLY Ernest Caldwell 5.00
____NATURE'S WAY TO NUTRITION & VIBRANT HEALTH Robert J. Scrutton 3.00
____NEW CARBOHYDRATE DIET COUNTER Patti Lopez-Pereira 2.00
____REFLEXOLOGY Dr. Maybelle Segal 7.00
____REFLEXOLOGY FOR GOOD HEALTH Anna Kaye & Don C. Matchan 10.00
____YOU CAN LEARN TO RELAX Dr. Samuel Gutwirth 5.00

HOBBIES

____BEACHCOMBING FOR BEGINNERS Norman Hickin 2.00
____BLACKSTONE'S MODERN CARD TRICKS Harry Blackstone 7.00
____BLACKSTONE'S SECRETS OF MAGIC Harry Blackstone 7.00
____COIN COLLECTING FOR BEGINNERS Burton Hobson & Fred Reinfeld 7.00
____ENTERTAINING WITH ESP Tony 'Doc' Shiels 2.00
____400 FASCINATING MAGIC TRICKS YOU CAN DO Howard Thurston 10.00
____HOW I TURN JUNK INTO FUN AND PROFIT Sari 3.00
____HOW TO WRITE A HIT SONG AND SELL IT Tommy Boyce 10.00
____MAGIC FOR ALL AGES Walter Gibson 10.00
____STAMP COLLECTING FOR BEGINNERS Burton Hobson 3.00

HORSE PLAYERS' WINNING GUIDES

____BETTING HORSES TO WIN Les Conklin 10.00
____ELIMINATE THE LOSERS Bob McKnight 5.00
____HOW TO PICK WINNING HORSES Bob McKnight 5.00
____HOW TO WIN AT THE RACES Sam (The Genius) Lewin 5.00
____HOW YOU CAN BEAT THE RACES Jack Kavanagh 5.00
____MAKING MONEY AT THE RACES David Barr 10.00
____PAYDAY AT THE RACES Les Conklin 7.00

__ SMART HANDICAPPING MADE EASY William Bauman 5.00
__ SUCCESS AT THE HARNESS RACES Barry Meadow 7.00

HUMOR

__ HOW TO FLATTEN YOUR TUSH Coach Marge Reardon 2.00
__ JOKE TELLER'S HANDBOOK Bob Orben 10.00
__ JOKES FOR ALL OCCASIONS Al Schock 7.00
__ 2,000 NEW LAUGHS FOR SPEAKERS Bob Orben 7.00
__ 2,400 JOKES TO BRIGHTEN YOUR SPEECHES Robert Orben 10.00
__ 2,500 JOKES TO START'EM LAUGHING Bob Orben 10.00

HYPNOTISM

__ CHILDBIRTH WITH HYPNOSIS William S. Kroger, M.D. 5.00
__ HOW YOU CAN BOWL BETTER USING SELF-HYPNOSIS Jack Heise 7.00
__ HOW YOU CAN PLAY BETTER GOLF USING SELF-HYPNOSIS Jack Heise 3.00
__ HYPNOSIS AND SELF-HYPNOSIS Bernard Hollander, M.D. 7.00
__ HYPNOTISM (Originally published 1893) Carl Sextus 5.00
__ HYPNOTISM MADE EASY Dr. Ralph Winn 10.00
__ HYPNOTISM MADE PRACTICAL Louis Orton 5.00
__ MODERN HYPNOSIS Lesley Kuhn & Salvatore Russo, Ph.D. 5.00
__ NEW CONCEPTS OF HYPNOSIS Bernard C. Gindes, M.D. 15.00
__ NEW SELF-HYPNOSIS Paul Adams 10.00
__ POST-HYPNOTIC INSTRUCTIONS—SUGGESTIONS FOR THERAPY Arnold Furst ... 10.00
__ PRACTICAL GUIDE TO SELF-HYPNOSIS Melvin Powers 10.00
__ PRACTICAL HYPNOTISM Philip Magonet, M.D. 3.00
__ SECRETS OF HYPNOTISM S.J. Van Pelt, M.D. 5.00
__ SELF-HYPNOSIS—A CONDITIONED-RESPONSE TECHNIQUE Laurence Sparks 7.00
__ SELF-HYPNOSIS—ITS THEORY, TECHNIQUE & APPLICATION Melvin Powers 7.00
__ THERAPY THROUGH HYPNOSIS Edited by Raphael H. Rhodes 5.00

JUDAICA

__ SERVICE OF THE HEART Evelyn Garfiel, Ph.D. 10.00
__ STORY OF ISRAEL IN COINS Jean & Maurice Gould 2.00
__ STORY OF ISRAEL IN STAMPS Maxim & Gabriel Shamir 1.00
__ TONGUE OF THE PROPHETS Robert St. John 10.00

JUST FOR WOMEN

__ COSMOPOLITAN'S GUIDE TO MARVELOUS MEN Foreword by Helen Gurley Brown .. 3.00
__ COSMOPOLITAN'S HANG-UP HANDBOOK Foreword by Helen Gurley Brown 4.00
__ COSMOPOLITAN'S LOVE BOOK—A GUIDE TO ECSTASY IN BED 7.00
__ COSMOPOLITAN'S NEW ETIQUETTE GUIDE Foreword by Helen Gurley Brown 4.00
__ I AM A COMPLEAT WOMAN Doris Hagopian & Karen O'Connor Sweeney 3.00
__ JUST FOR WOMEN—A GUIDE TO THE FEMALE BODY Richard E. Sand M.D. 5.00
__ NEW APPROACHES TO SEX IN MARRIAGE John E. Eichenlaub, M.D. 3.00
__ SEXUALLY ADEQUATE FEMALE Frank S. Caprio, M.D. 3.00
__ SEXUALLY FULFILLED WOMAN Dr. Rachel Copelan 5.00

MARRIAGE, SEX & PARENTHOOD

__ ABILITY TO LOVE Dr. Allan Fromme 7.00
__ GUIDE TO SUCCESSFUL MARRIAGE Drs. Albert Ellis & Robert Harper 10.00
__ HOW TO RAISE AN EMOTIONALLY HEALTHY, HAPPY CHILD Albert Ellis, Ph.D. 10.00
__ PARENT SURVIVAL TRAINING Marvin Silverman, Ed.D. & David Lustig, Ph.D. 15.00
__ SEX WITHOUT GUILT Albert Ellis, Ph.D. 7.00
__ SEXUALLY ADEQUATE MALE Frank S. Caprio, M.D. 3.00
__ SEXUALLY FULFILLED MAN Dr. Rachel Copelan 5.00
__ STAYING IN LOVE Dr. Norton F. Kristy 7.00

MELVIN POWERS MAIL ORDER LIBRARY

___ HOW TO GET RICH IN MAIL ORDER Melvin Powers 20.00
___ HOW TO SELF-PUBLISH YOUR BOOK Melvin Powers 20.00
___ HOW TO WRITE A GOOD ADVERTISEMENT Victor O. Schwab 20.00
___ MAIL ORDER MADE EASY J. Frank Brumbaugh 20.00
___ MAKING MONEY WITH CLASSIFIED ADS Melvin Powers 20.00

METAPHYSICS & NEW AGE

___ CONCENTRATION—A GUIDE TO MENTAL MASTERY Mouni Sadhu 10.00
___ EXTRA-TERRESTRIAL INTELLIGENCE—THE FIRST ENCOUNTER 6.00
___ FORTUNE TELLING WITH CARDS P. Foli 10.00
___ HOW TO INTERPRET DREAMS, OMENS & FORTUNE TELLING SIGNS Gettings 5.00
___ HOW TO UNDERSTAND YOUR DREAMS Geoffrey A. Dudley 7.00
___ MAGICIAN—HIS TRAINING AND WORK W.E. Butler 7.00
___ MEDITATION Mouni Sadhu 10.00
___ MODERN NUMEROLOGY Morris C. Goodman 10.00
___ NUMEROLOGY—ITS FACTS AND SECRETS Ariel Yvon Taylor 5.00
___ NUMEROLOGY MADE EASY W. Mykian 10.00
___ PALMISTRY MADE EASY Fred Gettings 7.00
___ PALMISTRY MADE PRACTICAL Elizabeth Daniels Squire 7.00
___ PROPHECY IN OUR TIME Martin Ebon 2.50
___ SUPERSTITION—ARE YOU SUPERSTITIOUS? Eric Maple 2.00
___ TAROT OF THE BOHEMIANS Papus 10.00
___ WAYS TO SELF-REALIZATION Mouni Sadhu 7.00
___ WITCHCRAFT, MAGIC & OCCULTISM—A FASCINATING HISTORY W.B. Crow 10.00
___ WITCHCRAFT—THE SIXTH SENSE Justine Glass 7.00

RECOVERY

___ KNIGHT IN RUSTY ARMOR Robert Fisher 5.00
___ KNIGHTS WITHOUT ARMOR (Hardcover edition) Aaron R. Kipnis, Ph.D. 10.00
___ PRINCESS WHO BELIEVED IN FAIRY TALES Marcia Grad 10.00

SELF-HELP & INSPIRATIONAL

___ CHANGE YOUR VOICE, CHANGE YOUR LIFE Morton Cooper, Ph.D. 10.00
___ CHARISMA—HOW TO GET "THAT SPECIAL MAGIC" Marcia Grad 10.00
___ DAILY POWER FOR JOYFUL LIVING Dr. Donald Curtis 7.00
___ DYNAMIC THINKING Melvin Powers 7.00
___ GREATEST POWER IN THE UNIVERSE U.S. Andersen 10.00
___ GROW RICH WHILE YOU SLEEP Ben Sweetland 10.00
___ GROW RICH WITH YOUR MILLION DOLLAR MIND Brian Adams 10.00
___ GROWTH THROUGH REASON Albert Ellis, Ph.D. 10.00
___ GUIDE TO PERSONAL HAPPINESS Albert Ellis, Ph.D. & Irving Becker, Ed.D. 10.00
___ GUIDE TO RATIONAL LIVING Albert Ellis, Ph.D. & R. Harper, Ph.D. 15.00
___ HANDWRITING ANALYSIS MADE EASY John Marley 10.00
___ HANDWRITING TELLS Nadya Olyanova 10.00
___ HOW TO ATTRACT GOOD LUCK A.H.Z. Carr 10.00
___ HOW TO DEVELOP A WINNING PERSONALITY Martin Panzer 10.00
___ HOW TO DEVELOP AN EXCEPTIONAL MEMORY Young & Gibson 10.00
___ HOW TO LIVE WITH A NEUROTIC Albert Ellis, Ph.D. 10.00
___ HOW TO MAKE $100,000 A YEAR IN SALES Albert Winnikoff 15.00
___ HOW TO OVERCOME YOUR FEARS M.P. Leahy, M.D. 3.00
___ HOW TO SUCCEED Brian Adams 10.00
___ I CAN Ben Sweetland 10.00
___ I WILL Ben Sweetland 10.00
___ KNIGHT IN RUSTY ARMOR Robert Fisher 5.00
___ MAGIC IN YOUR MIND U.S. Andersen 15.00
___ MAGIC OF THINKING SUCCESS Dr. David J. Schwartz 10.00
___ MAGIC POWER OF YOUR MIND Walter M. Germain 10.00
___ NEVER UNDERESTIMATE THE SELLING POWER OF A WOMAN Dottie Walters 7.00

___ PRINCESS WHO BELIEVED IN FAIRY TALES Marcia Grad 10.00
___ PSYCHO-CYBERNETICS Maxwell Maltz, M.D. 10.00
___ PSYCHOLOGY OF HANDWRITING Nadya Olyanova 10.00
___ SALES CYBERNETICS Brian Adams 10.00
___ SECRET OF SECRETS U.S. Andersen 10.00
___ SECRET POWER OF THE PYRAMIDS U.S. Andersen 7.00
___ SELF-THERAPY FOR THE STUTTERER Malcolm Frazer 3.00
___ STOP COMMITTING VOICE SUICIDE Morton Cooper, Ph.D. 10.00
___ SUCCESS CYBERNETICS U.S. Andersen 10.00
___ 10 DAYS TO A GREAT NEW LIFE William E. Edwards 3.00
___ THINK AND GROW RICH Napoleon Hill 10.00
___ THINK LIKE A WINNER Walter Doyle Staples, Ph.D. 15.00
___ THREE MAGIC WORDS U.S. Andersen 15.00
___ TREASURY OF COMFORT Edited by Rabbi Sidney Greenberg 15.00
___ TREASURY OF THE ART OF LIVING Edited by Rabbi Sidney Greenberg 10.00
___ WHAT YOUR HANDWRITING REVEALS Albert E. Hughes 4.00
___ WINNING WITH YOUR VOICE Morton Cooper, Ph.D. 10.00
___ YOUR SUBCONSCIOUS POWER Charles M. Simmons 7.00

SPORTS

___ BILLIARDS—POCKET • CAROM • THREE CUSHION Clive Cottingham, Jr. 10.00
___ COMPLETE GUIDE TO FISHING Vlad Evanoff 2.00
___ HOW TO IMPROVE YOUR RACQUETBALL Lubarsky, Kaufman & Scagnetti 5.00
___ HOW TO WIN AT POCKET BILLIARDS Edward D. Knuchell 10.00
___ JOY OF WALKING Jack Scagnetti 3.00
___ RACQUETBALL FOR WOMEN Toni Hudson, Jack Scagnetti & Vince Rondone 3.00
___ SECRET OF BOWLING STRIKES Dawson Taylor 5.00
___ SOCCER—THE GAME & HOW TO PLAY IT Gary Rosenthal 7.00
___ STARTING SOCCER Edward F Dolan, Jr. 5.00

TENNIS LOVERS' LIBRARY

___ HOW TO BEAT BETTER TENNIS PLAYERS Loring Fiske 4.00
___ PSYCH YOURSELF TO BETTER TENNIS Dr. Walter A. Luszki 2.00
___ WEEKEND TENNIS—HOW TO HAVE FUN & WIN AT THE SAME TIME Bill Talbert . . . 3.00

WILSHIRE PET LIBRARY

___ DOG TRAINING MADE EASY & FUN John W. Kellogg 5.00
___ HOW TO BRING UP YOUR PET DOG Kurt Unkelbach 2.00
___ HOW TO RAISE & TRAIN YOUR PUPPY Jeff Griffen 5.00

LIBROS EN ESPAÑOL

___ CARISMA—CÓMO LOGRAR ESA MAGIA ESPECIAL Marcia Grad 10.00
___ CÓMO ALRAER LA BUENA SUERTE A.H.Z. Carr 10.00
___ EL CABALLERO DE LA ARMADURA OXIDAD Robert Fisher 10.00
___ EL CABALLERO DE LA ARMADURA OXIDAD (con cubierta gruesa) Robert Fisher . . . 20.00
___ LA PRINCESA QUE CREÍA EN CUENTOS DE HADAS Marcia Grad 10.00

Available from your bookstore or directly from Wilshire Book Company.
Please add $2.00 shipping and handling for each book ordered.

Wilshire Book Company
12015 Sherman Road
No. Hollywood, California 91605

For our complete catalog, visit our Web site at http://www.mpowers.com.

WILSHIRE HORSE LOVERS' LIBRARY

____ AMERICAN QUARTER HORSE IN PICTURES Margaret Cabel Self 5.00
____ APPALOOSA HORSE Donna & Bill Richardson 7.00
____ ARABIAN HORSE Reginald S. Summerhays 7.00
____ ART OF WESTERN RIDING Suzanne Norton Jones 10.00
____ BASIC DRESSAGE Jean Froissard 7.00
____ BEGINNER'S GUIDE TO HORSEBACK RIDING Sheila Wall 5.00
____ BITS—THEIR HISTORY, USE AND MISUSE Louis Taylor 10.00
____ BREAKING & TRAINING THE DRIVING HORSE Doris Ganton 10.00
____ BREAKING YOUR HORSE'S BAD HABITS W. Dayton Sumner 10.00
____ COMPLETE TRAINING OF HORSE AND RIDER Colonel Alois Podhajsky 15.00
____ DISORDERS OF THE HORSE & WHAT TO DO ABOUT THEM E. Hanauer 5.00
____ DOG TRAINING MADE EASY AND FUN John W. Kellogg 5.00
____ DRESSAGE—A STUDY OF THE FINER POINTS IN RIDING Henry Wynmalen 15.00
____ DRIVE ON Doris Ganton 7.00
____ DRIVING HORSES Sallie Walrond 7.00
____ EQUITATION Jean Froissard 7.00
____ FIRST AID FOR HORSES Dr. Charles H. Denning, Jr. 7.00
____ FUN ON HORSEBACK Margaret Cabell Self 4.00
____ HORSE OWNER'S CONCISE GUIDE Elsie V. Hanauer 5.00
____ HORSE SELECTION & CARE FOR BEGINNERS George H. Conn 10.00
____ HORSEBACK RIDING FOR BEGINNERS Louis Taylor 10.00
____ HORSEBACK RIDING MADE EASY & FUN Sue Henderson Coen 10.00
____ HORSES—THEIR SELECTION, CARE & HANDLING Margaret Cabell Self 5.00
____ HOW TO CURE BEHAVIOR PROBLEMS IN HORSES Susan McBane 15.00
____ HUNTER IN PICTURES Margaret Cabell Self 2.00
____ ILLUSTRATED BOOK OF THE HORSE S. Sidney (8½" x 11") 10.00
____ ILLUSTRATED HORSEBACK RIDING FOR BEGINNERS Jeanne Mellin 5.00
____ KNOW ALL ABOUT HORSES Harry Disston 5.00
____ LAME HORSE—CAUSES, SYMPTOMS & TREATMENT Dr. James R. Rooney 15.00
____ POLICE HORSES Judith Campbell 2.00
____ PRACTICAL GUIDE TO HORSESHOEING 5.00
____ PRACTICAL HORSE PSYCHOLOGY Moyra Williams 10.00
____ PROBLEM HORSES—CURING SERIOUS BEHAVIOR HABITS Summerhays 5.00
____ REINSMAN OF THE WEST—BRIDLES & BITS Ed Connell 10.00
____ RIDE WESTERN Louis Taylor 7.00
____ SCHOOLING YOUR YOUNG HORSE George Wheatley 7.00
____ STABLE MANAGEMENT FOR THE OWNER—GROOM George Wheatley 7.00
____ STALLION MANAGEMENT—A GUIDE FOR STUD OWNERS A.C. Hardman 5.00
____ YOU AND YOUR PONY Pepper Mainwaring Healey (8½" x 11") 6.00
____ YOUR PONY BOOK Hermann Wiederhold 2.00

Available from your bookstore or directly from Wilshire Book Company.
Please add $2.00 shipping and handling for each book ordered.

Wilshire Book Company
12015 Sherman Road
No. Hollywood, California 91605

For our complete catalog, visit our Web site at http://www.mpowers.com.

A Personal Invitation from the Publisher, Melvin Powers...

There is a wonderful, unique book titled *The Knight in Rusty Armor* that is guaranteed to captivate your imagination as you discover the secret of what is most important in life. It is a delightful tale of a desperate knight in search of his true self.

Since we first published *The Knight in Rusty Armor,* we have received an unprecedented number of calls and letters from readers praising its powerful insights and entertaining style. It is a memorable, fun-filled story, rich in wit and humor, that has changed thousands of lives for the better. *The Knight* is one of our most popular titles. It has been published in numerous languages and has become a well-known favorite in many countries. I feel so strongly about this book that personally extending an invitation for you to read it.

The Knight in Rusty Armor

Join the knight as he faces a life-changing dilemma upon discovering that he is trapped in his armor, just as *we* may be trapped in *our* armor—an invisible kind that we use to protect ourselves from others and from various aspects of life.

As the knight searches for a way to free himself, he receives guidance from the wise sage Merlin the Magician, who encourages him to embark on the most difficult crusade of his life. The knight takes up the challenge and travels the Path of Truth, where he meets his real self for the first time and confronts the Universal Truths that govern his life—and ours.

The knight's journey reflects our own, filled with hope and despair, belief and disillusionment, laughter and tears. His insights become our insights as we follow along on his intriguing adventure of self-discovery. Anyone who has ever struggled with the meaning of life and love will discover profound wisdom and truth as this unique fantasy unfolds. *The Knight in Rusty Armor* is an experience that will expand your mind, touch your heart, and nourish your soul.